Yamamoto's Dilemma

Pacific War: Volume 1

Yamamoto's Dilemma

Pacific War: Volume 1

Carl L. Steinhouse

This Japanese Admiral planned the attack
on Pearl Harbor but warned Japan could not win the war.
They did not listen to him. And American Admiral Nimitz
saw to it that they did not win!

STONEWALL PRESS

PAVING YOUR WAY TO SUCCESS

Published in the United States of America

ISBN: 978-1-64460-117-4 (*sc*)
          978-1-64460-116-7 (*e*)

Library of Congress Control Number: 2019934434

Stonewall Press books may be ordered through booksellers or by contacting:

Stonewall Press
4800 Hampden Lane, Suite 200
Bethesda, MD 20814 USA
www.stonewallpress.com
1-888-334-0980
orders@stonewallpress.com

1. Historical
2. War and Military
19.02.15

CONTENTS

AUTHOR'S NOTE

In Japan, personal names take the form of family name first followed by the given name. To avoid confusion, the author adopts the Western/American form of given name first and family following. In Japan, friends address each other generally by their family name. That is the custom and not a sign of disrespect or impoliteness, and I follow that custom in this book.

This book, Volume I, takes us up to the time of the death of Admiral Yamamoto. Volume II, if I survive old age, will take us to the end of the war. Volume II, partially researched, has yet to be put down on paper with pen (or more accurately, into a digital file by computer key board).

Carl L. Steinhouse
2018

Japanese idiom: Hakko Ichiu:
"The world under one Japanese Imperial roof."

American idiom, probably from the Old West:
"Don't bite off more than you can chew, buster."

EXCERPT FROM THE BOOK

Konoye spread his arms sending Yamamoto a silent *What can I do?* sign. The prime minister sighed. "Admiral, Tojo and Nagano are hell-bent for war and I've tried, but there seems little I can do to stop them. The emperor seems inclined to give them their head. Tell me, what do you think our chances are in a war with America?"

Yamamoto frowned. "I've been asked the question regarding Pearl Harbor often and my answer is always the same, prime minister-san. If we follow my plan to surprise bomb and torpedo the American Fleet and facilities at Pearl Harbor, we'll set them back for a while—no doubt about it—and we'll be successful for six months, and maybe a year or even a little longer. But after that I cannot guarantee, as their industrial might gears up and their large population is called up to serve in the military. Then, prime minister, I think we will be in trouble."

PREFACE

THE WORD SAMURAI MEANS "those who serve" and in old Japan, most samurai held their land for a more senior overlord to whom they owed military service and allegiance. The samurai learned the art of sword fighting at an early age. When the country became united in the late 15th century, the samurai came out on top; they were the only ones permitted to carry a sword and were paid in rice by their feudal lords. The samurai's sword, called a *katana*, was a master-crafted blade, very strong, sharp, and durable. The sword was usually accompanied by a shorter sword, a *wakizashi*, whose blade was crafted equally fine. The samurai, expected to be brave, tough-willed individuals, were skilled swordsman and riders, fiercely loyal to their lord, and willing to face death at any moment. Indeed, their moral code stressed frugality, loyalty, martial arts, and honor unto death.

In the civil war of 1868, also known as the Bosshin War, the Imperial forces defeated the samurai of Nagaoka and one clan on the losing end was the samurai family of Sadayoshi Takano. Takano, always provided for generously by his regional lord, was now on his own—now no more than a peasant trying to eke out a living. Later in the 19th century, many samurais were conscripted into the military as officers. The military, particularly the Army, playing on the samurai code, glorified death and loyalty unto death as its ideal and the former samurai accepted that. But the Army also involved harsh training and plenty of punishment, together with instilling the idea of Japan's racial superiority and sense of invincibility, the *Bushido* or the spirit of Japan.

During the 1800s, the importance of martial arts and the art of war declined and so did the status of the samurai. They became bureaucrats, teachers, and artists, abandoning their swords and their fighting.

1906

Looking at a resurgent Asia under Japanese leadership which, if it gained force, could overwhelm Western civilization, Americans, particularly on the West Coast, feared being caught up in the "yellow peril" and the San Francisco *Chronicle* pressed our leaders to do something. They did. The city's school board ordered all Japanese Nisei children to attend school in Chinatown.

The Japanese government responded hotly and angrily, saying this discrimination and prejudice was impossible to overlook; some in government even talked of war. Teddy Roosevelt secretly warned the Philippines to guard against a Japanese attack. The war talk ended, but not the Japanese resentment, whose leaders felt that at some point they were destined to battle the United States. This position gained even more support when Congress banned the immigration of Japanese into the United States by passing the blatantly racial Exclusion Act in 1924. But Russia still remained Japan's number one potential enemy. Now, however, the United States became the number two enemy and China had dropped to number three.

The resentment festered into the 1930s. Why, many Japanese politicians and military leaders asked, was it acceptable for the English and Dutch to occupy countries in Asia, and America to grab the land of the American Indians, yet become outraged when Japan did the same in Manchuria and China? War with the Western powers is inevitable, many Japan's leaders felt, and planning for it became an important activity for the military.

PREQUEL

1884-1898, City of Nagaoka, Honshu

SADAYOSHI TAKANO, THE FORMER samurai, who lived in the city of Nagaoka on Honshu, one of the main islands of the Japanese homeland, had his seventh and last son on April 4, 1884 and, after many months, his wife confronted this disinterested father—after all, seven is a lot of children—and one more than he really needed.

"If you give him nothing else,' she cried, "the boy needs a name. Please, Sadayoshi, give him one!"

"Who cares?" he grumbled. But the nagging finally wore Sadayoshi down. He also knew, in his heart, that she was right, and he threw up his hands.

Then he smiled. It dawned on him that he was fifty-six years old when this boy was born. "Isoroku," the father proclaimed, "we shall call him Isoroku!"

"What? You are calling him Fifty-six?"

Sadayoshi stood there defiantly, hands across his chest. "That's my decision. No further discussion is necessary, nor will any be tolerated!"

✸✸✸

During the funeral of his half-brother, his father called aside Isoroku, then fourteen years old.

"Isoroku, as the seventh and last child in this family, you must realize that you will not inherit anything from me. Since I lost my status as a samurai, just like a peasant, I barely eke out a living. When you graduate school, you are strictly on your own."

Isoruku nodded his understanding, said nothing in reply, and simply turned away from his father.

Like every child in Japan, Isoroku learned *kodo*, the Imperial Way, where the Japanese concept of *on*, the obligation and devotion to the emperor and his own family, was ingrained into the child.

So, what does Isoroku Takano have at all to do with this story you might ask? Be patient, I will answer. Have faith, it will all become very clear.

1885-1919, Texas and Elsewhere

Less than one year after the birth of Isoroku Takano, on the other side of the wide Pacific Ocean, Chester William Nimitz, on February 24, 1885, came into this world, son of Chester Bernard and Anna Nimitz. Baby Chester's father died before he was born, so Chester's grandfather, a German hotelier in the Texas hill country, served as a father figure for the boy's first five years. Having Germanic ancestors, Chester grew up fluent in both the English and German languages.

His grandfather, a former captain in the Confederate Army, encouraged Chester to work hard in school—the school: The United States Naval Academy. The Academy, impressed with his academic credentials, accepted him for enrollment in in 1901.

Chester adored his grandfather and loved to tell—and proudly regale—his fellow students about the old man's exploits—many of them undoubtedly tall tales.

"Your grandfather did all of those things?" one classmate asked Chester during an evening of story-telling in the billets.

Chester nodded. "Here's the best one: when Grandpa visited New York City, he saw a very realistic show involving a drastic tenement fire. He returned to his hotel and he worried what he would do if there was a fire. His hotel room was, after all, several floors up. Once in his room, he checked for an escape route and saw outside his bedroom window a rope, with a sign, in bold letters, FIRE ESCAPE. By this time, Grandpa was already in his nightshirt. But he decided to try out this "fire escape" anyway, and down the rope he slid, confident no one would see him in his nightshirt in the dark. Grandpa got down okay but had trouble, when he decided to climb up the rope. He tired before he could go up two floors and, in a state of both exhaustion and embarrassment, slipped into an open window while the female occupant began shrieking upon seeing this apparition in just a nightshirt appear out of nowhere. By then, everybody in the hotel was alerted and all Grandpa could do was to agree to pay for drinks at the bar for all."

The classmate shook his head. "Wait a minute. If he was still in his nightshirt, when he went down to the bar to buy drinks for all, where the hell in his nightshirt did he find the bucks to pay for the drinks?"

Chester cracked a wicked smile. "I guess that's a story for another evening."

Chester graduated the Naval Academy with distinction in 1905.

After graduating, Ensign Chester William Nimitz, found himself, in 1908, assigned to duty on the submarine, *Decatur*. It was not his choice for an assignment, but given the small size of those vessels, it did give Nimitz more of a chance for command experience. Always an experimenter, he attacked the problem of gasoline engines on these underwater crafts, where a spark could ignite the fuel and sent the sub down to the bottom. More than one American submarine ended up that way. Thus began his campaign to replace the gasoline engines in submarines with diesels—he became one of the reigning experts in that field.

Nimitz quickly acquired his own command—the bigger *Snapper* submarine. By 1911, in recognition of his work on diesel engines, the Navy ordered him to the shipyard in Quincy, Massachusetts, to oversee the installation of diesel engines in the submarine *Skyjack*, which became the first diesel-powered submarine.

After marrying Catherine Freeman, daughter of a ship broker, he took the *Skyjack* to sea and as the vessel performed some surface drills, one seaman slipped overboard. Nimitz, in the conning tower at the time, without hesitation, dove into the water and, overcoming a strong current, successfully pulled the seamen to safety.

By 1919, Nimitz, now a lieutenant commander, took over the command and supervision of the building and operation of the new submarine base at Pearl Harbor.

1901, Naval Academy at Eta Jima, Japan, and Thereafter, for Isoroku

Isoroku, in the meantime, obtained his education from Christian missionaries. Though he never became a Christian, through this education he did learn some English and was exposed to American culture and ways in his preteen years. Isoroku attended Nagaoka Middle School, where his teachers toughened him up on long marches and prepared him well for future military service. A good part of his educational training taught him the "Cho-Chu spirit," which emphasized individual responsibility, a trait that stayed with him for all his life. Life wasn't easy for him. His family, poverty stricken, made Isoroku determined to obtain some sort of scholarship. As an adult, Isoroku was shorter, at five-feet-three, than most of his contemporaries and he weighed only 125 pounds. He loved and trained hard at gymnastics and eventually built up his strength and athleticism. This bull-necked, broad-shouldered man, developed the confidence he needed to succeed in life. He also turned out to be a very emotional person and could burst into tears at some sad occurrence, including the death of someone he knew and cared for.

His hard work and determination paid off He placed second among the three hundred competing for entrance to the Imperial Naval Academy at Eta Jima. The Academy is set in a bay, on an island in the Inland Sea, backstopped by a large protective mountain.

Isoroku entered the Academy in 1901, making the Takano family extremely proud—and yes, even his hard-to-impress father. In school, Isoroku showed himself to be a leader and had an impish spirit that made him well liked among his peers. But one thing he would not do with his peers is drink. One reason: he could not hold his liquor and got very ill after more than one drink. He may have been a teetotaler, but he was a teetotaler who loved to gamble at games of chance—and he was good at it, usually coming out ahead. The gambling spirit of boldness and aggressiveness marked his subsequent naval career.

Isoroku likes to tell the story about the time Vice Admiral Tanimura Toyotaro bet him in the officers' dining room of the Navy Ministry that Isoroku could not pass a lighted match through the hole in a ten-sen piece without putting out the match. Of course, Isoroku took the bet, but however many times he tried, he lost. There was, in fact, a knack to it: the hole in a ten-sen piece varied somewhat in size, and Tanimura always kept one with a large hole in his pocket, giving Isoroku one with a small hole. Not knowing this, Isoroku, very frustrated, persisted in trying until he finally succeeded in getting the match through the ten-sen piece with the small hole—something that Tanimura could not do. When Tanimura admitted defeat and revealed the secret, Isoroku felt cheated. He was not happy and told Tanimura so.

Isoroku's mornings were filled with exercise and running to build military discipline and the afternoons were filled with military learning. It was not an easy life, especially as a freshman, who were regularly beaten by upperclassmen as an accepted form of discipline. Many simply became timid in their obedience which, I suppose, was the aim of the Academy.

The airplane, at this time only in the process of being developed, was not appreciated for its potential military uses, mostly because those uses were not yet obvious. So, Isoroku, at Eta Jima, specialized not in aircrafts, but in gunnery and, in 1904, graduated as an ensign, joining the new cruiser *Nisshin*, just at the time Japan had initiated a surprise attack against the Russian fleet near Port Arthur under the leadership of Vice Admiral Heihachiro Togo. After that battle, the Russians sued for peace. During the battle, in his capacity as gunnery officer, a Russian shell exploded near Isoroku, wounding him in the right leg and left hand where he lost his index and middle fingers. In his later frequent visits to the geisha district in Tokyo, he became known to the geishas as "Eighty Sen." Why? Because the charge for a regular ten-finger manicure was 100 sen (one yen) but his regular geisha charged him less than a yen—only eighty sen because he had only eight fingers. I guess she felt fair is fair and those geishas certainly had a sense of humor. A serious young man on duty, Isoroku did not shun the pleasures of off-duty life, particularly his visits to the geisha houses and the gambling establishments. Even more important to Isoroku, he had caught the eye of Admiral Togo and his naval career was off and running.

While Isoroku was advancing in his Navy career, after the Treaty of Portsmouth in 1905 limited Japanese military ship building, there were reports received of rampant discrimination against Japanese immigrants on the American West Coast. So the Japanese military establishment came to look on America as the primary potential future enemy of Japan and the Navy adopted war plans with that assumption in mind. Even the Soviets, Japan's perennial enemy, became of secondary importance in Japanese military thinking and planning.

But Isoroku had no such thoughts at this time even though in the future, he'd be in the group of Japanese naval officers selected to be sent to the United States several times, with an eye toward preparation for potential hostilities with the Americans.

The Emperors of Japan

By 1911, Isoroku was in command of a division of men aboard his ship. This was the year the beloved Meiji emperor died and Hirohito's father, Taisho, became emperor. But Taisho was in poor health and mentally unstable and, since 1921, Crown Prince Michinomiya, otherwise known as Hirohito, now 19 and born in 1901, had to act on his father's, the disabled emperor's, behalf on government matters. On Christmas day in 1926, Emperor Taisho died and, with his death, his oldest son—and the Meiji's emperor's grandson—Michinomiya Hirohito, became emperor, and in the process, he also became a living god and the 124th Son of Heaven. The shy, slight, short Emperor Hirohito would be revered and considered to be a descendant of the sun goddess Amaterasu, an important Shinto religious deity. The Japanese Constitution provided that "The emperor is sacred and inviolable." In other words, he cannot be removed for any reason and cannot be responsible for going beyond the limitations of the law in the exercise of his sovereignty. No court can try him because he is not subject to any law. The Japanese believed they were unique because of this and tended toward a militaristic state, having never lost a war in their entire existence.

Hirohito, left, and brothers in 1921

Emperor Hirohito's education was militaristic, his school modeled on the War and Naval Colleges, and he was taught by military instructors, especially on the lessons learned from the Russo-Japanese War. As he matured, he developed a passion for marine biology and, after marrying distant cousin, he sired seven children. Hirohito, morbidly shy, rarely ventured outside his Tokyo-located, huge, stone-walled Imperial Palace spread over 240 acres, and encircled by a wide moat. Hirohito, highly intelligent, kept himself informed on every detail of government.

Until 1945, Hirohito had never actually addressed his subjects, probably because of his squeaky, high-pitched voice. His proclamations were all printed and distributed throughout Japan. Thus, most of his subjects didn't even know what he sounded or looked like! His reign would be known as *Showa*, which in English is "Enlightened Peace." Ironically, as it turned out, the first eighteen years of this mild, seemingly peaceable, Hirohito's reign was anything but. An unlikely looking emperor, being short and round-shouldered, he shuffled around the palace in a wrinkled, sloppy outfit, peering through very thick glasses and seemingly, totally without vanity. A very frugal man, Hirohito distained from buying clothes and even the books he so enjoyed reading. Nevertheless, his subjects regarded him as a demi-god and his children were warned not to stare at his face, for they may go blind if they do.

Isoroku Takano Becomes a Yamamoto—His Early Years

During this time, Isoroku, appointed to the Naval College and recognized as someone to be promoted very quickly, became a lieutenant commander. After graduating the college in 1916, his parents died. This led him to a wealthy family and, in the Japanese tradition, he joined that family because it had no male heir to carry on its name. His family already had several older brothers to carry on the Takano name. Isoroku, on his part, benefitted financially from becoming part of the well-off family of Tatewaki Yamamoto who, in a rebellion against the emperor, lost his head—literally—and he had no sons. So Isoroku would now carry on the Yamamoto family name. The practice, not uncommon in Japan, was very convenient for both the Yamamoto family and Isoroku.

As part of this ritual, Isoroku formally renounced his family name of Takano and legally became Isoroku Yamamoto. He made that name famous in the naval history of World War II in the Pacific-and, not incidentally, in the geisha houses of Tokyo, which he frequented when ashore. At age thirty-three, on August 31, 1918, he married Reiko Mihashi, the daughter of a rich farmer, the nuptials held at the Navy Club in Shiba. It was a convenient, if loveless, marriage. They would have four children, two boys and two girls. His first child was a boy, thereby discharging his obligation to the Yamamoto family to leave them with a male heir to carry on their family name.

But that is not to say Isoroku lacked for romance—certainly not. He frequented the geisha quarter in Tokyo's Shimbashi district; he and the geishas who worked there enjoyed each other's company. They described him as something of a clown and very funny. By the mid-1930s, however, and already an admiral, he fell in love with a particular geisha, a famous beauty named Chiyoko, who worked in Tokyo under the professional name of Umeryu, or "Plum-Dragon". By 1935, she was his closest confidant and that relationship would last for the rest of his life. They would often meet at a country inn, checking in under false names. He'd often telephone Chiyoko Kawai and serenade her. The other geishas were amazed that she should spend so much time with this admiral, a suitor who clearly could not afford her.

Yamamoto had cruised the world, courtesy of the Japanese Navy, visiting China, Australia, Korea, and the West Coast of the United States. In 1919, as a commander, he travelled to the United States, first class, visiting the West Coast, Washington, D.C., and ending up at his ultimate destination, Boston, where he studied English at Harvard University. He stayed there until 1921. He devoured everything American, from composer George Gershwin to boxer Jack Dempsey. And his love of gambling could be satiated by bridge, poker, and roulette. He had the reputation of a bold gambler who rarely lost. He wasn't the only Japanese naval officer touring the United States. Others were also sent to the United States. The feeling of Tokyo's military leaders: Japan should know its enemy. Yamamoto was to study America's petroleum industry because the Japanese Navy constantly worried about having enough fuel and felt it to be one of its greatest problems. Unlike most Japanese, who acquired their English from Japanese teachers, he learned it directly from the horse's mouth, so to speak—American teachers—so that while most Japanese had trouble pronouncing their ell's, Yamamoto did not. He had exceptional command of the English language and its pronunciation.

In December 1919, Yamamoto became a full commander in the Imperial Navy while continuing to absorb all things American. Now, aviation had peaked his interest, studying carefully General Billy Mitchell's claims, publicized in the American newspapers, that his planes could sink battleships. The American Navy publicly rejected that idea as preposterous—but not Yamamoto. In a demonstration, Mitchell had sunk an old battleship. This impressed the young Japanese officer. In an interview with a *National Geographic* writer, Yamamoto, quite presciently, opined that "the most important ship of the future will be a ship to carry airplanes." His language was quoted in the magazine.

As Yamamoto advanced in the Navy, this belief would become one of his mantras, even though he had been trained in the tactics of battleships, destroyers, and cruisers. The problem was the heads of the Navy were blackshoe men—meaning they were strictly battleship, cruiser and destroyer men—what they call surface sailors—with not one brownshoe—the naval aviators—among them! When he returned to Japan, Yamamoto tried carefully to explain to his disbelieving superiors that "I could destroy your battleships with torpedo planes that flew off one of my aircraft carriers! Of that there is no doubt in my mind, I assure you, gentlemen. You should know that the fiercest serpent could be overcome by a swarm of ants. And that's what my planes are; swarms of ants, ready to sink and kill!"

While visiting Europe in 1923, Yamamoto was promoted to captain. Upon his return to Japan, the Navy assigned him to command the cruiser *Fuji*.

CHAPTER ONE

Early Career of Yamamoto

Fall of 1924, Kasumigaura Naval Air Station Barracks

AFTER HIS TOUR ABOARD the *Fuji*, Captain Yamamoto arrived at Kasumigaura Air Station, appointed as executive officer and director of studies. Arriving at his new assignment, none of the students at the base had any idea of who he was. He was a captain and soon to become second in command at the Air Station.

The short man, barely five-feet-three, portly, with close cropped hair did not impress he students, full of themselves as pilots in training.

Yusuo a second-year student, shook his head. "He won't last long. Where did they find him? He's barely five feet tall! How is that roly-poly guy going to command *us?*"

Kazuki, in the same class, laughed. "We'll make short work of him, even if he is a captain. What does that dumb guy know about flying anyway?"

Yusuo nodded. "We'll see what happens at the school assembly tomorrow."

The Next Morning, at School Assembly

Yamamoto watched calmly from the stage as he looked over the students filing into the assembly hall. When they were all seated he moved up to the lectern.

The hum of conversation, and some snickers, filled the room. Yamamoto quickly stopped it.

"I am Captain Isoroku Yamamoto, your new executive officer, and you'd better pay attention."

That stopped the hum.

"The first thing I will talk on are the dress regulations. You may have thought you joined a boy's adventure club where you can dress anyway you like and be satisfied looking and dressing like a bunch of bums."

Yamamoto pointed to his own scalp, gray and shorn to the skull. "If you want to stay in this aviation class, you will get rid of all long hair and look like me. You will not dress sloppily but act like the naval aviators you will become—that is if you are skilled enough and lucky. You might not appreciate it yet, but flying is a dangerous and deadly business. It is not a gift from the gods to you. You don't fly by instinct but must rely on your instruments and that you can only do by learning how—every day—in your classes.

"This will be no picnic for you. It will involve intense physical training, impossible navigation problems, night flying and, I can't stress this too strongly, absolute obedience in the cockpit. If you can't cut it in any of these areas, you will be banished and never allowed back on this base at Lake Kasumigaura. This is no game. If you don't wise up, you're out!"

The students quickly found him to be deadly serious. Over the next eighteen months, Yamamoto transformed the playboy school into an elite training facility, graduating only the very best, first-rate, pilots. He had installed oxygen masks in the planes for his flyers and pushed his engineers to study ways of extending a plane's life.

But Yamamoto would not ask his cadets to do anything he wasn't willing to do, so he too took flight training, becoming a Navy pilot and, at the same time, developing a better understanding of carrier pilot problems, an understanding other types of naval leaders did not possess. In the process, he became a superb leader in naval avionics.

But one thing he would not do with his cadets is drink alcohol. "When I was an instructor at the Naval Academy" he explained quite frankly to them, "one evening, I went out drinking with my students, and I got so drunk I ended up in a ditch and there I slept until the next morning! That told me I can't take alcohol and, from then on, I stopped drinking—totally."

Captain Yamamoto also had the responsibility to keep track of and observe all the activities of the United States Navy, particularly as to whether it was adhering to the Naval Treaty of 1922, which called for the destruction of certain types of warships. In carrying out all his responsibilities he came to appreciate the power of the naval aviation arm and pushed for the building of more aircraft carriers, which Japan did, including converting some cruiser warships into carriers (permitted by the Treaty), and then, pushed for the first ship, built from the keel up, strictly as an aircraft carrier. Yamamoto noted, relying on his sources in the United States, that the Americans were also both building some carriers from scratch and converting several cruisers into carriers.

January 1925, Washington, D.C.

Yamamoto arrived in Washington, in his position as a Japanese naval attaché. Kiyoshi Hasegawa, the departing naval attaché, welcomed his replacement.

"Before I leave for Japan," Hasegawa informed the new arrival, "I am going to visit Havana."

Yamamoto eyes widened. "I hear it's the loosest city in the Western Hemisphere; that anything goes—gambling, women, cigars. You name it, they have it. May I join you? I hear they play roulette there in the gambling houses—and I love the gambling tables, especially roulette!"

Hasegawa smiled. "Be my guest, I'd love the company."

Yamamoto gambled, won, and came back with a large bunch of Havana cigars to give out to his visitors in his capacity as naval attaché.

Yamamoto gambled at bridge with his American counterparts and they respected his abilities and his intellect. So much so that they convinced naval intelligence to maintain a dossier on him. But his job was not all play. While he enjoyed the game of bridge immensely, playing with American naval officers gave him an opportunity, which he did not pass up, to learn much about the U.S. Navy.

One surprised American lieutenant told Yamamoto during a bridge game, "I am surprised at your abilities at the game of bridge. It is not a Japanese game and I have found very few Japanese with your abilities at this card game."

Yamamoto smiled. "Cards are no great mystery to me. As you may know, our language has no alphabet and each word or syllable is represented by a specific character. So, I have to keep *five thousand* ideographs in my head." Now Yamamoto laughed out loud. "Compared to that, it's a child's play for me to remember fifty-two cards."

He did not let gambling interfere with his duties, one of the most important of which was to observe all the activities of the U.S. Navy, particularly its adherence to the Naval Treaty of 1922, calling for the reduction of naval warships. His major concern was in carriers and aviation. Thanks in part to his influence, Japan led the world in carrier building.

The Naval Treaty of 1922 encouraged the building of carriers because it allowed any nation to convert a ship under 33,000 tons to an aircraft carrier without penalty. Thus many cruisers, rather than being destroyed under the Treaty, were converted to carriers and perfectly legal under the agreement. The U.S. carriers *Lexington* and *Saratoga*, which would play an important part in the coming war, were actually converted cruisers. By 1942, these carriers had been significantly upgraded with radar technology and better and more antiaircraft guns.

USS Lexington

All his activities were not solely business. He studied the life and writings of Abraham Lincoln. He could identify with him as a man born in poverty like himself, living in a simple log cabin not much different from his parents' modest dwelling in the city of Nagaoka. But it was the character of Lincoln that appealed most to Yamamoto. An emancipator of the poor, of woman, of slaves, of humanity—this Yamamoto admired enormously. Lincoln, like himself, made many mistakes. But this made him human and gave him the ability to lead people, enhancing his appeal.

On Yamamoto's return home, he discovered many in the Navy were not happy with the 6/10 terms of the treaty. Admiral Mineichi Kato confronted Yamamoto.

"How could you accept a limitation of 6 ships for us and 10 ships for our enemy," Kato asked accusingly. "The Americans are offering us the crust of the pie without the filling," he huff "You should have held out for a 7 to 10 ratio."

"First of all, it's the same ratio we've always had," Yamamoto retorted with some irritation. "If you had thought about it and studied our budgets for the past few years, you'd understand that naval spending, before the treaty, had ballooned to thirty-one percent of our budget, almost bankrupting our government. Now, with the treaty, that spending has been reduced to twenty-one percent!" Yamamoto, not one to back away from a good fight, stood jowl to jowl with Kato. "You should be thanking us, not carping and criticizing. Do your homework before you open your mouth!"

Hirohito's Japan was not as calm as it seemed. Packed with 80 million people, it was one of the most crowded nations in the world. Poverty was widespread and government corruption rampant, often stirring up unrest. The victories over the Russians at the turn of the century went to the heads of the military and, accordingly, Army and Navy spending ballooned, uncontrolled by the civilian government. The military, so powerful a political force, enjoyed virtual freedom from civilian control.

Yamamoto knew the power of the military over our civilian ministers actually hurt Japan. The generals and admirals have access to Emperor Hirohito that is denied to the civilian members of the government. Under the Constitution, the military can prevent the formation of a cabinet it does not like by simply refusing to release its officers to hold portfolios in the government with the result that no cabinet can be formed. If it is displeased with the government, the military can cause its dissolution simply by recalling its cabinet representatives. It left the civilian leaders at the mercy of the military and guaranteed the military the absolute right to interfere legally in politics. It is not a good system, Yamamoto knew. He felt some part of the military, specifically the Imperial Army, is leading our nation down a very dangerous path.

Yamamoto's concerns would soon evidence themselves on the rise of the Kwantung Army, to be Japan's Army in China. It would become a law unto itself and out of control, making war in China on its own authority, and brooking no interference by Japan's civilian government. Yamamoto and the Navy leaders were not happy about that, but for now, there was little they could do. In effect, the government found itself powerless to restrain the Army and, in the end, found itself having to justify the military's actions to the world.

The young Army officers were a serious problem—often they were ultranationalists who would brook no opposition and were not afraid to gun down anyone who got in their way. They could become a danger even to their own politicians—and a danger it was because while their goals were usually vague, these ultranationalists pursued them with a passionate fanaticism. Assassinations often went unpunished or lightly punished. The more hard-headed generals used the threat of these ultranationalists to cow the civilian ministers and extort whatever they wished from them. Tojo was one such Army leader—and it was these leaders who were to guide the Imperial Japanese Army during the threatened world war.

Less xenophobic and less politically influential than its Army counterparts, the Imperial Navy faced a never-ending crusade to obtain a greater share of the national budget and, but for the Army, it would, because Japan, an island nation like Great Britain, could only be attacked from the sea and even Japan's Imperial Army could do nothing unless its troops could be delivered safely to the Asia mainland or elsewhere. In short, the Army depended on the Navy without giving the Navy its due!

1927 was a year of change. It was on Christmas day of 1926 that the Japanese Emperor Taisho died, and his eldest son, Hirohito, began 1927 as the god-like emperor. Also in 1927, Charles Lindbergh flew solo across the Atlantic further supporting the importance of aviation, Japan had launched the thirty-thousand-ton aircraft carrier *Akagi*, followed by the large carrier, *Kaga*.

Emperor Hirohito

On his return to Japan, Yamamoto lectured the Japanese military on the need to understand the Americans, which, he felt, it was failing to do.

One opportunity arose on his visit to Naval headquarters in Tokyo. It seems that while Yamamoto was enjoying himself in America, Japanese naval strategists were tackling the problem of confronting the superior American fleet. Japan began building ships designed to give it the advantage over the Americans. They scrapped any comfort and defensive armament for their sailors for maximum speed and power, together with superiority in long-range guns and torpedoes.

Yamamoto met with one of the top naval strategists at Naval headquarters in Tokyo, who explained the Navy thinking: "If there is a war with the United States, the Americans, with their superior number of ships, will try to take the battle close to our home waters. And then we will have them facing our superior ships, assuring us every possible advantage in such a situation."

Yamamoto shook his head, at the strategist's ignorance. "Look, I learned a lot about the Americans serving as naval attaché in Washington. You do realize, don't you, that the United States had an incredible industrial base that supports their technological advances? I have seen personally their assembly lines and if they put their minds to it, they could become a mighty military machine, even dwarfing the enormous arms race of the Great War in 1914. We, on the other hand, don't have one tenth the production capacity that is available to the Americans. Why, their vast agricultural heartland alone could feed many armies!

"Just look what a retired American naval officer did," Yamamoto continued. "Lieutenant Commander Richard Byrd flew over the North Pole, relying *solely* on navigation instruments developed by the Americans. We must develop such scientific instrumentation before we even consider confronting the United States."

Yamamoto sighed. "No, we can't beat America and therefore, should not pick a fight them now or in the near future."

But much of Japan's military, like the strategist he could not convince, were not so pessimistic of their chances. Distaining, in 1918 to endorse the international protocol banning chemical and biological warfare, the next year it also refused to sign the full Geneva Prisoner of War Convention. The ministers accepted the arguments of the Army and Navy leaders that the clause was too lenient because the emperor's soldiers would never allow themselves to be captured—military regulations prohibited it, requiring them to kill themselves if necessary. It was, as it turned out, a decision that greatly impacted their treatment of prisoners of war and the military wounded in World War Two.

CHAPTER TWO

Japan Flexes Her Muscles

**1929 to 1933, Aboard the Aircraft Carrier, *Akagi*;
Attending the London Disarmament Conference**

Captain Yamamoto assumed command of the *Akagi*, a sleek, fast, 30,000-ton aircraft carrier, converted from a battle cruiser, and carrying seventy-two planes, and launched late 1927, followed by its sister ship, the *Kaga*. The Japanese naval hierarchy had begun to take notice of that brash naval officer who supported building up Japan's naval aviation capabilities. Not only could he handle this large vessel with skill, he had also a fine relationship with the crew and pilots. He instituted the training of his pilots in night flying and night landings, convincing them to trust their instruments. The powers in Tokyo took notice. As captain of the ship, Yamamoto had one sacred duty that American ship captains did not—to make sure, if his ship was sinking, to take down the emperor's photo and see that it is safely bundled into a lifeboat. Only then would the captain feel free to go down with his ship.

While on the Japanese carrier, command of the air unit rested with the captain of the ship. Once in the air, the responsibility became that of the attack leader. Usually, there was a great deal of tension between the two, but Yamamoto tried hard to work closely with his attack leaders, thereby avoiding those tensions.

He spent only a year as captain of the *Akagi*. In 1930, Yamamoto was promoted to rear admiral and was selected to attend the Naval Disarmament Conference in London. His growing convictions about carrier aircraft were now being heard and, in 1933, he was appointed Commander of Carrier Division One. He had assembled torpedo planes and long-range bombers, all capable of flying off a carrier deck. But most of all, he needed a decent fighter plane for his carriers to protect the bombers from enemy planes. He worked with Mitsubishi to produce one and it came up with a Navy fighter it called the Zero, named such because it had a double zero on its fuselage in honor of the 2600th anniversary of Jimmu (1940). Yamamoto tried the fighter plane out and liked it. The plane was built around radial engine developing 951 horsepower on takeoff. Considering that the plane was lightly armored, the engine had to provide extreme maneuverability, which it did, permitting it to fly rings around the then existing Allied fighter planes. Being faster and more maneuverable that the American fighters it turned out perfect for a dogfight. On the other side of the ledger, because of its light armor and lack of self-sealing fuel tanks, it did not take much to bring the Zero down—but only if you could get and keep the plane in your gun sights! Yamamoto gave the go-ahead and soon these planes were being produced in impressive numbers. But if the Japanese productions lines were modern, their plane delivery system—ox carts—certainly was not!

The one thing Yamamoto regretted about his Zero is that it provided the Army with an effective weapon to kill the Chinese and ruthlessly crush nationalist aspirations in Korea. He never intended the plane's use for such aggression and it frustrated him greatly.

1934, London, Southampton

After the Great War, during which the Japanese were allies of Britain and the United States, Japan ended up coerced into the 5-5-3 Naval Limitation Treaty whereby it was limited to building three capital warships for every five built by the Americans and British. In the post-war years, Japan pushed for vigorously for a higher ratio, whereby it could build more capital ships, but to no avail. Tokyo sent Yamamoto to London as their chief delegate. He arrived in Southampton on the morning of October 18, 1934 and called a press conference. In front of the assembled reporters, and in perfect English, Yamamoto began. "Japan can no longer submit to the ratio system. We cannot compromise on that point. I repeat, there is no possible chance of compromise. We need a new treaty—or none at all."

A reporter yelled a question. "Then, Admiral, what's the point of meeting?"

Yamamoto smiled. "An excellent question. I suppose the only point is to advise the other signatories to the treaty that we are giving notice at this time, as required by the treaty, that there will be no renewal of the treaty, at least with Japan as a member. As far as I am concerned, the ratio system and this treaty are dead!"

Thus Japan had now officially given notice on the scheduled expiration of the treaty, on its part.

Yamamoto, once a strong supporter of the treaty, now had some doubts on the limitations the treaty imposed on Japan. Now Vice Minister of the Japanese Navy, Yamamoto called the naval ratio imposed on Japan as "this national degradation." But he was conflicted because still, he knew that the Treaty has provided benefits of preventing an unrestricted race to build bigger navies.

He led, on behalf of Japan, the negotiations regarding the treaty. Though he had a total command of the English language, he used Japanese in his negotiations. That gave him extra time to note his adversaries' reactions during the translation.

The American negotiator pressed Yamamoto. "Admiral, why has Japan, a strong supporter of the treaty, now changed its mind?"

Yamamoto looked the questioner in the eye. "Simply, the advances made in aviation and the refueling of ships at sea had so shrunk the oceans that it was impossible to maintain a strategic balance under the treaty, even in Japan's home waters, and that, to me, was unacceptable.

"Let me make it very clear to my compatriots from America and Britain that Japan will pull out from the current treaty and leave—unless you Western Powers are willing to negotiate a new treaty without limitations."

They were not, so he picked up and left.

But between sessions Yamamoto developed a good rapport with the Americans, especially with his capable American English, skillful banter, and small talk. Notwithstanding being unable to agree with his position on behalf of Japan, they still liked him.

On his way back to Japan, Yamamoto stopped in Berlin, with a courtesy call to his Ambassador and German Foreign Minister Joachim von Ribbentrop. He declined, however, an invitation to meet with Hitler, who, by now, had been in power for two years.

He did not stick around for any further invitations but boarded the Trans-Siberian Railway to take him most of the way home to Japan.

1936-1937, Tokyo, Naval Headquarters

On returning to Japan after he told the British and American representatives that the Treaty, without serious changes was dead, Yamamoto admitted that he was conflicted on that position because he, unlike his superiors, realized that by the Treaty, Japan was able to avoid an arms race against the Americans, a race, given their less developed economy, it would surely lose. Unfortunately, these brutal economic realities went right over the heads of Japan's leaders and the fleet faction of the Imperial Navy violently opposed the treaties and any renewals of them. So, given orders to scrap the Treaty, that is precisely what a reluctant Yamamoto did. Nationalism simply overcame logical economics when Japan advised it would withdraw from the Treaty in 1937.

The 'treaty faction' of the Navy, which Yamamoto supported, opposed the 'fleet faction', and favored coming to an accommodation with the United States on ship building.

The fleet faction, controlled by the political right-wing within the Navy, including many influential admirals, wanted nullification of the Washington Naval Treaty and permit unlimited naval growth to build the most powerful navy possible, thus challenging the naval supremacy of the United States and the British Empire.

Yamamoto had the opportunity to lecture his 'fleet faction' fellow officers. "The most important matter is a country's will to defend itself, not necessarily military strength alone. Remember the fate of the Spanish Armada? The British, with numerically inferior numbers, used the weather to defeat the Spaniards. And how the divine winds, the *kamikaze*, had struck the forces of Kublai Khan and destroyed most of his enormous invasion fleet and saved Japan from the Mongol invaders. Our *kodo*, or imperial way, shall power us regardless of the limitations imposed by the treaties."

But the fleet faction remained unconvinced and the debate, throughout the early thirties, continued about building more and better ships. Some of the fleet faction did not limit themselves to debate but tried to take get their way through assassinations and attempted assassination and, at one point, wounded Prime Minister Osachi Hamaguchi.

As soon as the naval limitation treaty lapsed at the end of 1936, a great naval expansion got underway in Japan, with the building of two super battleships, the *Yamato* and the *Musashi*, which were the world's largest and most heavily armed battleships with record size 18-inch guns. Great stress was placed on building super ships like this. But Yamamoto, now Navy vice minister, locked horns with the battleship admirals who saw no future in the aircraft carrier.

Yamamoto confronted his boss, Admiral Osami Nagano, head of the Navy Ministry. "You must realize, Admiral, that no navy, including ours, can be successful in future wars if its fleet is not built around ships carrying planes. We need aircraft carriers and we need them now! The whole shape of naval warfare is changing before our eyes. The old system is outmoded."

Nagano knitted his brow. "What do you mean, outmoded? With these super battleships, we're almost invincible! They will help us win the decisive battle."

The concept of *haiku*, that is, achieving total victory by one decisive battle, has been around a long time in the Japanese culture and clearly influenced its military leaders.

Yamamoto shook his head. "Impressive super battleships? Maybe to the layman. But invincible? Certainly not! Those battleship admirals, and opposing the building of aircraft carriers, will be our undoing. The opposition to aircraft carriers are asses, pure and simple! Let me show you why."

Yamamoto stood up and moved to the center of the room. There, he spread his arms as if he were an airplane. "Picture it, Admiral. The aircraft carrier could send out scout aircraft hundreds of miles." With his arms still spread, he roamed around the room. "When the enemy is found, we will then send out the bombers that have been warmed up and just waiting to take off from our carriers." Yamamoto moved, as if in take-off position. "We can take the fight to the enemy before their surface ships were close enough to do battle. We have built bomber planes that can take off from carriers and could fly hundreds of miles to the enemy carrying 2000-pound bomb loads. Battleships could be bombed out of existence before they knew we were there or close enough to fire their own guns, no matter how big and long-range those guns were." He hovered over an ash tray sitting on a table and dramatically, swiped it onto the floor. "The battle could be won—or lost—without our fleet ever seeing an enemy surface vessel—or they seeing us!"

Nagano rubbed his chin. "What you say may be true. Also, the ships we are building, I realize, are more powerful than ever before. But aren't they effectively tethered to land bases by their insatiable need for fuel? There's your problem, Yamamoto!"

Yamamoto nodded. "Absolutely! It's a problem I hope we can solve, But not by building bigger and bigger fuel guzzling battleships that are easy prey for warplanes."

15

"The fleet faction," Nagano reminded Yamamoto, "the aggressive faction of the Navy, says we could get copper from the Philippines, petroleum from the Dutch East Indies and Indo-China, and rubber from Malaysia."

Yamamoto thought for a moment. "Perhaps, but the last thing we want is to precipitate a war with Britain, France, and the United States, and moving Japanese troops into those countries would almost surely do that. I don't have to remind you that we are putting ourselves in the position of opposing the combined power of the United States and Britain, two of the strongest naval powers on the seas!"

Admiral Nagano grunted. "You may get a war whether you like it or not. If so, we must win the decisive battle at sea and it is leaders like yourself, well-versed in naval tactics and having supreme self confidence in your own abilities, to get others to carry out your orders. That, Yamamoto-san, will win us the day."

Yamamoto nodded. "But we are not helping ourselves by our Army's involvement in that quagmire they euphemistically call the 'China Incident.' It's really a full-scale war against billions of Chinese and we have no control over our own Kwantung Army over there and the Kwantung Army has little control over the fall-out in China, which comes back to bite us in the butt."

Admiral Nagano frowned. "Yes, the right hand, the Army, does not tell the Navy, the left hand, what it is doing. With that I agree. The 'Incident' in China looks like a lot more than that, and the Army is having trouble controlling things now; and they are trying to sweep it all under the rug. But look at the bright side—we do now control all of Manchuria and its raw material resources."

Yamamoto laughed, derisively but without humor. "Let's call it what it is: an all-out war. And let's face it, the resources we need for war—fuel and rubber—we don't have. Our excursions into China are killing our relations with the Americans. Now the Army is using chemical weapons on humans in the city of Harbin in Manchuria. How unconscionable!"

Nagano shrugged. "The emperor has sided with the Army. It is out of my hands."

Yamamoto slammed the table with his open palm. "I am so angry over wasting our resources in China like this. In protest, I'm giving up smoking my expensive cigars from England and Cuba! You can have them if you want."

Nagano smiled. "I smoke cigarettes, not cigars. But you should not get so upset over something you have no control."

"Perhaps," Yamamoto retorted, "but when this craziness is over, I going to smoke until it comes out of my ass!"

Nagano laughed. "If you give the cigars to me, I'll keep them for you until this China shit is all over."

Then Nagano's eyes narrowed. "At the War Ministry, our general staff people were very annoyed because it seems the Army policy on China, without consultation, has already been decided. There's just nothing you or I can do. The Army has no real desire for a solution. They succumbed to the demands of their lower-ranking officers who want to go to war. They love it! Those young turks almost overthrew the government last year, nearly killing the prime minister and assassinating several high-ranking officials including the Lord Privy Seal Makino. After the emperor declared martial law in Tokyo, the Imperial Guards put down the rebellion. But the danger persists that they might rise up again."

Indeed, around 1932, many small landowners and shop keeping families were facing hard times and they joined the services and became Army and Navy officers. When poverty haunted their families, the young officers turned rebellious, taking their frustrations out on the politicians, courts, and even their own superiors. Joining secret cabals, these young officers called for action by assassination as well as territorial expansion for raw materials and food. Nagumo feared these young Turks and he looked at Yamamoto. "You have to be careful. Stop broadcasting your critical views about the Kwantung Army and particularly to the fleet faction of the Navy, who are all pining for war against the United States."

"Like hell, I'll stop," Yamamoto said angrily. "You think I'm not aware that you are part of the 'fleet faction?' You know very well that Japan would be committing national suicide going to war against the United States. I will not stop warning our people, unless I'm ordered to. Just this year, the Hirota government, dedicated to peace and civilian government control, fell because of a dispute with an Army that's not interested in peace. The Army has got all the politicians by the neck with the simple control mechanism after it got the government to pass a constitutional amendment that the war minister in the cabinet must *be an active Army officer*. If the Army doesn't like what the government is doing, it can dissolve it by simply having its officer resign from the cabinet—no cabinet, no government. No one in the Army would serve in a new Hirota government, so he had to resign. That maniac, General Hideki Tojo, was promoted to head the Kwantung Army. If you think things were bad in China before, now Tojo is calling for further preemptive strikes in China before Chiang Kai-shek grows stronger. The Army has already created an incident at the Marco Polo Bridge in Beijing and is using that as an excuse to go on the offensive. And the damn *Zaibatsu*, the Japanese cartels, like Mitsubishi and Mitsui, oppose the naval treaties and support all these conflicts and yearn for even more because it means increased business in trucks, tanks, planes, and ships." Yamamoto shook his head in frustration.

Yamamoto waited, but Nagano did not react.

So, Yamamoto continued. "Well, in the meantime, I will continue my work on improving our aircraft. My training as a naval pilot should prove most helpful because I know what our flyers need. Our Zero fighter, I am confident is the best in the world and can fly circles around the best planes the American and British have. And now we are getting deliveries of a twin-engined attack plane that can fly long distances with a heavy bomb load. And we have almost finished developing the giant four-engine Kawanishi flying boat."

Nagano raised his eyes. "Flying boat?"

Yamamoto nodded. "Yes, they will be used for long-range searching so that our bombers could bomb targets hundreds of miles away or attack an enemy fleet, before they knew what hit them. That, Admiral Nagano, is why battleships are becoming obsolete and wars will be won by carriers and their attack planes. And if it

18

comes to that, that is how we will win the decisive sea battle against *any enemy*. I agree with American General Billy Mitchell that naval warplanes were far superior to these obsolete battleships and the future of the Navy is in aircraft carriers."

Nagano looked at Yamamoto. "I am concerned. Since you were appointed vice minister of the Navy, the fleet faction has expressed its unhappiness at your appointment because first, you were instrumental in negotiating the now moribund Naval Treaty, which limited our ship building, and second, because of your oft-stated beliefs that it would be suicide to go to war with the United States. You must be careful. Many in the military right-wing are not above attempts at assassination."

"What do you suggest?"

Nagano shrugged. "Just be careful and aware of the dangers in this current climate."

But Yamamoto continued to work behind the scenes and, later in the year, he had a new boss, Admiral Mitsumasa Yonai, a former Commander-in-Chief of the Combined Fleet and a political moderate. But these were not moderate times in Japan. Yamamoto continued to oppose the Army's attempts to oust the moderate civilian government. The political climate became charged and both Yonai and Yamamoto were threatened with assassination by the ultranationalists, who were slowly gaining control.

The German influence was strong in the Army and the ultranationalists pushed to join with Germany and Italy in what would be called the Tripartite Pact.

Sponsored newsreels presented Hitler as a heroic figure and Hitler's book, *Mein Kampf,* was becoming a best seller in Japan (of course, Hitler's unflattering references to Asians was conveniently edited out). And indeed, in 1940, Hitler looked unbeatable in Europe. The prime minister asked for unanimous support since it has already been decided to join the Pact. But a furious Yamamoto persisted, still arguing against joining the pact and thereby avoiding war with the United States. Yamamoto went so far as to submit to the government his opposition to the Pact, in writing:

A war between Japan and the United States would be a major calamity for the world, and for Japan it would mean, after several years of war already, acquiring yet another powerful enemy— an extremely perilous matter for the nation. If, after Japan and America had inflicted serious wounds one each other, the Soviet Union or Germany should step in with an eye to world hegemony, what country would be able to check it? If Germany should prove victorious [in the war with Britain] Japan might look to its goodwill as a friendly nation, but if Japan at the time happened to be in a wounded state, its advances would carry no weight; a friendly nation can only look for friendly treatment so long as it has powerful forces of its own. The reason why Japan is respected, and its hand frequently sought in alliance is that it has actual power in the shape of its naval and other forces. It is necessary therefore that both Japan and America should seek every means to avoid a direct clash, and Japan should under no circumstances conclude an alliance with Germany.

This only served to inflame the conflict between the Army and the Navy and things seemed on the verge of a civil war; Navy detachments were called ashore to protect their high officers.

CHAPTER THREE

War on the Horizon; Yamamoto Takes over the Imperial Combined Fleet

1937, Washington, D.C., United States Naval Headquarters

STRANGELY, IN 1937, YAMAMOTO was of one mind with Admiral Ernst King, who himself had commanded the American heavy aircraft carrier *Lexington* in the early thirties. King argued with passion that the battleships belonged to a bygone era and that the next war will be fought with airplanes from aircraft carriers—and he was no more believed by his superiors, than was Yamamoto, in Japan. King became a vice admiral, and the Commander, Aircraft, Battle Force in 1938 and, in an eerie prelude, staged his own successful simulated naval air raid on Pearl Harbor, thereby showing that the base was dangerously vulnerable to aerial attack, although again, he was not taken seriously until Dec. 7, 1941. In the fall of 1940, King became head of the Atlantic Fleet.

Late 1937, Yangtze River, Up River from Nanjing, China

The Japanese Kwantung Army had just captured Shanghai and began marching on Nanjing. The Japanese general signaled Navy flyers to attack "enemy vessels" on the Yangtse River. The young Navy pilots, chomping at the bit for action, were only too glad to flex their muscles and the fact that the target vessel flew a large

American flag went by the boards as the naval flyers bombed and sank and American gunboat, the *USS Panay* and three steamers of the Standard Oil Company. At the same time, Japanese Army artillery on shore attacked three British ships on the river.

A furious Navy Vice Minister Yamamoto knew he would be facing storm of anger from the United States. He rushed to the American Embassy where Ambassador John Grew was preparing to leave, in the expectation that he would be recalled at any time. Grew, appointed by Roosevelt, had been a classmate of the president at Groton and Harvard. His affection and rare understanding of all things Japanese, as well having a wife who grew up in Japan and had an excellent command of the Japanese language, made him the ideal choice for ambassador to Japan.

Grew invited Yamamoto into his office. Grew, a tall man with bushy, heavy eyebrows, a moustache and graying hair, stared at his guest through narrowed eyes, waiting.

Hat in hand, Yamamoto looked crestfallen. "Ambassador, I am deeply apologetic for the sinking of the *Panay*."

Grew accepted his apologies, but Yamamoto knew his own protestations were not felt by those young Navy flyers themselves. They were jubilant at what they accomplished and some of their senior officers were no better.

Yamamoto wasted no time, recalling Admiral Mitsunami to Tokyo, the officer in charge of the task force that sunk the *Panay*. Navy Minister Yonai and Yamamoto confronted Mitsunami.

"What were you thinking when you permitted the attack on the American gun boat? We are not at war with the United States, but thanks to you, we may yet be!" Yamamoto growled.

Mitsunami shrugged. "The Army requested the action against the aggressive gunship, so I felt we had no choice."

"No choice?" Yamamoto asked angrily. "What precisely was the *Panay* doing that threatened the Army or your forces?"

"Personally, I cannot answer that. I do not know. I depended on the Army's report and request to take out the vessel."

Yonai shook his head. "So, admiral, to 'protect' the large Army garrison from the small gunboat, you committed an act of war against a non-belligerent. Does that about sum it up?"

Mitsunami just sat there, silent, his eyes cast downward.

"Admiral," said Yonai, "you are relieved of command and may I suggest you retire from the Navy, while you still can! You are dismissed."

Mitsunami stood up, hat in hand, and silently left the room.

"I would have cashiered him out of the Navy right on the spot," Yamamoto growled.

Yonai frowned. "I know that you, as well as myself, are part of the 'treaty faction' of the Navy, which seeks accommodation with other countries like the United States and Britain. But face it, there are more of the Navy siding with the "fleet faction', which would like nothing better than to go to war against the Americans and British. So, I would not excite them by firing Mitsunami outright. Let's just stick him where he can do no harm!"

June 1939, Tokyo, Naval Headquarters

The fleet faction of the Navy and other rightists stepped up their campaign against Yamamoto so that he could no longer meet his favorite geisha, Chiyoko, on the weekends, at her Tokyo house, as often as he desired. He feared for her safety when she was in his presence. Instead, he stayed at a friend's house, where he could get his clothes cleaned and play spirited games of mahjong, tossing the tiles and singing in a loud voice, without anyone objecting. Occasionally, when he couldn't fall asleep, he would call Chiyoko in the middle of the night and, in his deep voice, serenade her with some song he'd just learned. As a matter of fact, he had a quite good singing voice and she loved hearing from him in that manner—even it was in the wee hours of the morning.

July 1939, Tokyo, Naval Headquarters

Navy Minister Admiral Yonai called his vice minister into his office "Yamamoto, sorry for the interruption, but I need to speak to you."

Yamamoto smiled. "That's okay, I was just writing poetry and practicing my calligraphy."

"You've done a lot of that art. You must be very good at it."

Yamamoto shook his head. "Not really. A friend of mine, Admiral Shiozawa, was browsing in an art shop and came across a framed piece of calligraphy signed by me. 'How much?' he asked the shopkeeper. 'Eighty yen,' the shopkeeper replied. My friend frowned. 'Eighty yen? But that calligraphy is not very good and not worth buying at that price.' The shopkeeper shrugged. 'I agree, it's not very good, but the frame cost me 90 yen and you are getting a big ten-yen bargain by buying it for 80 yen!'"

Yamamoto roared with laughter and Yonai joined in.

Yonai's features turned serious.

"What's the matter?" Yamamoto asked.

"Prime Minister Hiranuma Kiichiro's government is about to fall over the issue of the Tripartite Pact with Germany and Italy. He doesn't want the pact, but his Army cabinet minister does. You know that under our constitution, if the Army minister resigns from the cabinet, the cabinet—and his government—fall."

Yamamoto nodded. "I know, it is a stupid system that gives the Army inordinate power over any existing government. If it doesn't like what the prime minister is doing, the Army man simply resigns and that ends the government and requires a new prime minister."

Yonai gave Yamamoto a sad look. "Because of your vociferous opposition to the Tripartite Pact with Germany, there have been numerous threats on your life. The Army said it is sending military police to 'guard' you. But I don't trust them; I think the guards themselves might be a danger to you."

Yamamoto frowned. "I am not surprised. Too bad the Navy does not have their own military police—it's a weakness we will have to cure. But those Army Military Police—I don't trust them either not to try to get rid of me—they are wolves in sheep's clothing!"

Yonai nodded in agreement.

Yamamoto shifted in his chair. "So, Minister, what do you suggest?"

"This is what I am going to do. I am appointing you Commander-in-Chief of the Combined Fleet and sending you out to sea where you will be safe from any assassination attempt. You will become the top officer in the Imperial Navy, taking over from Admiral Zengo Yoshida."

Yamamoto nodded. "I am not afraid of those Army thugs."

Yonai looked Yamamoto in the eye. "That's an order, Yamamoto!"

Yamamoto shrugged. "I never liked these land-based jobs, anyway. I'm a sailor, and I suppose it is on a ship that is where I should be."

Yonai smiled. "Good. Those bastards can't get at you aboard your own ship.

"Admiral Fukudome is Your chief of staff. Soon we will replace him with Admiral Matome Ugaki."

Yamamoto nodded. "A good man, I can trust Ugaki."

Admiral Matome Ugaki

Since his stint as second in command of the Kasumigaura Naval Air Training Corps, Yamamoto saw to it that naval air power was stressed and became the focus of training. As Commander in Chief of the Combined Fleet, he saw to it that Japan became the strongest nation in naval air power with a program under which the carrier force supplanted the battleships as the major offensive weapon in the Imperial Navy and greatly improved the Navy's pilot training program. Earlier, in 1933, in his stint as head of the Navy's technology department, his 'shore job', he worked with the Nakajima Company to develop a torpedo plane that was tough and lethal. The Americans called it the 'Kate.' He worked also with Mitsubishi to develop the G4M twin engine bomber that could carry a heavy bomb load for a very long range and thereby cover the vast reaches of the Pacific and its spread-out islands. To the Americans, the bomber was the 'Betty.'

Though his stint in the tech department was a shore job, he had spent little time at his own home, preferring the officer's club or, a very special geisha house, or the frequent visits to the home of Admiral Gentaro Yamashita to 'talk navy' and banter with Yamashita's lovely wife, Tokuko.

As Yamamoto left Tokyo to take the position of Commander-in-Chief of the Combined Fleet, he arranged to have the Navy Shore Patrol guards whisk him out of town before the Army Military Police could come in to "protect" him.

August 1939, Aboard the Battleship *Nagato*, Anchored in Hashirajima Bay

Yamamoto, a gymnast in school, never lost his love for that sport. Since he was a young lieutenant on a destroyer and later, an officer on a cruiser, he often would place his hands briskly on the ship's railing and do a handstand. Indeed, he continued to show off his handstands in dangerous places, such as poising himself on the guard rails on deck where a slip would put him overboard and continued this practice even after he became an admiral.

In the tumultuous period of 1939, Admiral Yonai became prime minister and Yamamoto returned to the Combined Fleet, now busy as its commander-in-chief, stationed at Hashirajima. Being there and out of Tokyo, Yonai felt, should keep him out of danger. It was getting tiresome of having Yamamoto fearlessly stand up to each threat of assassination, even from the fleet faction of his own Navy.

The Island of Hashirajima lies just twenty miles south of Hiroshima. The anchorage, large enough to hold the entire Combined Fleet and still accommodate merchant ships who commonly ply those waters. The ships lie at anchor among many little islands in the bay. It is well protected by antiaircraft batteries located on these many islands. Hashirajima acts as the headquarters of the Combined Fleet. For Yamamoto, it was far enough away from the assassination dangers of Tokyo. Hashirajima, close to Hiroshima, lay even closer to the great naval arsenal and shipyards of Kure. It was also just a few steps away from the Naval Academy.

Sailors on the ships anchored around the island could see the great battleships of the First Fleet, the symbol of the Japanese Navy's great power, which seemed to take over the bay.

Yamamoto admittedly felt a sense of relief being out of Tokyo and even more so, safely out of politics. He ate well, even though the China Incident was in its third year and for the general population, there were food shortages cropping up throughout Japan.

But politics, needless to say, tried to intrude while he commanded the Combined Fleet from his flagship. He continued to lobby for some accommodation with the United States. But his arguments fell on deaf ears. *Okay,* he thought, *that ends dabbling in politics for me. As Commander-in-Chief of the Combined Fleet, I intend to avoid politics.*

From that moment on, Yamamoto simply refused to discuss anything touching on politics.

Cornering one of his staff officers, Rear Admiral Shigeru Fukudome, after dinner, Yamamoto let out some of his frustrations. "Fukudome, the Tripartite Pact would put Japan into fighting a potentially ruinous war with the United States with little chance of winning. Let us say we attack the Americans; we will, undoubtedly, be in for a long war of attrition. We are not going to have the luxury of one decisive battle like we did with the Russians in 1905 at Tsushima. That's pure day dreaming." He waved away that idea with his hand, sweeping it across his body in a wide arc.

"You know what will happen?" Yamamoto asked.

Fukudome did not answer, but gave his full respectful attention to this man, now his boss—this man that spent so much time in the United States—this man that knew the Americans like no other Japanese military man did.

"The Americans will not be rushed into some sort of decisive battle," Yamamoto explained, "or accommodate our current plans to let them come to us to be intercepted in our home waters where we are close to our supplies and fuel. I know the Americans better than that. They will take as much time as they need to build up overwhelming naval and air power, and then return to the Pacific very methodically, by island-hopping their way to Japan."

Fukudome cut in. "But we have better, faster ships."

Yamamoto shrugged. "It won't matter, they'll overwhelm us in numbers—in both ships and planes." He sighed. "You know how heavily populated our cities are? And the tinder box constructions of our homes? We are so vulnerable to air raids, it's frightening. Eventually, the Americans will occupy islands in the Pacific close enough to our mainland to level our cities with their bombers."

"Keep letting them know in Tokyo how you feel," Fukudome said.

Yamamoto frowned. "I do, but with each passing month, the government becomes more radical and war-like. We are like the school boy that lives for the moment, behaves thoughtlessly and damn the consequences! Just look at our Army in China. We keep winning battles but General Tojo can't find a way to win the war against a billion Chinese. We are expending lives and materiel at an alarming rate. Now, with the effective guerilla tactics being used by the Chinese, our Army is reduced to committing atrocities on the civilian population. They want to keep it under wraps, but they can't.

"The Americans insist that we evacuate all our troops from China. You know our Army will never go along with that. I fear war is inevitable, so I am resigned to doing my very best to fight the Americans and obtain the best terms possible for peace."

Fukudome shrugged. "All we can do is mind our own business. There is a bright side to our conflict in China, you know."

28

Yamamoto looked at his chief of staff waiting for the inevitable explanation.

Fukudome smiled. "Thanks to the China war, the Army and the Navy have been able to stockpile weapons and ammunition to be able to confront the United States. Our Army has expanded to 41 divisions and look at all the warships we were able to build. We have the best fleet in the Pacific!"

Yamamoto looked doubtful. "Perhaps, for maybe a year, and possibly two. After that, their industrial base will swamp us with new warships and planes."

Fukudome pointed with his right index finger to make a point. "Maybe we can force them into a peace by then!"

"I sincerely doubt it," Yamamoto replied. "I know the Americans, you don't, and I expect the Americans will fight back with all the fury at their command."

Yamamoto sighed. "You know, don't you, that any war with the Americans is going to fall on *our* shoulders, not the Army's! It's a war on the Pacific Ocean where there is no Army. And if Japan signs the damn Tripartite Pact, war with the United States is for sure! And everyone will be looking to us."

"I agree totally," Fukudome replied. "We can gain nothing by a military alliance with Germany and a war with the United States would be suicidal given all their natural resources of coal, aluminum, iron, and most important, oil, the life blood of the modern navies since we switched from burning coal and wood to crude oil."

Yamamoto smiled ruefully. "You sound like me. But you are right, it's a war we could not win," he said softly.

"What can we do?"

Yamamoto rubbed his chin. "I have been giving this considerable thought. Since our leaders, if they so decide, will wage war on America, without our consent, we must give ourselves at least some advantage by a surprise attack. The way I see it, the American Asiatic Fleet is weak with just a handful of ships well past their prime and no battleships, an old carrier, *Langley*, now of little use except to transport planes. Their flagship is a cruiser! But the Pacific fleet is another story with ten battleships and several carriers. Now, I was thinking, if we could knock out the Pacific Fleet for a year, then we could move to take over much of the central and south Pacific and maybe even Australia. But it the attack would have to be a total surprise."

Fukudome frowned. "But where could we find most of the Pacific Fleet in one place?"

Yamamoto smiled. "In Pearl Harbor! If we can destroy most of their Pacific Fleet there in a decisive battle and eliminate American sea power in the Pacific especially the aircraft carriers, then we have a chance of coming out ahead in a war. War with the United States is just plain foolish and if we must take them on, then this is the way we must do it."

Later that Day

After dinner, Yamamoto visited his chief of staff in his room on the *Nagato*.

Fukudome, seeing his commander-in-chief enter, picked up a book sitting on his desk. "Have you read this?'

Yamamoto read the title. *Mein Kampf.* He nodded.

"It is dangerous to ally ourselves with Germany. Hitler is clearly out for world conquest," Yamamoto observed dryly. "And he doesn't think much of the Jews, Arabs, Blacks or us Asians. And this is who we are aligning Japan with? Of course, the government keeps all this from the people, complicating our task of trying to oppose the Tripartite Pact."

Fukudome nodded. "But even the Army and our own fleet faction in the Navy are pushing for the alliance."

Yamamoto nodded. "And there's damn little we can do about it, I can tell you that much!"

CHAPTER FOUR

World War Two Begins in Europe; Japan Moves Against China; If the Brits Can Do It, Japan Can Do It!

Spring of 1940, Tokyo, Office of Prime Minister Konoye

GENERAL TOJO POINTED TO the map of Europe. "Since the start of the war in Europe, when Germany was provoked into invading and conquering Poland…"

Konoye smiled. "Provoked?"

Tojo shrugged. "Well that is what Hitler claims. Why shouldn't we believe him?

"But that is beside the point. What is significant for us is that Hitler has easily overrun most of Western Europe. Even France has surrendered! What an opportunity this is for us to move into French Indo-China and its vast reserves of raw materials!"

Konoye rubbed his chin. "Hmm, you may be right! The French Vichy government is hardly in position to deny us, especially if we join the Tripartite Pact with Germany and Italy. If they try to deny us, we'll simply take it anyway, by force. They are in no position to defend the territory."

"The war in Europe will be over very shortly," Tojo predicted. "German troops are sweeping away all opposition."

Konoye eyed Tojo. "Except the British."

Tojo smiled. "Take it from me, as an Army leader. The British cannot hold out on their small island much longer."

"We might even be able, in a little while, to move on Malaysia and its rubber and oil resources," Konoye suggested, getting into the spirit of things.

"Especially if America extends its embargo, as it is threatening to do," Tojo added.

Konoye nodded in agreement. "Especially then!"

"We must step up preparations for war with America," Tojo pushed, his tone more of a demand.

Konoye's eyes narrowed. "The emperor will make the decision on war. But I agree, we should be prepared. The burden in any such conflict will fall on the Navy with the Pacific as the battleground."

"Of course," agreed Tojo. "Contact Admiral Yamamoto. We'll need his help to handle the American Navy."

"I still think I should try to meet with Roosevelt secretly to seek an accommodation," the prime minister said.

Tojo glared at Konoye. "It won't do any good, we have already tried, and the Americans are intransigent. Besides, the Army and the Navy have already decided that war is inevitable, and we are preparing as we speak."

Nagano, the Navy chief, silent up to now, jumped in. "General Tojo is correct, the time for negotiations is over. We must attack while the Americans are still not prepared for war."

Konoye shook his head. "Well, I, for one, will not abandon any chance for peace that arises."

Ugaki and the Kamikazes

September 28, 1940, Aboard the Battleship *Nagato*, Anchored in Hashirajima Bay

Yamamoto shuffled the papers on his desk until he found what he was looking for. He pulled out the document, a cable from the prime minister. He waved it in front of his new Chief of Staff Admiral Matome Ugaki. "Against my advice, our government has joined with the Germans and Italians against the Western Powers in the Tripartite Pact."

Yamamoto shook his head. "A big mistake, Ugaki, a very big mistake that is going to drag the Americans into the war. And by this pact, we will be obligated to fight the Americans and other Western Powers."

Ugaki shrugged. "Perhaps you are correct, but I am not so sure. Just look how the Germans are rolling over all their opponents. The war in Europe may be over before we know it!"

Yamamoto frowned. "Don't count on it. The Americans will never let Britain lose to Hitler. They'll enter the war first, just like

33

they did in the last big war. And if they do, the pact we just signed will have us fighting the Americans, as well!"

Ugaki shook his head. "You're too much of a pessimist. The war in Europe will keep the Americans occupied for a long time."

Yamamoto's eyes narrowed as he glared at Ugaki. "And what if Hitler attacks the Soviets?"

"It won't happen. They have a non-aggression treaty", Ugaki insisted.

Yamamoto issued a harsh laugh. "It didn't stop Hitler before, and it won't stop him now. He hates the Communists with a passion. His pact with them is a short-term convenience, one which he won't hesitate to break when he feels the time is ripe."

Yamamoto, with his elbows on his desk, placed his head in his two hands. Then he looked at Ugaki. "The prime minster, despite my warnings that we will face disaster and, undoubtedly egged on by that maniac Tojo, has ordered us to prepare a plan for a war with the United States—so the fat is in the fire and that, my dear Ugaki, is what we will do. We will have to figure out how to knock out the American Pacific Fleet before it gets its guard up. I don't like it, but there's no going back now."

Yamamoto went fishing in a wide drawer and pulled out a large map of the Pacific Ocean. "You know, since April, I was sure this day would come, and I began planning for a quick, surprise strike against the American fleet at Pearl Harbor."

Ugaki's eyes widened. "In Hawaii? I can't begin to think of all the problems that will entail."

Yamamoto nodded. "I know it's a gamble, but I feel the odds are in our favor. At first I struggled with the idea of luring the American fleet out of San Diego into the Pacific and then discovered the American admirals did it for me; they moved virtually all the Pacific Fleet to Pearl Harbor! What a set up for us if we make a surprise attack on Pearl with naval warplanes from our carriers and with our submarine fleet I have watched our airmen practice with very good results in the air attack training. I know we can pull it off

Yamamoto returned the map back to the drawer. "Our people in Honolulu have been carefully monitoring the American fleet there. Our consulate there has detected a definite pattern. The fleet leaves Pearl on Mondays and Tuesdays and returns for the weekend. Most everything is closed down on Saturday and Sunday while the American sailors enjoy themselves in Honolulu. They are making it easy for us. If we fiercely attack and destroy their fleet in Hawaii at the outset of the war, I hope we can sink the morale of the U.S. Navy so low it will take a long time to recover."

"It seems rather risky. Isn't there a danger that while their fleet is sailing out of Pearl, they may discover our task force?" Ugaki asked.

Yamamoto shook his head. "Not likely, because we have determined that they practice maneuvers within forty-five minutes of Honolulu, so they don't venture far enough out to discover our approaching task force, which will be well beyond that."

"Granted, you may achieve surprise, but our torpedo planes simply cannot effectively launch in those shallow harbor waters! The torpedoes would bury themselves in the harbor mud," Ugaki protested. "Everyone knows that!"

Yamamoto shrugged. "I have our ordnance people working on it and there is good reason to believe we will solve that problem."

September 1940, Tokyo, the Imperial Palace

Premier Konoye requested a conference at the Imperial Palace after the director of the cabinet planning council, Naoki Hoshino, raised the question, once again, of Japan's resources to wage war.

At the conference, Hoshino stated his concern. "If we confront the United States militarily, I can only see that we will have extreme difficulty in securing the fuel supply the Navy must have."

General Tojo sighed. "We have gone over this many times. The Army will guarantee the sufficiency of the oil supply by moving into Borneo, Java, and Sumatra. We will have more than enough for the Army and the Navy."

Hoshino frowned. "You mean you intend to move militarily in that direction also?"

Tojo shrugged. "Of course; but only if diplomatic efforts fail. In that case, military force will become necessary. But don't concern yourself, it will not be prolonged. Western presence in those areas is very weak. Once we settle the China question, which I anticipate will occur very soon, the whole issue will be moot. We will then absorb China into the Greater Asia Co-Prosperity Sphere with us as the leader of all east Asia. Our troops are already moving into Indo-China with the assent of the Vichy government, while the Germans sweep away the countries of Europe, including Britain."

"Assent of Vichy, or the Germans?" Hoshino asked, somewhat sarcastically.

Tojo smiled. "Does it really matter? The entire region is under the German influence."

"The United States will retaliate!"

"I am not so sure of that," Tojo replied. "But let them, if they so choose. They will not stop us!"

October 1940, Aboard the Battleship *Nagato*, Anchored in Hashirajima Bay

Yamamoto enjoyed the comfort of safety aboard the *Nagato*. Back in Tokyo, with the heads of the Navy, he found himself amid the rightists, who would watch his every act, just waiting for the opportunity to take him out. Oh, there were some young flyers, hot heads, who worshipped every move made by their hero, Hitler, and they doubted their commander-in-chief had the courage to lead the Combined Fleet. But here, amid some 40,000 officers and men concerned for his safety, Yamamoto felt secure.

He called in his chief of staff Ugaki. "Admiral, we are going to hold maneuvers involving the entire Combined Fleet. We'll see how ready they really are."

Ugaki smiled. "Good, we have the vast range of the Pacific Ocean in which to practice!"

Yamamoto shook his head. "It's very tempting, I know, but we have to face reality. We will be experiencing a serious oil shortage.

You know how much fuel we consume when our ships are operating at general quarters. We simply cannot sail our Navy all over the Pacific with the bunker oil we have available. We will conduct maneuvers close to home where we won't consume as much fuel. We will concentrate on fleet night attacks. I know this is an area of weakness for the Americans. It is essential that our flyers learn to search for the enemy fleet at night and get comfortable with after-dark landings."

"I see that despite our opposition, our leaders have signed the Tripartite Pact," Ugaki observed.

Yamamoto shrugged. "With Tojo pushing hard to sign the pact, and the toadies in Tokyo unwilling to stand up to him, we had little chance out here in the field to stop this runaway train. It looks like war with the Americans, for sure. We can't win the war in China, yet we are willing to take on a much stronger opponent— the United States. It doesn't make sense. The American Congress won't vote to go to war, but we will provide the *casus belli* Roosevelt could never have provided by himself. And thereby, we are taking on one of the most populous countries with military and industrial powers far exceeding our own. Does that make sense?"

Ugaki grunted. "That Yamamoto, is why you have been assigned out here in Hashirajima Bay—simply to keep you from asking those questions and from being assassinated!"

Yamamoto frowned. "I expect a war with the United States will be a disaster for us, maybe not at first, but yes, in the long run, we will lose."

October 1940, Washington D.C., the White House

Secretary of State Cordell Hull, waved in by Roosevelt, took a seat in the Oval Office The president did not rise to greet him. Indeed, it was not expected he ever would, given the paralysis of his legs when struck down by polio. Other than speeches to Congress where Roosevelt wore heavy braces and hung on to the podium for dear life, Hull had never seen the president stand.

Roosevelt took the cigarette holder out of his mouth and placed it and the remains of his cigarette in the ashtray on his desk.

"Cordell," the president began, "it looks like we can't any longer hold off taking action against Japan. It has now allied itself with Germany, and the puppet French Vichy government controlled by the Germans, who has let the Japs enter Indo-China; and now Japan is threatening to take the Dutch East Indies by force. We can't have that!"

Cordell pressed his lips together, then looked at Roosevelt. "What are you thinking?"

The president stared at the ceiling. "Oh, a boycott. Cut off American scrap metal. If that doesn't get their attention will add many strategic commodities including arms, ammunition, aviation gasoline and many other petroleum products, machine tools, scrap iron, pig iron, iron and steel, copper, lead, zinc, aluminum, and a variety of other commodities important to their war effort."

"They don't get much arms and ammunition from us," Hull observed.

Roosevelt shook his head in agreement. "That's true, but they do get plenty of petroleum products from us. But let's start with scrap metal and see what happens."

As Hull got up to leave, the president started talking again so Hull paused. "Also, I plan to call up the Army of the Philippine Commonwealth into the service of the United States and recall General MacArthur out of retirement and to active duty."

Hull's eyes widened. "MacArthur? That egomaniac?"

Roosevelt nodded. "They love him in the Philippines and I can't think of a better way of getting them prepared to fight."

Hull frowned. "With one American Army division and the Filipino Army ill-trained and lacking modern weapons and tools? I hear some of the Filipino soldiers don't even have shoes!"

The president shrugged. "I can only work with what I have. Hopefully, they can hold out long enough for us to get help to them. At least it will delay the Japs!"

"And sacrifice an American division," Hull mumbled, half under his breath.

Roosevelt looked up. "I heard that. I have a lot of problems, Cordell, but hearing isn't one of them. I'll have you know I have authorized the transfer to the Philippines, of a fleet of our new B-17 heavy bombers; you know, the ones they call the 'Flying Fortresses.'"

November 11, 1940, Bay of Taranto, Italy

The British flagship, the aircraft carrier *H.M.S. Illustrious*, circled the Greek Island of Cephalonia, two hundred miles southeast of the Italian naval base at Taranto. Aboard, Admiral Sir Andrew B. Cunningham pored over the high-altitude reconnaissance photos taken by the speedy Martin Maryland aircraft, capable of outrunning the Italian Arrow fighters. The latest photos confirmed that the Italian fleet was still at anchor in the Taranto harbor—battleships, cruisers and destroyers. Cunningham knew that without radar, the Italians would not be aware of the presence of the British fleet two hundred miles away unless an Italian ship happened to spot it, and as far as he knew, that hasn't happened.

The planning hadn't been easy. Torpedoes had to be devised that would not run deep and thus bury themselves harmlessly in the mud in the shallow bottom of Taranto's harbor. The defenses at the base included dozens of antiaircraft batteries, barrage balloons, metal nets and powerful listening devices. The listening devices would pick up the drone of the attacking airplanes, which would be the first warning of the raid. Cunningham had thirty Farley Swordfish biplanes to launch. They were slow and outdated but highly reliable and capable of taking plenty of punishment. Moreover, it was highly unlikely they would encounter any Italian fighters, because the Italian pilots did not fly at night. The Swordfish planes would go out in two waves, an hour apart.

As the sun set, Admiral Cunningham ordered Captain Dennis Boyd, commander of the British carrier *Illustrious*, to prepare for the attack, to commence at 2100 hours.

November 14, 1940, Taranto, Office of Admiral Riccardi

Lieutenant Takeshi Naito, the Japanese assistant air attaché in Berlin, introduced himself to Italian Admiral Riccardi. The admiral did not have time for such visitors, but since Japan was an ally, he listened politely and answered the lieutenant's questions concerning the British attack, depth and size of the harbor, and the ability of the British to use, so effectively, torpedoes in the shallow water, sinking of three of the seven Italian battleships. Naito seemed most interested in the battleships and the ability of the British planes to sink them.

Riccardi wondered at the Japanese interest in an event so far from the Pacific but he didn't dwell on it. He had too much work to do to restore his decimated fleet

November 20, 1940, Tokyo, Office of Admiral Yamamoto

Six days later, Admiral Isoroku Yamamoto reviewed Lieutenant Naito's meticulous notes again. He smiled and silently thanked the British. For years, Yamamoto had planned and proposed an attack on the United States naval base at Pearl Harbor in Hawaii. He considered that to go to war with the United States, as his superiors were determined to do, was unwise; but if it was to have any chance of success, Japan would have to knock out the American fleet in the Pacific at the very beginning. Pearl Harbor presented such an opportunity, but he'd been unable to convince his superiors of its feasibility.

If the British could successfully launch torpedoes in shallow harbor waters, the Japanese could find a way to do it also. Japanese planes, he knew, were vastly superior to the antiquated Swordfish and our Navy could mount an attack with ten times the number of aircraft. The harbor at Taranto was not dissimilar to Pearl Harbor, and if the British could do it against an enemy with which it was already at war and which was on its guard, surely Japan would have even greater chances of success against a country at peace, with few defenses manned, especially on Sunday mornings. He put down

Lieutenant Naito's report. Now he had the ammunition to convince his superiors that if they insisted on war, a surprise attack on Pearl Harbor was both feasible and imperative.

December 1940, from Commander-in-Chief Yamamoto's Flagship *Nagato* anchored at the Japanese Naval base at Hashirajima Island, in Hiroshima Bay

Yamamoto grimaced, speaking to his Chief of Staff Admiral Matome Ugaki. "It's crazy. We cannot simply ignore the economic power of the United States. Fighting them is like fighting the whole world. I tried to tell that to our new minister of war, Hideki Tojo, but you know him, he's bad news and always ready to fight-and lose—a war anywhere. He did not listen in China where he got us into a quagmire, and he won't listen now. And our Navy chief, Osami Nagano is no better—also spoiling for a fight he doesn't understand!"

Ugaki looked confused. "So, it has already been decided?"

Yamamoto shrugged. "I'm afraid so. Not having any choice, I will fight the best war I can. Meanwhile, I expect to die aboard my flagship, the *Nagato*, while Tokyo will be burnt to the ground three times. If it was up to me, I would withdraw from China and abrogate the Tripartite Pact and go our own way without Germany or Italy."

"But you know that's not going to happen. What if we do go to war?" Ugaki queried.

Yamamoto sighed. "With America? Oh, I can surprise them at their fleet assembly point at Pearl Harbor and bloody their noses. But I keep telling Tokyo that while I can raise havoc with the Americans for oh, six months, or maybe, even a year, but if the war goes on for two or three years," he shrugged, "then I have no confidence Japan can survive. Unfortunately, our leaders are not listening; they are moving headlong into this war with the United States. In the end, it will be ruinous for us. We seem to have taken leave of reality. However, it seems to be the wish of the entire country, even one sick of the war with China. With this nationalistic fervor holding sway, our leadership has lost their ability to look at these actions in a cool, reasoned way, and to realize the nature and outcome of such a gargantuan war."

"Well," Ugaki offered, "at least thanks to you, we now have the most powerful carrier force in the Pacific in the world! Our torpedo design is generations ahead of the Americans and their allies, our gunnery abilities are far superior, and the new Zero fighter will fly rings around anything the Americans and British can put up to challenge us—even better than the Germans! But torpedoes in the shallow waters of Pearl Harbor?" Ugaki shook his head. "Not likely."

Yamamoto smiled. "You're wrong, Ugaki. The British recently did it at the Taranto Italian Naval Base with an aerial torpedo attack in the harbor's shallow waters and sank many of the Italian ships there, including *three* battleships. The attack was carried out by carrier planes. I received a detailed report from our naval attaché— the British apparently attached special fins that did the trick in those shallow waters. There's no reason why we can't do the same."

"Do we have such torpedoes?" asked a skeptical Ugaki.

"We will," Yamamoto explained. "I went to Rear Admiral Takijiro Onishi, our ordnance specialist, and asked him to study the problem and come up with such a torpedo. He put his head together with Commander Fumio Aiko, our torpedo expert. Aiko had already studied the harbors in Manilla, Singapore, Vladivostok, and Pearl Harbor and found the average depth to be from seventeen to twenty-five feet. He determined that our torpedoes could sink no more that twelve feet without burying in the mud."

"Twelve feet? An impossible task!" Ugaki snorted.

"Well, Aiko worked with it out Aeronautical Bureau of the Navy Ministry and they came up with a torpedo fitted with wooden fins that they felt could work. I told Admiral Fukudome to study such an attack with planes coming in low with these modified torpedoes."

Ugaki shook his head. "The Navy Ministry will never go for it. It's too risky and a tremendous gamble."

Yamamoto smiled. "Yes, that's what they said, but I happen to be fond of games and gambles. You know what they say: 'A cornered rat will bite a cat.' This is my idea and I need your support."

Ugaki's eyes narrowed and he focused on Yamamoto. "And the Navy Minister agreed?"

Yamamoto shrugged. "Not yet, but I warned them in no uncertain terms that if they did not agree, that I would quit—retire and spend the rest of my days with my geisha in the various gambling houses in Monte Carlo and around the world. I mean it, too! I explained that this will be our only chance to knock out a major portion of the American Pacific Fleet, which should give us some breathing room and give us a tactical respite. We'll use that time to fortify our defenses from the Kuril Islands to the central Pacific then on to the southeast Asia area. By then we should have the resources to wage a war of attrition. Sometime in the future, we may be able to negotiate a settlement with America. No guarantees, mind you, but frankly, I'm not sure the Americans by themselves have the fortitude to fight a two-front war if Germany completes its conquest of Europe, as I think everyone anticipates."

"Anything else you want to tell me?" Ugaki asked suspiciously.

"Well..." Yamamoto paused for a moment. "I also insisted that we give the Americans at least one-hour notice of Japan's declaration of war to precede the attack."

"And the prime minister and Tojo agreed?" Ugaki asked.

"Oh, Prime Minister Konoye hemmed and hawed, and War Minister Tojo screamed at me a bit, but I think they'll come around to my way of thinking if they want me to supervise the attack."

"Sounds like blackmail to me," Ugaki muttered.

Yamamoto laughed. "Well, maybe just a little coercion. And, you'll be interested in this, I asked for six carriers with which to bomb Pearl Harbor!"

"They're giving you *all six?*"

Yamamoto shook his finger. "They'd better! Otherwise we won't have enough firepower to take out the American Fleet. We need at least all six carriers—including the big ones—the *Akagi, Kaga, Hiryu,* and *Soryu.* I also made that a condition of my remaining in the Navy, and I think they'll eventually give them to me because I also have the support of Lieutenant Commander Minoru Genda of the First Naval Air Wing, who said that success would depend on concentrating multiple carriers into a single task force, so we can launch one coordinated strike. And the more power in the force, the greater the chances of success."

Ugaki nodded. "He's a good one to have on your side. The naval chiefs think highly of him. He's a naval air force ace from his time in the China war."

"I agree," Yamamoto said.

"But if they give you the six carriers, we won't have any carriers for our attack in southeast Asia and the Philippines!" Ugaki pointed out.

"That's true," Yamamoto replied. "But think about it; we don't need carriers in that area because those battlegrounds are well within the reach of the Army's land-based warplanes in China. So, the Army will have its own air support. Hawaii, on the other hand, is nowhere near any of our bases and our land-based planes are simply not in the equation for such an attack."

Ugaki rubbed his chin. "I must admit, your approach makes sense, when you put it that way. The thing that concerns me, though, is how we are going to move so many ships so far—from Japan to Hawaii—without being detected?"

"That's a chance we'll have to take," Yamamoto said. "If we take the long way around, that is, by the extreme northern route where there is very little commercial or military traffic at that time of year, we shouldn't stumble onto any steamers. If we do, we'll just have to take them out before they can warn anyone. If we keep radio silence all the way, I like the odds we will not be discovered before our planes are already over Hawaii. It's a gamble, I admit, but I think it will pay off-big."

Ugaki frowned. "I don't know. The northern route will be shrouded with fog for much of the way and that's a lot of ships, over forty, to keep track of and keep in any sort of formation."

Yamamoto spread his arms. "That's why our ships have searchlights to signal with! We have trained for such sailings and I am confident the commander of the fleet can keep them in formation and not bumping into each other!"

"Have they considered landing our forces in Hawaii?"

"Admiral Onishi pushed for it," Yamamoto replied, "but Tojo refused to provide Army troops for such a venture and besides, we'd be stretching our lines of supply beyond our abilities. It's simply too far away from our nearest bases in the Pacific and we'd need three divisions of troops from the Navy. It's just not practical."

"How do we know that American ships will be in the harbor when we attack?"

"Because that's what the Americans do every weekend—bring the ships in and give the sailors shore leave."

Ugaki shrugged. "I still think it's a gamble."

Yamamoto grinned. "It's gambling, but I like the odds. I hope a crushing blow at Pearl Harbor will move the Americans shortly to sue for peace!"

December 14, 1940, Tokyo, American Embassy, Office of the Ambassador

Ambassador Grew rang for his secretary. She came in immediately.

"Sit down and take a short letter to the president."

She seated herself and had her steno pad and pencil at the ready, as she always did when called into the Ambassador's office.

"Address this to the President of the United States," Grew instructed. "Dear Frank: It seems to me increasingly clear that we are bound to have a showdown someday with the Japanese, and the principal question at issue is whether it is to our advantage to have that showdown sooner or have it later."

December 23, 1940, Washington D.C., The White House, the Oval Office

The president handed Ambassador Grew's letter to Harry Hopkins, who quickly read it.

"What do you think?" Roosevelt asked.

"I agree with Grew's conclusion," Hopkins responded, "but I'm not sure how we can act on it."

"Ah, there you have the conundrum," the president said. "Congress won't let us go to war, not with all those isolationists in Congress—unless, of course, we were attacked. So, we can't fire the first shot. Puts us at a disadvantage, doesn't it? We already have embargoed every product to Japan that we can. Now, all we can do is keep on the alert."

Mid-January 1941, Tokyo, Aboard the Battleship *Nagato*, Anchored in Hashirajima Bay

"So how was your meeting with the General Naval Staff in Tokyo?" Ugaki asked.

Yamamoto sighed. "Not sure yet. We went through this last September and they are *still* studying the feasibility of what they are now calling my 'daring and aggressive plan.'"

Ugaki nodded. "It is certainly that!"

"It has to be, to be a surprise and accomplish its purpose, especially with the strong American naval forces amassed in the Hawaiian waters." Yamamoto spread his arms out wide. "Like talking to a brick wall. The Naval General Staff still sees itself as committing more naval strength to the invasion of southern Asia and are reluctant to weaken those forces by giving us those six carriers to use against American Fleet in Hawaii."

"They do have a point there," Ugaki suggested.

Yamamoto shook his head. "Not really. We must recognize that a serious potential threat is posed by the American fleet in the Pacific and committing too much naval strength to South Asia will leave us weakened in the western Pacific at least temporarily. I think the Americans would attack us in the western Pacific before we could regroup the fleet to fight off such an attack. I insisted, therefore, that we dispose of the danger by my plan for a surprise air and submarine attack on Pearl Harbor to cripple their fleet *before* they are alerted by our invasion in South Asia. Besides, as I pointed out earlier, the South Asia force has the Army land-based planes in China to support them, they don't need our carriers. We do, because we have no land bases close enough to Hawaii to obtain such support."

"I understand. But I am still concerned about how can our fleet travel so far to Hawaiian waters without being detected?" Ugaki posed.

"Very carefully, in absolute radio silence and using the least travelled route, even if it takes us much longer to get there.

"Admittedly, Vice Admiral Nagumo and Rear Admiral Ryunosuke Kusaka felt the proposal was far too speculative; that I was a gambler."

"Sounds like a reasonable concern," Ugaki said. "How did you respond?"

"I told them I understand their fears, but I want them to stop arguing with me and make every effort to put the plan into effect. War itself is a gamble and no plan is fool-proof and you must take risks to obtain great gains—and destruction of the Pacific Fleet at Pearl Harbor would be a great victory!"

Yamamoto rolled his eyes in frustration. "Then the Navy staff assigned the blackshoe Kusaka the responsibility for drawing up a workable plan. Me, I would have preferred a regular pilot to do it."

"You obviously prefer a brownshoe officer." Ugaki noted.

"Yes, we need their air experience for designing an aerial attack," Yamamoto explained.

Ugaki shook his head. "I still don't see how we can do it. Our ships don't have the range to reach Hawaii without running out of fuel."

"The fleet will be accompanied by fuel tankers with sufficient capacity to get there and back," Yamamoto said in his finest lecturing tone. "If the Americans can do it, so can we!"

Ugaki frowned. "Tankers are notorious plodders. They will slow the fleet down!"

Yamamoto nodded. "True enough, but we are in no hurry, if we leave a lot of time to get there."

"I suppose,"Ugaki mumbled,"but I still don't see how, considering the great distance the fleet has to travel to be in a position to attack, how we won't be discovered by the Americans."

Yamamoto, irritated, moved to the wall map. "As I explained several times, we will use this northern route." Yamamoto tapped his pointer on the map. "We have studied it and no ships use this route in November and December because of the rough ocean. Accordingly, I feel that inadvertent discovery would be highly unlikely. It is also important that our South Asia attack doesn't jump the gun *before* we attack Pearl Harbor and put the American Fleet on a war footing and on the alert."

Ugaki shook his head, thinking to himself, *We've got a great leader, but he has a gambler's heart.*

"Don't you worry about those six aircraft carriers. We'll get them," Yamamoto assured. "I sent Kuroshima to Tokyo to speak to the Navy head, Admiral Tomioka, who initially resisted my plan but quickly caved after Kuroshima told him that I definitely would resign immediately if I did not get the six carriers for the attack on Pearl Harbor."

"It's still a desperate gamble." Ugaki insisted.

Yamamoto smiled. "Well, if you want the tiger's cubs, you have to go into the tiger's lair!"

CHAPTER FIVE

Japan on Offensive in Asia; America's warnings

Late January 1941, Tokyo, American Embassy, Office of Ambassador John Grew

ED CROCKER, FIRST SECRETARY at the embassy, settled into a club chair in the ambassador's office spreading his long legs out on the carpet. "Mr. Ambassador, I heard from my contact at the Peruvian Embassy, Dr. Rivera, who has a few friends in the Japanese Navy. And they say there is a rumor going around that that the Japanese Navy is planning "a surprise mass attack on Pearl Harbor."

Ambassador Grew's eyes widened. "How much stock do you put into this rumor?"

Crocker pressed his lips together and thought for a moment. "Well, he's been surprisingly accurate in other information he's passed on to me before. I would not ignore it."

Grew nodded. "No, I suppose I can't ignore it. I'll cable Washington and warn them."

Same Day, Washington, D.C., Joint Chiefs of Staff

The duty officer slit open the message from the Naval Intelligence Center reporting on the rumor in Japan of a surprise attack on Pearl Harbor. Naval Intelligence advised that "based on known data regarding the present disposition and employment of Japanese

Naval and Army forces, no move against Pearl Harbor appears imminent or planned for the foreseeable future."

The duty officer saw no urgency in this message and routed it through the normal office distribution procedures, which did not include a copy to Naval Headquarters in Pearl Harbor.

Admiral Stark, commander-in-chief of the naval forces, ultimately did pass it on to the naval command at Pearl, with the comment, "I place no credence in these rumors. No move against Pearl Harbor appears imminent or planned in the foreseeable future."

Admiral Kimmel, who had just replaced Admiral Richardson as CINCPAC head, just filed the message away.

June 1941, Aboard Commander-in-Chief Yamamoto's Flagship *Nagato* anchored at the Japanese Naval base at Hashirajima Island, in Hiroshima Bay

Yamamoto looked grimly at his two guests, Admiral Ugaki and Air Commander Minoru Genda. "I just got word that that the Germans have launched a massive surprise attack on the Soviet Union. So much for Foreign Minister Matsuoka's non-aggression pact with the Soviets in April!"

Ugaki snorted. "And so much for Hitler's word of honor. He had a peace pact with the Soviets that he simply broke without a qualm!"

Yamamoto shook his head. "The pact was and is a bad joke. I warned Tokyo—do not conclude the Tripartite Pact with Hitler. The Tokyo gang must have had their heads up their asses! I can tell you, I will continue warning against this Tripartite Pact with Hitler and Mussolini. But they won't listen."

"But with General Tojo in Tokyo championing it, and you out here, out of sight..." Ugaki did not finish the sentence. He didn't have to.

"That's why the government in Tokyo was so willing to appoint me commander-in-chief of the Combined Fleet. It gets me out of their hair!" Yamamoto growled. Thus his face brightened. "But to tell you the truth I'm happy they did. Shore duty in Tokyo stinks and it is so stifling."

Yamamoto continued. "I just hope this Pact doesn't push us into the German war on the Soviet Union also. We will have our hands full just fighting the Americans and British! I hear the German Foreign Minister Ribbentrop is pushing our foreign minister to enter the war against the Soviets."

"The Pact," Ugaki tried to explain, "obligates us to join in a war only if Germany or Italy *were attacked*. That clearly has not been the case here."

"I certainly hope so," Yamamoto grunted. "But with General Tojo and Admiral Nagano, you just never know." He sighed. "You just never know," he repeated.

"Tell me this," Ugaki inquired. "If you rely on the torpedo planes to sink the battleships at Pearl, how are you going to get the inbound moored vessels, protected by the ships tied up on the outside?"

Yamamoto smiled. "It's taken care of." He nodded his head toward Genda, who was given the task of creating the plan for the air assault on Pearl Harbor.

Genda looked at his two superiors. "We know we need a diverse attack and that's what my Aichi dive bombers and high-level warplanes are for. They can lay the bombs right on the inside ships. They dive from up high, come down very low and drop those bombs right on the decks of the inside ships. And what bombs! Ordnance has begun converting 16-inch armor-piercing shells into aerial bombs to be delivered by those planes. With our plan, none of their ships will be safe—if they are anywhere in the harbor! Of course, my priority targets will be the carriers.

"And no one can match our long-range torpedo bombers. The planes will be able to reach the enemy while American planes still are out of range of our ships. My fighter planes, also long-range, will tag along to rid the skies of any hostiles. My pilots, with over 300 hours experience over China, are the best in the world."

"What if the enemy fleet comes out to meet us, assuming we have been discovered before we attack?" Ugaki asked.

Yamamoto looked him square in the eye. "Then we must meet them with all the power at our disposal and destroy them with one stroke! That is why we will have a fleet of submarines also to engage the enemy and sink any ship trying to escape from Pearl Harbor during the attack. Sort of a double insurance!"

Genda smiled. "There are some who think an attack on Pearl Harbor is too risky; that we should stay in our home waters to await the Americans."

Yamamoto laughed harshly. "Our enemy is not above approaching our home waters and launching a bombing attack to burn down our cities. Even if we were successful in our South Asia operation, can you imagine the public reaction to the Navy for being bombed by the Americans? No, if we stay in our home waters and the bombing of our cities happen, it will destroy Japanese national morale beyond recovery!"

Genda nodded. "I agree. Your plan is difficult, but certainly not impossible if we use a diverse attack and not rely solely on torpedoes. Also, I know you are concentrating on the ships moored at Pearl Harbor, but another priority should be against the American land-based planes in Hawaii. This is necessary to protect our carrier force."

"Of course," Yamamoto said, "we must be sure to make that part of our plan of attack."

"Surprise will be a most important aspect of our attack." Genda said.

"Fuel fund appropriations for the American Navy shows no increase, so American preparations appear to be lackadaisical" Yamamoto reported. "That gives us a good chance. I have no qualms about assaulting one that is asleep just because they are careless and ensures us a victory. It's not our fault they are unprepared," Yamamoto sniffed. "Our naval leaders tend to belittle American strength but the so-called 'Japanese Spirit' they tout is not a monopoly of this country. It is a big mistake to underestimate the Americans. I know, I've been there many times."

Same Day and Place, Two Hours Later

Commander Genda waved Commander Mitsuo Fuchida, his best combat pilot in the Imperial Navy, to a chair in the empty ready room.

"Fuchida," Genda began, "war is coming between Japan and the United States, and we will stage a surprise attack on the American Fleet in Pearl Harbor. I would like you to be our fleet leader for that attack."

Fuchida's eyes widened as he processed this astonishing news. "Attack Pearl Harbor? Wow! I would be honored to do so."

Genda gave him no time to digest this piece of news. "You are the man to lead the first wave of aerial attackers. Many of the details have yet to be worked out and I will be relying on you to help me out."

Fuchida nodded. "And who is commanding this action, Yamamoto?"

Genda shook his head. "No, Admiral Nagumo will lead us."

Fuchida screwed up his face. "Nagumo? A blackshoe admiral who's not an airman? It seems to me he's too conservative for such an audacious undertaking."

"That's not your decision," Genda remonstrated.

Fuchida reflected on the news and smiled. "So, as I understand it, we are going to attack their citadel, widely touted as impregnable, by using torpedoes not net perfected for this mission."

"I think we have perfected a torpedo which will run true in the shallow waters of the harbor without burying itself in the mud bottom," Genda said.

"We cannot rely solely on torpedoes and our dive bombers' missives are too light to penetrate the heavy armor of the American battleships," Fuchida insisted.

"Our engineers are solving those problems," Genda assured. "You just concentrate on the battle tactics of the aerial attack."

"What about torpedo nets, how are we going to get around them?" Fuchida asked.

"Believe or not, the Americans at Pearl Harbor have not been deploying them."

Fuchida shook his head. "It's hard to believe that the Americans would ignore such an elementary precaution! But we can't assume they won't put them in place. We could destroy the nets with suicide planes."

Genda shook his head. "Only as a last resort. That's why we need a diverse attack to include dive bombers and high-level bombers," Genda explained.

"We'd need them anyway because with the double mooring at that base, only the outboard moored ships will be vulnerable to torpedo attack," Fuchida said.

Genda smiled. "I knew you are the man to lead the attack—and to train our pilots for the task at hand."

Fuchida straightened up in his chair. "I won't let you down."

July 1941, Tokyo, Naval Headquarters

The Navy minister called a special meeting of the senior admirals in the Imperial Navy.

The Navy minister did not waste any time getting to the point. "The policy of the government now is leaning toward going to war against the Americans and the British. I am asking for all your support for that policy."

The Navy heard many excited cries of "We are ready," from the audience.

But some members were not enthusiastic. Admiral Yoshioka thought it was a bad idea. "If we confine ourselves to an attack in the southern region of Asia, even the Philippines, the Americans will be angry, but not likely go to war and, even if they did, they would be open to negotiations. But if we surprise attack Pearl Harbor, the Americans will go insanely mad and there will be no hope for any compromise or agreement."

Yamamoto, as head of the Combined Fleet, slowly stood up and looked around the room.

The Navy minister looked puzzled.

His back to the Navy minister, he told the admirals, "If we don't destroy their fleet at Pearl Harbor, the Americans will not compromise. Period."

Then Yamamoto turned to face the Navy minister, and asked, "But tell me Minister-san, and the rest of you admirals in this room, where are we going to get the resources to conduct this war?"

The Navy minister did not answer, so Yamamoto continued. "Do you know that our fleet consumes enough fuel to deplete our stocks in less than a year? And what about rubber and iron ore, of which we are grossly deficient?"

"That, Admiral Yamamoto, has all been considered by our leaders and they assure that supplies of those materials will readily available in southeast Asia," the Navy minister huffed.

Yamamoto stared at the Navy minister. "So that means we go to war not only with the Americans, but with the British and Dutch, as well, since Malaysia and the Dutch East Indies are the only places where we will find sufficient quantities of rubber and fuel!"

"It is," the Navy minister sniffed. "a policy question for the emperor, the prime minister, and his staff. What I want from you gentlemen is your approval."

"The consensus at the imperial conference a few days ago," the Navy minister reminded, "is to move troops and planes into the southern part of French Indo-China and that this would provoke the United States into war. Even if it did, the mandated goals are worth the risk. The emperor has sanctioned this policy."

Yamamoto glared at the Navy minister. "And what about the Kwantung Army in China?"

"Tojo says it will be ready for war with Russia, but only if the Germans are able to quickly destroy Russian resistance in the West. But His Majesty did not think we were ready for a full-scale war with both the Soviets and the United States."

Yamamoto laughed harshly. "Well, at least someone is showing a little common sense!"

"Well," replied the Navy minister, "the Army and Navy leaders are spending much more time with emperor. He often resolves debates between the two services. It looks like he is taking over the decision-making process and about to become commander-in-chief! Frankly, it's a huge effort to keep His Majesty informed, forcing us to delegate important planning work down to our subordinates. I'm not too happy with that."

But Yamamoto was not yet finished with Tojo. "So, as I understand it, my only options are to support Tojo's crazy war or resign my commission, is that correct?"

The Navy minister nodded. "That's about it. Follow the government policy or get out!"

And that, thought Yamamoto, was my reward for building, in the Navy ministry, the most powerful naval air force in the world. I've been a full Admiral since November 1940. Maybe, just maybe, it really is time to retire.

Yamamoto looked at the Navy minister. "I've been thinking about retiring. Perhaps I should take your advice and retire—now."

The other admirals were appalled that the planner of the Pearl Harbor attack might leave. The Navy might just leave the responsibility, heaven forbid, up to one of them to carry out Yamamoto's daring plan!

Admiral Nagano stood, glaring at Yamamoto. "You know we have been planning this war since American interference in our war with Russia in 1905. And when they made us a second-class power limiting the size of our Navy by the Treaty of Portsmouth. We even sent you to the United States several times to observe and learn about the Americans. Have you forgotten already? You cannot retire now, on the eve of the greatest war in Japan's history. It would be traitorous to abandon us now! There is much work to be done, and only you can do it, since it is your concept and idea, and we are depending on you to finalize all the details."

Yamamoto smiled inwardly. *They think they know what they are doing, yet they are fouling up my plan by putting the cautious, unaggressive Admiral Nagumo to lead the expedition. He certainly would not have been my pick to lead—a typical blackshoe admiral with no aviation experience.*

But that's who the Navy General Staff picked, and I am stuck with him. I certainly did not appreciate being called a traitor, but perhaps Nagano has a point. I planned this raid, pushed my bosses into approving it. I suppose I can't really abandon my fellow admirals at this juncture. But they should have put me in as commander of this attack on Pearl Harbor.

The Navy minister then obviously felt he may have pushed Yamamoto too far. Yamamoto could see his boss back pedaling.

The Navy minister turned to face Yamamoto. "Now admiral, don't do anything in haste that you will regret later. You have had your say, and it was considered. Now it is up to you to carry out your plan for a surprise attack."

Admiral Chuichi Nagumo

Later in the Day, Still at the Navy Ministry

"Excuse me, Admiral," the young naval aide said, poking his head in the door of the office in which Yamamoto was sitting and relaxing. "A bunch of young naval officers are demanding to see you."

"Demanding?"

"Yes sir, and they are pretty insistent."

"Then by all means," Yamamoto exclaimed with a smile, waving his arm in a sweeping motion toward himself, "show them in!"

The naval aide looked dubious. "Shall I call the guards to stand by outside the door?"

"Oh no! Come, come, let them in. I can take care of myself."

Six young naval officers entered the office

Yamamoto stood and faced the obvious leader of the group, cheek to yowl. "And what can I do for you, young man?"

The leader hesitated, not expecting such an aggressive stance from the outnumbered admiral. "Well, uh, sir, it seems to be most unseemly for you, an admiral in the Imperial Navy, especially one that is Commander-in-Chief of the Combined Fleet, to be consorting, on a regular basis, with women in the geisha quarter of Tokyo."

The young officer then backed way a few steps, but Yamamoto matched him step for step and still stayed in right the young man's face.

Yamamoto smiled. "So, you object to the choice of my own leisure time with geishas, eh?" Then he stepped backed and surveyed the group as a whole. "Well, any of you," his eyes swept around the room taking in all the nervous young officers, "that doesn't fart, or shit, and has never screwed a woman, step forward and to you, I am willing to listen!"

No one moved.

Yamamoto raised his voice a notch. "Then get out this office and go about your assigned duties and stop trying to be the Navy's moral police!"

The officers backed out of the room in the face of Yamamoto's glare and disappeared out of the building.

Yamamoto had been tempted to tell them that thanks to him, Japan has built the most powerful naval fleet in the Pacific Ocean but decided he had made his point without having all the bragging.

The telephone rang. Yamamoto picked up the receiver. He shook his head sadly. *Well*, he thought, *the fat is really in the fire now.*

We moved our troops into French Indo-China and now the Americans, British and Dutch have announced an embargo on oil exports to Japan. We are facing a war with all three of those countries plus Australia and New Zealand. The Navy Chief of Staff Nagano predicted a seventy to eighty percent chance of victory in a war with the Western Powers. He must be drinking too much sake—or he's hooked on opium!

End of July, Tokyo, Navy Ministry

An angry Captain Sadatoshi Tomioka, chief of the Operations Section in the Navy Ministry, confronted Yamamoto's staff officer, Captain Kuroshima. Tomioka often referred to Kuroshima as that "foggy staff officer", but never to his face.

"Your boss is shortchanging the operation into South Asia by demanding *all* our carriers for what might be a wasted effort. They'll be lucky if the fleet gets halfway to Pearl Harbor without being detected; either that or they'll find Pearl Harbor empty of ships. Then what are you going to do, Mr. Bigshot?"

Kuroshima balled his hands into fists and stepped right up to this annoying adversary.

Admiral Nagano stepped between them. "Now, now, we are not going to have any fisticuffs are we?"

Kuroshima swung his head up. "You are correct Admiral, I don't have to justify my boss or myself to this chronic complainer. If we don't take care of America, your push into South Asia won't amount to anything! Your boss knows that and so should you. Your fleet has land-based warplanes stationed in China for support. You don't need the carriers. Where are we going to have the support of land-based planes in the middle of the Pacific?"

Disgusted, Kuroshima turned on his heel and stalked out of the office.

August 1941, Tokyo, Home of Prime Minister Konoye

Yamamoto took the train from the anchorage at Hashirajima to Tokyo, for a meeting at the request of Prime Minister Konoye. As he watched the landscape roll by his thoughts wandered to the upcoming meeting and got to thinking.

I wonder why Konoye wanted to me at the prime minister's private residence and not in his office Ugaki, not comfortable with me travelling to Tokyo in view of the earlier assassination threats wanted to send a few guards to accompany me. But I'm not going to let those rightist bastards restrict my movements! I can take care of myself. Besides, after I meet with the prime minister, I plan to visit my lovely Chiyoko Kawai in Tokyo's geisha district. He smiled. *I certainly don't need guards for that. What an encumbrance that would be!*

Kuroshima's report on his run-in with Captain Tomioka— interesting. He handled it well. Tomioka, I am sure, just represents the jealousies of those of the fleet going to South Asia.

A few hours later, Yamamoto arrived at Konoye's residence. He looked it over. *Certainly a modest residence for a prince.* Konoye had been an heir to the ancient Fujiwara clan and, on the death of his father Astumaro, Konoye, at age 12, became a prince. It had given him plenty of social standing, but his family had little in terms of money or assets. So, Yamamoto was not surprised at the prince's small residence. But with that hereditary title, he did automatically become a member of the House of Peers, Japan's upper house of parliament, like the British parliamentary system.

Konoye's wife greeted the admiral at the door. Yamamoto, as expected, took off his shoes and carefully lined them up with the other shoes left at the door—his compulsion for neatness always kicked in.

He followed the wife to the prime minister's den. She slid open the shoji screen and stepped aside while Yamamoto entered. She retired discretely, sliding the screen door closed behind the admiral.

"Welcome, Admiral," as Konoye stood and bowed. Yamamoto bowed in return, his bow being just a little lower, in recognition of Konoye's status as a prince and his own as a commoner.

They both sat down on cushions.

Konoye spread his arms sending Yamamoto a silent *What can I do?* sign. The prime minister sighed. "Admiral, Tojo and Nagano are hell-bent for war and I've tried, but there seems little I can do to stop them. The emperor seems inclined to give them their head. Tell me, what do you think our chances are in a war with America?"

Yamamoto frowned. "I've been asked the question regarding Pearl Harbor often and my answer is always the same, prime minister-san. If we follow my plan to surprise bomb and torpedo the American Fleet and facilities at Pearl Harbor, we'll set them back for a while—no doubt about it—and we'll be successful for six months, and maybe a year or even a little longer. But after that I cannot guarantee, as their industrial might gears up and their large population is called up to serve in the military. Then prime minister, I think we will be in trouble."

Prime Minister Konoye looked at Yamamoto, eye to eye. "Are you saying we cannot win a war with the United States?"

"Yes. If we are lucky we may be able to sue for a peaceful settlement if we make the war too costly for them. But win a war? I don't think so! I spent many years in America—went to school there—and I can tell you that the great nations, like America, have superiority over our small nation in terms of raw materials and financial staying power."

Yamamoto shrugged. "It's simply a fact of life!"

Konoye shifted uncomfortably on his cushion. "So, no glorious victory?"

"If you tell me to fight I will be able to go wild in the first six months, and maybe even a year. But if there are glorious victories in the end," Yamamoto said softly and with a sigh, "I fear they will be our enemies', not ours. In other words, if the war is prolonged for two or three years while America's industrial builds their warships and planes, then I have no confidence in Japan's ultimate victory."

Konoye sighed. "Thank you, Admiral-san. Let me see what I can do with that knowledge. The military hawks warn me that each day, twelve thousand tons of irreplaceable oil is being consumed and if we run out, we'll be helpless as a stranded whale."

"I can't argue with that," Yamamoto replied, shaking his head.

"You know," said Konoye, "many are opposed to your surprise attack plan."

Yamamoto nodded. "I do know, Prime Minister. Captain Tomioka just unloaded on my staff officer, Captain Kuroshima." The admiral's eyes narrowed. "As far as I am concerned, Captain Tomioka is full of shit. With land-based planes at his disposal, he doesn't need carriers. He's just against my plan to raid Pearl Harbor and this is his way to scuttle it—and it'll be over my dead body! If the Naval Command gives him any of my carriers, I'll resign! He wants to attack in South Asia—fine. But what would you do if we were engaged in South Asia for oil and the American fleet came from the east and launched bombing attacks on Tokyo and Osaka, burning them to the ground. Are you all right with that? Because I am not! Then move south is converting part of our powerful Navy into nothing but a ferry service for Army troops."

Yamamoto then calmed down. "Look, prime minister, we have conducted special exercises with our six aircraft carriers. Our torpedo squadrons practiced sinking ships at Kagoshima Bay, which happens to closely resemble Pearl Harbor in layout and shallow water depth. Our flyers were very successful at launching our torpedoes and hitting their targets. Very few torpedoes failed in those shallow waters, so I see no reason why they would fail at Pearl Harbor. We did it over and over. Our pilots are ready, and we can do it at Pearl Harbor. I have full confidence in them."

Konoye answered the ringing phone. He put down the receiver and smiled, putting his hand comfortingly on Yamamoto's shoulder. "I have just been advised by the navy secretary that your plan to attack Pearl Harbor has been approved by the emperor on the advice of the top admirals of the Combined Fleet."

So, Admiral Yamamoto, we are definitely going forward with your planned attack—that is, if the negotiations with the Americans fail. So, friend Yamamoto, there's no sense getting yourself in an uproar with every criticism."

Yamamoto nodded. "I guess you are right. I see Lieutenant Commander Mitsuo Fuchida, fleet commander of the *Akagi*, has been selected to lead the raid on Pearl Harbor. An excellent choice. He's one of our best aviators and very aggressive. I hope he'll balance out Admiral Nagumo, whom I consider one of the most conservative and unaggressive admirals in the fleet and a poor choice to lead this raid.

Konoye smiled. "I know what you mean. Nagumo's still complaining to me about taking the northern route, citing refueling problems and weather so foul he said he'll probably have to order his destroyers home thus depriving him of protection from American submarines. When I told him it was Yamamoto's responsibility, he snorted that you, Yamamoto, would be safe aboard the *Nagato* in Japanese waters with your maps and atlas while he, Nagumo, would be poking into the eagle's nest.

"But bringing the American fleet to Hawaii to show us that it's within striking distance of Japan has the corollary effect of bringing their fleet within striking distance of our carriers and enabling us to strike hard at all those ships sitting at anchor! I don't think even Admiral Nagumo can foul that up."

Early September 1941, Flagship *Nagato* anchored at the Japanese Naval base at Hashirajima Island, in Hiroshima Bay, Admiral Yamamoto's Office

Yamamoto reported on his meeting with Konoye. Admiral Ugaki listened intently. "I sent Premier Konoye a letter, warning him that 'It is not enough that we should take Guam and the Philippines or even Hawaii.' Then I added somewhat sarcastically, 'We would have to march into Washington and dictate the terms of peace in the White House.'"

The premier had given Yamamoto's letter to the press and American Naval Intelligence picked it up from the Japanese Domei News Agency. Little did the admiral know that by that letter, Yamamoto had just painted a big bullseye on his back as far as the Americans were concerned, even though this was simply his biting sarcasm, which he was so capable of expressing. But the American propagandists painted Yamamoto as a fanatical military man bent on personally leading Japanese forces into Washington—and the White House, no less—putting him in a hate category with Tojo himself.

Ugaki smiled at the thought, then turned serious. "Konoye is on his way out as premier. He'll never succeed in avoiding war because he's incapable of overriding Tojo and making diplomatic concessions needed to get our troops out of China. After all, we already spent more than fifteen billion yen in war costs and lost 150,000 men. An indication of the temper of the Japanese nation is shown by the recent special ceremony at the *Yasukuni Jinja* (shrine) in Tokyo, built in 1869, that commemorates those who have died in the service of the Empire, and where the spirits of fifteen thousand casualties of the China war were enshrined. Even the emperor paid a personal visit to the shrine that day. How do think we could simply withdraw from China with our tails between our legs?"

Ugaki's eyes narrowed. "Do you really think Tojo will permit that and let his dream of the Greater East Asia Co-Prosperity Sphere to go for nothing? Tojo can and will deadlock his cabinet by simply withdrawing the Army minister from the Cabinet. Konoye may be a prince, but he's a lousy politician!"

Yamamoto nodded. "I agree. Konoye won't be there much longer. I don't think he even wants it anymore, and with Tojo being recalled from China, and seemingly entering the higher councils of government, there will be a political shake up and I fear it will not be for the betterment of Japan. The Naval Section has absolutely no experience with the Americans. I lived there for many years, went to school there. Admiral Nagano is typical of the Naval Section. He is under the illusion we will defeat the Americans because they are weak and decadent and will not make the sacrifices necessary to win. Nagano wouldn't listen to me. He is afraid of Tojo, who is hell bent for going to war. I fear I am engineering the very situation I always wanted to avoid—a war with the West. The fact is our land, with its mountainous terrain and volcanic soil can barely support our population, which seems to increase greatly each year. How do I argue against moving into those countries bursting with the rich resources we crave? It might make common sense if only we did not have to go to war with America. And that, to me, my dear Ugaki, makes no sense at all."

September 29, 1941, Tokyo, Naval Headquarters

Chief of the Navy General Staff, Admiral Nagano, called Yamamoto to Tokyo for a conference. Nagano probed Yamamoto's mind on war with the Americans. Yamamoto was wary. *I'm well aware,* he thought, *that Nagano had not been an enthusiastic proponent of war with the West but preferred not to swim against the tide of Tojo and the young turks in both the Navy and the Army, chomping at the bit to go to war. He probably feared assassination if he opposed them too openly. I know that Nagano opposed my plans for the surprise attack on Pearl Harbor, but he backed down when I threatened to quit the Navy if the attack were not approved. If I am to be dragged into a war with the Americans, the Japanese Navy needs all the advantages I could give it at the start—and Pearl Harbor was just that start.*

"You really want my true feelings?" Yamamoto said querulously.

"I have spent many years in the United States and have seen their gigantic auto factories and their never-ending Texas oil fields. There is no way Japan could inflict a total defeat on the Americans. A war with the United States will ultimately be a catastrophe. A surprise attack will gain us a year or two, but not much more—if that. It will be a protracted war because the Americans will never give in, and slowly, the they will wear us down when our war materiel is exhausted, and we will be unable to replace our damaged ships and planes, and we will run out of food for our population. Shall I go on?"

Nagano sighed. "Yamamoto, you are my best admiral, but you will not survive in Japan if you don't keep your mouth shut!"

Yamamoto shrugged. "So, don't ask me!"

Nagano nodded.

CHAPTER SIX

Japan Prepares for War with the United States; American Boycotts Hurt

October 9, 1941, Aboard the Flagship *Nagato* anchored at the Japanese Naval base at Hashirajima Island, in Hiroshima Bay

ADMIRAL MATOME UGAKI LOOKED out from the railing of the *Nagato*, taking in the ships anchored in the naval base, more than 200 of them, extending out as far as the eye can see—a powerful sight indeed.

Ugaki then retired to the assembly room where all the captains, called aboard the *Nagato*, assembled to hear an address from him, the Chief of Staff

Ugaki stepped up to the podium, his usual severe and unsmiling self. His underlings called him 'the Golden Mask,' but never to his face. He was not known for his sense of humor.

"Captains of the Imperial Navy," Ugaki began. "This may be our last meeting while we are at peace. War against the West, against America, is coming, no doubt about it."

Someone in the audience asked about the diplomacy that was taking place.

Ugaki shook his head. "It's too late. We do not seek war, but the intransigence of the Americans leaves us no choice. They will not sell us oil; they will not sell us steel; they will not sell us rubber. They are slowly choking the Empire of Japan, leaving us no choice. We must strike swiftly, massively, or die! We are the Japanese Imperial

Navy and represent the empire's sword and shield! We will prevail! Banzai, banzai, banzai!"

As one, the captains all stood, repeating Admiral Ugaki's war cry.

October 13, 1941, Washington, D.C., the White House

As Hull entered the Oval Office Roosevelt looked up and waved the secretary of state to a chair in front of his massive desk.

Roosevelt took a drag on the cigarette protruding from his long silver holder. Then he let go of the holder and left it resting easily in the corner of his mouth. "Well, Cordell, what good news do you have for me today?"

"Nothing, I'm afraid. Obviously, the Japanese are furious with the total oil embargo you ordered in August. There does not appear to be much room for compromise now. Ambassador Nomura did just float the idea that if we do not insist on Japan withdrawing from China, we might have a basis to negotiate some sort of settlement."

Roosevelt took the long holder out of his mouth and vigorously stamped out the last glowing embers of his cigarette in the ashtray at his elbow. "No, we can't agree to that. They must agree to withdraw from all of China. You tell Ambassador Nomura that!"

Roosevelt then sighed. "Ever since the Japs signed that pact with Hitler, I knew we were just dealing with yet another fascist power! When Japan invaded Manchuria and the League of Nations did nothing, they just encouraged Hitler. It was a breakdown of global civility. Now, the Japs have joined with him. Just don't expect them to be reasonable."

October 14, 1941, Tokyo, Office of the Prime Minister

Prime Minister Fumimaro Konoye waved the cable he'd just received from Ambassador Nomura in Washington. "Bad news— Nomura cabled that the negotiations with the Americans are 'deadlocked'. I met with American Ambassador Grew and suggested that I meet with Roosevelt in Hawaii to hammer out an agreement. Grew contacted Washington and urged a meeting but admitted to the secretary of state that there was little likelihood of success with the Japanese government hamstrung by the Army's effective control. So Roosevelt refused, and State then advised Ambassador Grew that the president did not see any use to a meeting, especially since withdrawing from China is a condition of a meeting."

Army Minister Tojo growled. "That just about does it. They don't want to negotiate. Well, in this game, you must take risks, even if you cannot calculate the chances of success absolutely. There is no way we are withdrawing from any part of China."

Navy Chief of Staff Nagano nodded in agreement. "I agree, we cannot wait too much longer. What Roosevelt and his administration are demanding is unreasonable, vindictive and clearly, uncompromising. The Americans would relegate us to be a third-world power!"

Tojo banged his fist on the table. "This is an insult to the Japanese people and nothing but a bald-faced ultimatum! We must get the emperor's approval for war. Now is the time to strike, before America builds up her power!"

"I agree," Nagano chimed in. "The fleet is consuming 400 tons of oil an hour. We cannot keep this up much longer. We must strike soon to obtain our fuel and rubber materials from South Asia!"

"We cannot settle this matter by diplomatic negotiations—that much is clear," Tojo chimed in. "We must therefore petition the emperor to hold an imperial conference and decide upon war."

Konoye shook his head. "I think that attacking the United States is a grave mistake and I cannot support such a risky business. Even Admiral Yamamoto thinks so. The people should be told openly that they face ten to fifteen years of gashin-*shotan*."

Literally, the expression meant "sleeping on kindling and licking gall." But Tojo was not buying any of it. The general warned, "Stationing troops in China is a matter of life or death to the Army. Absolutely no concession can be made on that issue."

Just thinking about it made Tojo lose his temper. He began shouting, "Such concessions regarding withdrawal means the defeat of Japan at the hands of the United States and a stain on the

Japanese Empire. I will not have it! I am finished arguing with you! I will instruct my Army cabinet minister to resign and that, prime minister, will bring down your government."

Konoye shrugged. "That's your prerogative, General. Go right ahead; I am tired of all this crap and ready to step down, in any event."

Shortly thereafter, under Tojo's orders, the Army minister in the Cabinet resigned, bringing down the Konoye government. By regulation, the minister of war had to be a general on active duty, chosen by the Army. If he resigns, the current government must fall. If the Army and Navy refuse to name a minister, they could prevent a government from forming. And that is just what Tojo threatened—to refuse to name a war minister. This gave him the power to name his successor, so it was self-perpetuating. In essence, either the prime minister danced to the Army's tune or that prime minister was gone.

Konoye met with Lord Keeper of the Privy of the Seal Kido and handed him the written resignations of his cabinet. "Please give these to His Majesty."

Kido's eyes widened. "This comes as a great surprise."

Konoye shrugged. "Once the Army withdrew its member from the cabinet, I had no choice under the law, especially with the success of the German Army in the field"

"I suppose that's true."

The Lord Keeper of the Seal was the man to see in that situation because Kido, in that position, was the permanent confidential adviser to the emperor on all matters.

Two days later, the emperor summoned Army General Hideki Tojo, the command being relayed by the Lord Keeper of the Privy Seal. Hirohito then appointed this war hawk general, prime minister of Japan. Tojo accepted the post while also retaining his position as war minister.

Not everyone was happy. Admiral Okada, a former prime minister, asked the Lord Keeper of the Privy Seal, who, he knew, advises the throne and controls the schedule of the emperor, "Do you remember your own words in the past about the Army? Specifically, 'the Army used to shoot rifle at us from the rear; I hope they don't start using cannon.'"

The Keeper of the Privy Seal shrugged. "When the emperor makes his decision, we have to abide by it."

✵ ✵ ✵

After his investiture as prime minister, Tojo, one not to flout custom and tradition, travelled to southern Honshu to the city of Ise to visit and pray at the Shinto Ise Daijingū (Grand Shrine of Ise), dedicated to the sun goddess Amaterasu, from which Emperor Hirohito supposedly can trace his lineage.

Tojo would not become the typical dictator, possessing none of Churchill's spirit, Roosevelt's smarts, Stalin's ruthlessness, Mussolini's flair for the dramatic, and Hitler's evil genius—but strong enough to keep his people in line. He'd been a successful general with a sharp mind.

Tojo was determined not to bring Yamamoto back as Navy Minister. *The last person we need in that job is a peace monger,* he thought. *Besides, this was a time for conquest, not diplomacy!*

Early November 1941, Imperial Palace, in the Company of Emperor Hirohito

"So, this is the situation, Your Majesty," Tojo, the recently installed prime minister of Japan, explained. "The Americans are totally intransigent, with Secretary of State Hull insisting we evacuate all of China—the territory on which and for which many Japanese soldiers fought and died. As prime minister, I am absolutely opposed to any withdrawal from China. It simply cannot be done. And we cannot pull out of Indo-China either without endangering our supply routes from South Asia and putting them at the mercy of the Americans. At best, we can off to pull out our troops in twenty-five years."

Hirohito, in his squeaky voice, spoke for the first time at this meeting. "The Americans will never go for that. I recall you prognosticating in 1937 that we will subdue the Chinese *in four months*, yet here we are, many, many years later, no closer to victory!"

"But the Chinese territory is quite expansive, Your Majesty," Tojo said.

Hirohito looked sharply at him. "If that is expansive, as you put it, it seems to me that the Pacific Ocean is boundless, and if we open hostilities with the Americans and British, we will be fighting on that ocean. Being more immense than China, it's like putting your head in a lion's mouth! Don't you think?"

General Hajime Sugiyama, now Army Chief of Staff and a strong proponent of war against the United States, spoke up. "Your Majesty, China's a different animal. There is a great difference between a war in highly populated China with its vast hinterlands and a conflict on various sparsely-populated islands and peninsulas in the Pacific with basically only the Americans to oppose us. We can handle the islands easy enough, particularly those within our defense perimeter and close to our supply lines and far from our enemies' sources of supply. It will give us a tremendous advantage and the ability to turn back the American foes."

"How long do you think the war with the Americans will last?" Hirohito asked.

"The operations in the South Pacific could be disposed of in about three months," Sugiyama responded.

Hirohito stared at him. "You were the one that told me the China Incident would be would be settled in a short time and yet, here we are, four years later, and no closer to a conclusion! Are you trying to tell me the same thing again?"

Seeing Sugiyama at a total loss for words, Prime Minister Tojo stepped in at this point, changing the subject. "Your Majesty, Hitler is urging us to attack the British at Singapore and pledged if such a move got us into a war with America, Germany would come into the conflict at our side, creating a two-front war for the United States, thereby weakening their Pacific position considerably. Hitler thinks Britain cannot hold out much longer and feels that Germany and Japan together are more than a match for the United States. Germans think their soldiers are far superior to the Americans.

"Fortunately, Roosevelt underestimates us and has declared a 'Germany first' policy in any war. That, Your Majesty, will be their undoing in the Pacific! And as far as the English in Malaysia, French in Indo-China, and the Dutch in Indonesia, are concerned, they are very weak in southeast Asia and will not present much of a problem, and thus, we can secure the necessary, rubber, fuel oil, and metals to successfully fill our war needs."

"You will attack the British, too?" Hirohito asked.

Tojo smiled. "Absolutely! They have their hands full in Europe and Africa and will soon lose the war there. Even Australia and New Zealand, their lackeys, have send most of their troops to Africa!"

Hirohito sighed, and then nodded. "Very well, I leave it up to you. But keep me informed."

Tojo smiled. "And I assure you, Your Majesty, that every effort will be made to come to a diplomatic agreement with the alternative of war only as a last resort. But if we give too much, we will be asking for war! If no acceptable agreement is reached with the Americans by early December, I find that it will be necessary to go to war with the United States."

"It seems we have reversed the traditional image of our Navy as Japan's great wall. My shield has now become my sword!" With that, Hirohito gave Tojo a doubtful look, stood up, and disappeared behind a curtain leading to other parts of the Imperial Palace, while his visitors bowed deeply.

November 5, 1941, Aboard the Flagship *Nagato* anchored at the Japanese Naval base at Hashirajima Island, in Hiroshima Bay

"Well, the die is cast," Yamamoto told Ugaki. "I just issued Combined Fleet Order Number 1 that sets forth the plans to be followed for the surprise attack on Pearl Harbor and the simultaneous attacks on the Philippines, Guam, Wake Island, Hong Kong, and Malaysia. Hostilities will begin on the Sunday morning of December 8, Japanese time. That's December 7, Hawaiian time."

"Are they still negotiating?" Ugaki asked.

Yamamoto nodded. "I expect they'll keep negotiating to the end, but the emperor agreed to set an internal deadline of December 1. If there is no agreement by then, he decided, we will go to war.

Early November 1941, Washington, D.C., White House, Office of the President

Cordell Hull waved the cable in front of the president. "This is what I got from Tokyo, from Ambassador Grew, today."

"Just summarize it for me, I can't read another damn thing today!" Roosevelt grumped.

Hull nodded. "Basically, Grew warns that if our negotiations with the Japs flounder, he thinks Japan will swing to an all-out military attack against us—sort of a do-or-die attempt—risking, as he puts it, national hari-kari. The Japs feel they must make their country impervious to economic embargoes rather than cave in to foreign pressures. Grew wrote and I quote, 'In the meantime, let us be ready for anything and keep our powder dry.'"

The president took the cigarette holder out of his mouth. "And that means?"

"That means," replied Hull, "Japan may go headlong into a suicidal war with us."

Roosevelt shook his head. "That's crazy! But it might be true, given their history of surprise military attacks without a declaration of war."

Hull looked down at the cable. "Well, Grew warns us right here that Japanese sanity cannot be measured by American standards and the conflict may come with dangerous and dramatic suddenness."

The president sighed. "I just hope our military is ready for any eventuality."

"I heard from my man Hornbeck, in Naval Intelligence, one of the guys handling the MAGIC intercepts."

Roosevelt interrupted. "MAGIC intercepts?"

Hull smiled. "As you are aware, our Navy intelligence has long since broken the Japanese military code. Our own code name for those intercepts, which is kept highly secret, is 'MAGIC'."

The president nodded. "Go on."

"Hornbeck is convinced they are bluffing and would not dare fight us."

Roosevelt frowned. "I'm impressed with his code-breaking abilities, but that doesn't make him an expert on interpreting those messages. But I suppose we can sit on our hands for a while. Both General Marshall and Admiral Stark begged me not to do anything that might force a crisis because we have to deal with Germany first—a much stronger enemy. They reason if we defeat Japan, Germany remains undefeated and, while fighting the Japs, that could cripple our struggle against the more dangerous enemy, Germany. Marshall and Stark don't want me to issue any ultimatum against the Japanese, at least for three or four months, so that we can strengthen our defenses in the Philippines and Singapore."

"Sounds like a reasonable course of action though I am not so sure we can foreclose an attack on us much sooner," Hull said. "Another decoded message, this time from Japanese Ambassador Nomura to Premier Tojo, says relations between the two countries, and I quote, 'reached the edge.'"

November 11, 1941, Tokyo, Office of Prime Minister Tojo

Foreign Minister Shigenori Togo shook his head in frustration at the aggressive policies of the newly installed Prime Minister, Hideki Tojo. "I don't understand why you have to set in concrete a deadline of November 30. We ought to give our negotiators in Washington more leeway to reach agreement with the Americans."

"Because," Tojo retorted angrily, "we spent a whole day last week thrashing this out, and if you will recall, our military leaders felt strongly that we had go to war without delay if there was no significant progress by November 30. When I told the emperor that our empire stands at the threshold of glory or oblivion, I meant it."

"I agree with the foreign minister," Finance Minister Okinori Kaya said. "There is no sense in taking on the dangerous Americans if we don't have to. I respectfully suggest to the prime minister-san that a more flexible approach would be highly beneficial. Perhaps with a little more time, we can reach an accommodation."

A leading proponent of an early deadline, a furious Navy Chief Osami Nagano modulated his voice with great effort and inserted himself into the argument. "There is a saying: 'Don't rely on what won't come.' The future is always uncertain, and it would be a huge mistake to take the Americans for granted. In three years, the enemy defenses in the Pacific will be at its strongest and the number of enemy ships will have grown exponentially. Then, we will be in deep trouble, but not now—we must strike soon! I believe a crushing blow at Pearl Harbor will move the Americans quickly to sue for peace."

"If that's so, when can we go to war and win?" Kaya asked.

"Right now!" both Tojo and Nagano barked, almost in unison.

"The time for war will not come later, when the Americans are prepared!" Nagano added. "But we must have absolute secrecy to achieve a decisive early victory. We cannot outproduce them, but we can establish a strategical impregnable position and frustrate the enemy. When the emperor called me to the Palace and asked me personally about a possible war with America, I told His Majesty that our oil stocks are down and would last only two years and once war came, they would last a mere eighteen months. If we take the initiative now against the Americans, we can secure our oil supplies and win."

"What did His Majesty say?" Tojo asked.

"Well, the emperor asked, 'Will we win a decisive victory like we did at the Battle of Tsushima?' I had to explain that such a quick victory was not possible in these circumstances."

"His reaction?" Tojo inquired.

"His Majesty looked grim and just said, 'We will go to war if we have to, but it will be a desperate one.' He left me at that point and obviously, not very happy. He really doesn't want a war."

Army Vice Chief of Staff General Ko Tsukada, facing Tojo, angrily slammed his hand on the table. "Did you know that Roosevelt refused to meet with our Konoye? We keep bending and they keep giving us a cool reception. I don't think the Americans want peace. They are just playing for time to build up their forces. I absolutely insist, on behalf of the Army, that we stop dithering and that any negotiations beyond November 30 are useless. If there is no agreement with Roosevelt and Hull by that date, then we go to war with the United States, regardless of what happens in Washington thereafter! Admiral Yamamoto advises me he has solved all the problems of attacking Hawaii in the shallow waters of the Pearl Harbor and is very confident a surprise carrier torpedo and bombing attack will be successful. Once the Navy sets out for Pearl Harbor, there is no turning back. It is good that we attack now, because with Germany on the move in Europe and defeating all their opponents, if we do not seize the day, we will forever lose the chance to share in spoils of war."

Nagano thought: *It is best not mention that Yamamoto had also warned that Japan could not win a war with America. Yamamoto had pointed out that the oceanic offensive in the south Pacific may be fine but there are no concrete plans for guiding the war through the protracted stage, after the Americans have geared up and are ready to fight the long, drawn-out battle. The intense propaganda by the Tojo government directed to the Japanese public, and calculated to arouse them to war, is doing the job. The public never hears the dissenting voices, like Yamamoto's. It's a good thing, too! Our war-minded government doesn't need public opposition.*

Same Day, Tokyo, Naval Headquarters

The appointment of Tojo as prime minister put the lid on any hope of avoiding war, so it was time to get down to the business of making the best of it.

Yamamoto met with the commanders-in-chief of the various fleets and with the chiefs of staff

"We will attack Pearl Harbor in a surprise raid on December 8. I am ordering the main task force carrying out this assignment to assemble in Hitokappu later this month where they will set sail using the northern route to Hawaii. At that time of year, there will be no shipping in that part of the ocean and the accidental discovery of our fleet will be highly unlikely. Our war games at Saeki Bay, which closely mimics Pearl Harbor, proved to me that such a raid is feasible.

"Admiral Nagumo will command the strike force. If our negotiations in Washington show progress, I shall order the fleet to withdraw. In such a case, you are to turn around and return to Japan."

Admiral Nagumo jumped to his feet. "Assuming we can get close without being detected, you actually may order us to turn back, once we have gotten that far?" Nagumo shook his head vigorously. "It can't be done! It would damage the morale of our men and besides, having gotten that far, it would not be practical to turn around."

Yamamoto leaned forward on the table. "That has been decided, and those are your orders. If you feel you cannot carry them out . . ."

Nagumo interrupted. "Oh, I can carry out the orders, but have you considered the fuel problems? We can't reach Hawaii unless we get refueled along the way, and on the way back."

Yamamoto shook his head. "We have solved those problems. You will be escorted by large tankers, which will refuel your ships, coming and returning."

"Tankers will slow down the fleet," Nagumo complained.

Yamamoto, tired of Nagumo's arguments, had an edge to his voice. "Nagumo, your fleet is leaving early enough so that there is more than enough time to get to the strike point without moving at top speed."

"The elaborate and grandiose plan violates the military principles of simplicity, aim, and objective," Admiral Kusaka protested. "The fleet should be like a lion in a fight and concentrate on the most important and immediate objective, namely the conquest of southeast Asia and not, like an American cowboy, go dashing off like this after the elusive golden apples."

Yamamoto got up with a grim expression. "Just why do you think we spend so much time training military men?" he asked. "If there's any commander here who doesn't think he could turn back if he got the order, I forbid him here and now to go; he can hand in his resignation forthwith."

The room became as quiet as a tomb. Yamamoto stood up and stalked out.

The rest of the naval officers enjoyed a feast of surume (dried cuttlefish) and kachiguri (walnuts), customary fare while drinking to success in advance of the battle and praying for victory in the war.

A Few Days Later, Aboard the *Nagato*, Anchored in Tokyo Bay

"Tokyo has sent Ambassador Kurusu to Washington to assist Admiral Nomura in his talks with the Americans," Yamamoto advised Ugaki.

"Think it will help?" asked Ugaki.

"Not really. I don't think Tojo wants to find a common ground for peace. My guess is that Kurusu is a more devious, slicker, and experienced in negotiations but frankly, while Nomura will still be the front man, Kurusu is there as a ploy to keep the Americans off balance until our attack."

Yamamoto shook his head. "Speaking of the attack, I don't know why they chose Nagumo to lead the strike force against Hawaii."

Ugaki nodded. "I agree; he is certainly not an aggressive enough leader. When he plays cards, he does a lot of bluffing and I sincerely doubt he is prepared to advance in the face of death."

Yamamoto laughed harshly. "The mouse didn't even speak a word in opposition at the time of the outbreak of the China Incident, despite his being Chief of the Second Section of the Naval General Staff. He's afraid of Tojo and the Army! Instead of stoutly opposing that ridiculous venture and threatening to resign, he just kept quiet."

"He's not fit for this assignment," Ugaki opined.

"I agree." Yamamoto sighed. "I should be leading the strike, but orders are orders. They told me last week to prepare for war with the United States, Britain, and Holland, and then they tie my hands with weaklings like Nagumo.

"I was told the plans are, while we strike against Hawaii, also to attack Malaysia, the Philippines, and the Dutch East Indies simultaneously."

"We have a lot to do," Ugaki said.

Yamamoto just sat there silently, in meditation.

Ugaki waited and a few minutes later, Yamamoto opened his eyes. "I heard that the American president just signed an order arming his merchant ships and giving even more aid to England and transferring spare forces to the Pacific to add to England's naval strength, which already has four battleships and two carriers in southeast Asia. But our forces are the strongest and most resourceful in our long history. However, for a prolonged war, I think we will be in trouble."

"The Americans are weak in fighting spirit, unlike the Japanese military. Now is the time to strike! I am sure we will win," Ugaki trumpeted. "We have indoctrinated our sailors to a discipline that gives our fighting men a fear of shame for failure that extends not only to the sailor but his family, friends and neighbors. A fear of failure that is worse than death itself!"

Yamamoto shrugged. "I hope so, but we should not underestimate the Americans. They can fight when they have to."

Ugaki smiled. "But they don't know that a big dagger will be thrust into their throat in a few days!"

Same Time, Pearl Harbor, Office of Admiral Kimmel

Kimmel's Chief of Staff, Captain William W. Smith, knocked lightly and then entered the Admiral's office.

"What's up, Bill?"

Captain Smith frowned. "I have some disquieting news Admiral. The Japs appear to be withdrawing all their merchant vessels from the Western Hemisphere. That's the first sign of an impending conflict sir."

The admiral nodded. "You don't have to tell me! Tell my boss, Admiral Stark, who just advised me he has turned down my request for new destroyers and the two new battleships, the *North Carolina* and the *Washington*, just commissioned. Everything is going to fight Hitler and we're just the step child."

"We have plenty of battleships in Pearl, Admiral," Smith noted.

Kimmel shook his head. "Sure, old, slow, and vulnerable!"

November 17, 1941, Aboard Yamamoto's Flagship *Nagato*, in Saeki

The *Nagato*, sailed into Saeki, located just outside of Hiroshima. Yamamoto assembled the pilots on the deck of the super carrier, *Akagi*, and indulgently wished godspeed to these airmen who will be flying into the sights of the American guns, the same pilots that have pledged themselves to die for the emperor and their empire, particularly coming on the heels of Yamamoto's stirring speech.

At midnight of that day, Admiral Nagumo and his group of warships set sail for the Kuril Islands, to rendezvous with the rest of the attack fleet and from where the strike force will jump off, one group headed for Hawaii and the other, for the Aleutian Islands. Yamamoto watched with approval and he gave a stirring send-off speech as five I-class submarines also set sail, each with a midget submarine lashed down on deck, ready for release when close enough to enter, submerged, into the Pearl Harbor. The admirals knew the men in the midget submarines never expected to survive—they had gone through the ritual to seek death—*kesshitai no seishin*.

Yamamoto shook his head sadly at the whole Pearl Harbor attack scenario. He'd just penned to his good friend, Admiral Teikichi Hori, who could keep his confidence, "What a strange position I find myself in—having to pursue with full determination a course of action which is diametrically opposed to my best judgment and firmest conviction. That too, perhaps is fate."

Same Day, Washington, D.C., Office of the Secretary of State

Secretary of State Cordell Hull re-read yet another warning from Ambassador Grew of the atmosphere in Tokyo. Grew expressed his fear of sudden military action by the Imperial Navy, and not in China, an action to exploit all tactical advantages, including that of surprise.

It looked to the secretary like the negotiations with the Japanese diplomats were going nowhere rapidly. At this point, the only thing Hull could do is forward the message to the president, Army Commander-in Chief General Marshall, and Navy Commander-in-Chief Admiral Stark. Any breakdown in negotiations would leave matters in their hands now.

CHAPTER SEVEN

Climb Mount Niitaka!

November 23, 1941, Somewhere in the Northern Pacific Ocean, Aboard the Japanese Aircraft Carrier *Akagi*

THE OFFICERS OF THE all the warships in the attack force, including the captains of the submarines, came aboard the *Akagi* on orders from Admiral Chuichi Nagumo.

The admiral looked over the group, assembled in the largest room on the carrier. Nagumo did not waste time. "Our mission is to attack Pearl Harbor."

It was like a lightning bolt hit the room. The excitement was palpable and the buzz among the audience kept getting louder. Nagumo slammed his open palm of the podium and the room quieted down.

"I must tell you that the attack is not an absolute certainty. Our diplomats are negotiating to see if we can come to an agreement with the Americans. If we cannot, there is no alternative but to strike at Pearl Harbor. If the negotiations are successful, the attack force will be ordered back. I don't think there's much chance that we will be able to agree so I am appealing to each of you to do his level best to assure the success of our mission.

"I will now turn the fleet over to my chief of staff Admiral Ryūzaki Kusaka."

Kusaka stood and took the podium. "If the enemy discovers us before the attack minus one, Admiral Nagumo has been ordered to turn the fleet around and return to Japan. If we are discovered on attack day, then we will just fight it out and try to carry out our mission." Kusaka then went into details of the order of attack for the 370 planes involved in this mission.

Next to the podium, the naval aviator, Captain Minoru Genda, discussed the targets, the primary ones being the aircraft carriers and then the battleships. "We may have to content ourselves with sinking their battleships since our information is that all the carriers are out at sea.

"When our planes return, we will begin immediate preparations to meet any counterattack and all bombers will be armed with torpedoes. If such a sea battle does not materialize then we are thinking of launching a second strike against Pearl where our planes would carry bombs rather than torpedoes.

"The fifty-four fighters would remain near the task force as a protecting screen and for scouting purposes. Final attack plans will be prepared the day before the planned assault on Pearl Harbor, and you will be so advised at that time."

November 25, 1941, Washington D.C., the White House, Oval Office

Roosevelt finished reading the memorandum from Admiral Harold Stark, chief of naval operations. He put down the paper and looked up at his waiting visitors, General George Marshall and the president's personal in-house advisor and friend, Harry Hopkins.

"I asked Admiral Stark to lay out our naval operational options in the Atlantic and Pacific. This is his memorandum on the subject," the president explained. "Basically, he sees four options. First is to concentrate on a hemispheric defense; the second option is to prepare for an all-out offense in the Pacific and remain on the defensive in the Atlantic. The third is to make an equal effort in both areas; and the final option is to concentrate on defeating Hitler and remain on defensive in the Pacific."

"And what did he recommend?" Hopkins asked.

The president picked up the memo off his desk, pointing to the last paragraph. "Stark's opinion is that Hitler and the Germans are a far stronger enemy and a much closer military menace than Japan. I am inclined to agree with him."

"We did agree with Churchill for a 'Germany first' policy. Let's hope we won't have to fight a two-front war," Marshall said.

"The Nazis have already torpedoed one of our destroyers, the *Greer*," the president informed his visitors, "and I have issued orders, as commander-in-chief, that if any German or Italian vessel enters waters, the protection of which is necessary to our defense, they do so at their peril."

Hopkins grumbled, "Damnit, we should, but can't declare war on the Germans because as things stand now, we don't have the votes in Congress."

Roosevelt put up his hand. "We just must be patient; the opportunity will come. In the meantime, let's see that we build up our war industry and our armed forces. Let's be on a war footing even though we are not yet at war."

"We are not yet at war is true enough," General Marshall added, "but let's face it, the 'Battle of the Atlantic' has sure as hell started."

The president sighed. "Yes, it has."

"Will you approve sending some ships from the Pacific Fleet to the Atlantic?" asked Marshall.

"Yes, I don't see I have any other choice," the president replied.

Same Day, Honolulu, Japanese Consulate, Office of the Consul General

Consul General Kiichi Gunji finished packing in preparation for returning to Japan. His successor, Otojiro Okuda, listened carefully, watching Gunji snap close his luggage.

"You will have your hands full because this consulate is one of the busiest in the diplomatic service of our country, especially in the field of naval intelligence. Our agents have long been active in Hawaii," Gunji explained. "I would collect the information from them and forward my report on the size, disposition, and activities of the American Navy ships in Hawaii. Actually, you may be surprised to know that the Honolulu newspapers are just as important a source of intelligence as our agents."

"The daily newspapers?" Okuda's eyes were wide with astonishment.

Gunji nodded. "I don't know why the military permits it, but the newspapers dutifully report the comings, goings, and activities of the U.S. Fleet. When I first got here, I couldn't believe the information they printed about the size, numbers, and movements of the warships; they even give the *names* of the warships and the times of their arrival! You will have to scour the dailies every day." He picked up today's morning paper, flipped to one of the pages. "A few days a week you can find a report like this," his finger tapping on a particular article.

Okuda smiled. "The Americans are very accommodating in this regard."

"Yes, and that information will be very important to our intelligence service," Gunji said. "You have your work cut out for you."

Same Day, Kure, Japan, Aboard the *Nagato*

The fleet including Commander-in-Chief Yamamoto, arrived at Kure. While there, he received a secret message from his naval superiors that the negotiations with the Americans were going nowhere. The Americans demand that Japan evacuate Indochina and all of China and withdraw from the Tripartite Pact. Further, the Americans would not agree to stop helping Chiang Kai-shek. Americans were prepared to give no concessions whatsoever. *Well, that was that.* Yamamoto thought. *There would be no peace.*

"So, what now?" Ugaki asked.

Yamamoto replied, "There is only one way out and that is for us to make short work of the Americans."

In the meantime, Yamamoto arranged for train tickets for his love Chiyoko. He, disguised in thick glasses and civilian clothes, met her in Shimonoseki, not far from where he was stationed at

Kure. The couple checked into a lovely old inn, using false names and, happily for them, no one paid any attention to these apparently nondescript lovers.

November 27, 1941, Hawaii, Pearl Harbor Naval Base, Office of the Commander of the United States Pacific Fleet

Admiral Husband E. Kimmel, commander-in-chief of the United States Pacific Fleet, watched his visitor, Lt. General Walter C. Short, Army commanding general of the Hawaiian Department, settle into the easy chair. "Have you seen Secretary of War Stimson's dispatch to the secretary of the navy warning of a possible Japanese attack on Midway or Guam, and even a rumor of an attack on Pearl Harbor?" Kimmel asked.

Short nodded. "I got a similar message from General George Marshall. As far as Pearl as a potential target, that's all it is, sheer, unsubstantiated rumor. The Japs would never try such a daring raid so far from their home base. Look, the nearest land-based Japanese bombers are 2,100 miles away and with our Pacific island outposts and our carriers in that area I consider any attack, much less a surprise one, highly unlikely. If they attack, it'll probably be against the Philippines, Borneo, or Malaya."

Kimmel nodded. "They know, and we know, that it's not feasible to launch torpedoes from warplanes against our ships anchored in Pearl because the harbor waters are too shallow."

Short frowned. "But didn't I hear that the British did just that to the Italian fleet in the harbor at Taranto?"

"That's true," answered Kimmel dismissively. "But I'm sure the waters there simply cannot be as shallow as Pearl. The type of torpedoes the Japs have in their arsenal would, in these waters, bury themselves in the harbor bottom mud. Admiral Stark told me he feels any other conclusion is pure speculation."

"But didn't you issue orders last February of be on the lookout for a surprise air and submarine attack on our ships at Pearl?" Short asked.

Kimmel shrugged. "I was just covering all our bases."

Short looked at the Kimmel. "In that case, should we have so many of these big ships in Pearl at the same time?"

"I don't like to send my battleships out to sea without air cover and we have no carriers in the vicinity, at present. I think it's safe if we're right about the unlikelihood of an air attack. My boss, Admiral Stark agrees with me. I still remember," Kimmel said, "what happened to Admiral Richardson, my predecessor. The president relieved him of his command after he kept insisting that the Pacific Fleet shouldn't base a large contingent of vessels at Pearl Harbor because of vulnerability to Japanese carrier attack. Can you imagine what Roosevelt would do to me if I told him Hawaii was in danger of attack?"

Short laughed harshly. "If the Japs do bomb Pearl Harbor, we'd both end up with desk jobs in the Pentagon, if we were lucky—or the federal prison at Leavenworth, if we're not!"

"Still, I'd feel a lot better," Kimmel complained, "if our commander-in-chief did not order every fifth of our combatant fleet back to the Atlantic to buttress up Admiral King. Doesn't make much damn sense to me. But you know Roosevelt. He still thinks Germany is our main enemy and apparently our boss, Admiral Stark, agrees with him. I warned them in Washington that weakening our fleet in the Pacific removed a deterrent to war and an invitation for Japan to strike against us. If there is war, we will need an *increase* in strength if we are to undertake a bold offensive."

Then Kimmel shrugged. "But it was like talking to a friggin' blank wall." He slammed his fist on the desktop. "But this much I promise, we'll train our sailors rigorously to prepare for the possible conflict ahead. But the men need some relaxation time too, so I'm going to keep most of the ships around the Hawaiian waters berthed in Pearl on the weekends—strictly for morale purposes, you understand."

Kimmel shook his head. "Washington has ordered that we should not be the ones to fire the first shot of the war, but we can protect ourselves, if absolutely necessary. What the hell does that mean? We'll have to rely on your Army antiaircraft guns to protect the ships in the harbor from air attack. But frankly, I see the main threat coming from submarines trying to penetrate Pearl. And whether Washington likes it or not, I'm going to give orders to attack any unidentified sub they discover in these waters."

Short looked at the map of the Pacific on the wall. "Sounds reasonable to me. I'm going to concentrate on preventing sabotage by keeping my planes parked close together, so we can guard them better, and keeping them unarmed so that blowing up one plane won't set off the entire group. We have a whole ocean separating us and that should give us plenty of warning to get my antiaircraft defenses activated and my planes ready, and for you to get your ships out to sea, if the Japs attempt an attack. I can have the planes dispersed, armed, and ready to fly in thirty minutes."

Kimmel looked at General Short. "And if it's a surprise attack?"

Short shrugged. "All the way from Japan with a large fleet, without being discovered? I doubt that!"

"Just so you know. I have no planes here, except for those at the Marine Air Station at Kaneohe," Kimmel advised. "And all three of my carriers are away. The *Lexington* left for Midway, the *Enterprise*, under the command of Admiral Bill Halsey, is going to Wake Island to deliver Wildcats fighters to that airbase, and the *Saratoga's* on the West Coast. So your planes, General, for the time being, will be our first line of defense," Kimmel reminded.

Short smiled. "Don't worry. We'll be ready."

Kimmel, though uncomfortable with the cocky answer, decided not to comment.

Then Kimmel brightened and smiled. "Halsey wanted to know what to do if he encounters a Jap warship. I told him to use his God-damned common sense. He said those are the best orders he's ever received! What a character!"

Short nodded. "That's typical *Bull* Halsey, all right!"

Kimmel nodded. "Yeah, but I wouldn't advise you call him that to his face!"

"Not to change the subject," Short said, "but are you going to put up the anti-submarine nets near the entrance to Pearl?"

Husband "Kim" Kimmel shook his head. "Nah, with all those ships entering and exiting the harbor, it just doesn't make sense. Even though it bothers my boss, CNO Admiral Stark. He tells me to be ready for anything."

"But ready for what?" General Short wondered out loud. "The average American soldier was armed with an old 1903 Springfield rifle though the Army claims it has more modern rifle on order like the M-1. The Army's standard artillery piece is a modified French 75 mm cannon that commanders in the field called wholly inadequate. Radar is just beginning to be developed. A crude radar antenna system had just been set up on a mountain on Oahu and my soldiers were only first learning now how to operate it."

Short knew that the United States Army was geared to the employment of massive ground troops, best suited for a war in Europe. "I tell you, Kim, damn little consideration is being given to island warfare over vast stretches of ocean that characterize the Pacific and possible confrontation with the Japanese who, in the eyes of most American Army commanders, were markedly inferior to the modern German soldier and German weaponry. And that's just plain bullshit. Look what the Japs did in China. The Generals, preparing for a war against Hitler, look upon our possible Pacific conflict as a minor annoyance, and tend to forget about us."

Short paused, thinking, then continued. "And the Army Air Corps isn't much better, with less than 500 combat planes, most of which are probably obsolete—even its latest fighter , the P-40B, recently coming into production, I expect will ultimately prove to be vastly inferior to the new Japanese fighter, the Zero. And the Corps had a grand total of 50 B-17s in the Pacific its primary long-range bomber—many of them not in operable condition."

Kimmel commiserated. "Listen, in 1941, the Navy had just begun its major expansion. It has more respect than its sister services for the Japanese as a worthy fighting force, but it, too, has given top priority to the Atlantic and the coming European war. But if the Japanese attack first..."

Kimmel sighed. "The Navy built big ships with big guns, like battleships, for the anticipated big sea battle by surface ships, commanded by traditional 'blackshoe' officers. While naval leaders knew that aircraft and torpedoes were important, they relegated them to being secondary weapons, though the commanders and pilots of the aircraft carriers, the 'brownshoe' boys, knew better. A similar situation had existed in the Japanese Navy, but with Yamamoto on the side of the brownshoes, he made damn sure the Japanese experts were perfecting torpedoes with a speed of 49 knots and at maximum range of 22,000 yards, while American naval leaders were satisfied with torpedoes that ran at an inferior 26 knots, with a range of only 17,000 yards. Further, as American submarine and destroyer commanders, and pilots in torpedo planes, are discovering to their chagrin, a large percentage of American torpedoes are duds—in other words, defective. In our maneuvers, believe it or not, most them would not detonate or, if they did, they would detonate prematurely."

Kimmel paused, thought a while, then continued. "Nor were the American ships armed as well as the Japanese. While the American Navy armed its submarines and destroyers with torpedoes, Yamamoto saw to it that the Japanese also armed their heavy and light cruisers with a full battery of torpedo tubes. The American cruisers have none.

"But President Roosevelt is clearly distracted with Hitler and stunned at the German dictator's military successes after he began World War II by unleashing his war machine on September 1, 1939. In 40 days, mind you, he had accomplished what the German soldiers were unable to do in the Great War back in 1914."

"The Japs probably know that," Short interjected.

"Undoubtedly," Kimmel agreed. "You know, Britain urged the Americans to send a portion of their naval force to protect Singapore, but Roosevelt pointed out they can't have it both ways: to strengthen the Atlantic and Pacific theaters simultaneously. The decision was made to fight Hitler first, and that's what the president is determined to do."

✸✸✸

General Short did not become Army commander at Pearl Harbor because he was ignorant or deficient. In fairness to Short, he pointed out to General Marshall, who would soon become Chairman of the Joint Chiefs of Staff about the deficiencies of the Army materiel for the protection of Pearl Harbor.

"Even Admiral Kimmel, Commander of the Pacific Naval Forces, complained," Short told Marshall at an earlier conference.

Marshall had commiserated, but that was all. "Unfortunately, you are both right. But what you and Kimmel don't realize, it's not limited to Pearl. We are tragically lacking in materiel throughout the Army. The fact is that the Army at Pearl is better off than most of my Army units. What I see as the risks at Pearl are a surprise raid by air and possibly, by submarines. But frankly, I don't see it a Jap landing as a probability. The Philippines? Yes. But a landing in Hawaii? Not possible as long as we have air superiority.

"Let's face it," Marshall continued, "Hawaii is vulnerable because it is dependent on the mainland for food and fuel." Marshall shrugged. "If the Japs could cut that off well . . ."

Short nodded. "You don't have to spell it out."

Marshall looked at Short. "Your real danger, General, is sabotage."

Short had a puzzled look. "Sabotage as a risk?"

"Sure," Marshall replied. "Don't forget, Hawaii is populated with over 160,000 Japanese, about 38,000 of whom were born in Japan. We only have to look at what Hitler was able to do with discontented minorities in some countries in Europe."

"I will issue the appropriate orders," Short assured.

Same Day, Japan, Hitokappu Bay, at the Southern End of the Kuril Islands

The large Japanese task force assembled in Hitokappu Bay—over two hundred ships, ships as far as the eye could see. Its commander, Admiral Chuichi Nagumo, gave the signal and so began the orderly departure of the naval force from the anchorage, heading out to the North Pacific with its destination, Hawaii—its aim, war.

Yamamoto received Imperial Naval Order No. 12 from the Vice Chief of the General Staff to "Climb Mount Niitaka 1208," meaning the attack day has been set at December 8. Now, they only awaited the Imperial rescript from the emperor.

Yamamoto watched the fleet leave. He desperately wanted to lead this attack, but in his position as Commander-in-Chief of the Combined Fleet, in no way were his bosses going to permit him to be in harm's way, at least not on a mission so dangerous as this one, despite his pleading to command the attack on Pearl Harbor.

As the ships moved out in orderly fashion, Yamamoto thought back to his own opposition to a war with the United States. But once the emperor agreed to a war against the Americans, he, Yamamoto, immediately ended his personal opposition, for he would never speak against the throne. Now, he was the emperor's sword and would do everything in his power to defeat the United States. Yamamoto felt strange—but determined. And the tool he would use was the warplane.

November 29, 1941, Washington, D.C., the White House Cabinet Room

The president cleared his throat. "I called this cabinet meeting because there is a good possibility that we may be attacked by the Japanese on December 1."

"In two days?" asked an incredulous War Secretary Simpson.

Roosevelt nodded. "We just decoded a Jap message from Tojo in Tokyo." He picked up the paper and began reading. "'THIS TIME WE MEAN IT. THAT THE DEADLINE ABSOLUTELY CANNOT BE CHANGED. AFTER THAT THINGS ARE AUTOMATICALLY GOING TO HAPPEN.' That's it boys. There's little doubt they are going to attack somewhere and they are notorious for doing it without warning."

Simpson rubbed his chin. "Hmm, they'll probably attack Western interests in the Philippines and Malaysia."

"And we've got reports that Jap convoys are heading for Indochina or southeast Asia," Hull said.

The president's right elbow rested on the desk. He leaned his head in his hand. "Bastards. We have no choice. Cordell, send a message to Ambassador Nomura repeating the demand that they withdraw all their military forces from China and Indochina and abrogate the Tripartite Pact. Tell them if they do this, we will unfreeze their funds, make reciprocal trade agreements, reduce trade barriers, and give other economic concessions."

Hull frowned. "But the ambassador already warned Tokyo would see that as an insult."

Roosevelt shrugged. "Well, tell them that's as far as we can go. Just make sure the Japs fire the first shot so there is no doubt in anyone's mind who are the aggressors."

"Just remember," Hull reminded, "they offered to stop any advancement into southeast Asia, and to withdraw from China, upon concluding a peace treaty between our governments and restoring normal commercial relations and material shipments between the United States and Japan."

The president shook his head. "All those things? Impossible!"

December 2, 1941, Tokyo, Imperial Palace Audience Hall

Summoned to Tokyo by the Lord Privy of the Seal Kido, Yamamoto arrived at the Imperial Palace dressed in full regatta, with all his medals. Kido led the admiral into the audience hall, where the emperor sat on high up on a platform.

Yamamoto bowed deeply.

The emperor looked over the admiral, then read to him the rescript (Imperial Proclamation), tantamount to an announcement of war.

Yamamoto stood stock still, waiting.

The emperor, in his high squeaky voice addressed the admiral.

"In issuing this order, I am entrusting you with the duty of commanding the Combined Fleet. Remember, the prosperity of our Empire depends on them. With your trustworthy experience of many years of training of the fleet I expect you will satisfy my desires by displaying my authority and force necessary for victory over the enemy."

Once again, Yamamoto bowed deeply, then straightened up. "Your humble subject is filled with trepidation and inspiration, to have received your Gracious Precept prior to the opening of war. The officers and men of the Combined Fleet will swear to do their duty. With confidence we face the enemy."

Bowing deeply once again, he backed out of the room, clutching the emperor's order to go to war—a war he doubted Japan could win. He tried to shake the thought while in the presence of the emperor but couldn't. *No conceivable string of great victories could overcome the superiority that America will achieve, by 1943 or 1944—their industrial strength will be our undoing.*

December 2, 1941, Aboard the *Nagato*, Anchored in Tokyo Bay

Yamamoto arrived at his flagship, *Nagato*.

Ugaki greeted his commander-in-chief.

"It's official" Yamamoto announced. "I just came from a meeting at the Imperial Palace with the emperor and accepted the Imperial Rescript authorizing the attack on Pearl Harbor."

"No surprise there," Ugaki noted.

Yamamoto nodded. "No surprise, but a necessary step."

"Out of an abundance of caution, I am ordering our secret Navy code changed as of today."

"Good idea," Ugaki agreed.

Yamamoto walked over to the *Nagato* communications center with Ugaki. "Cable the Pearl Harbor Strike Force in code, 'Climb Mount Niitaka,'" Yamamoto ordered the communications officer on duty.

"Then send another to the fleet," Yamamoto issuing a second order, to the clerk. "Advise them that they are authorized to commence hostilities at one minute after midnight of December 8, Tokyo time."

"Mount Niitaka?" Ugaki inquired.

Yamamoto nodded. "The highest peak in the Japanese Empire, located in Formosa. It's the signal to the attack force that the raid is on."

Ugaki smiled. "So, the fat's in fire, eh?"

Yamamoto sighed. "That's right. Heaven help us!"

"Why?" Asked Ugaki. "Americans are a hollow shell softened by luxurious living and no match for the tough, discipled soldiers and sailors of Japan."

Yamamoto just shrugged. He knew the good-natured giant could be pushed only so far, and that Pearl Harbor would be that point, especially after a surprise attack! "Don't sell the Americans short. We have faced many worthy opponents like the Mongols, the Chinese, and the Russians. But in the Americans, I fear, we will be meeting the strongest and most resourceful opponent of all. Further, Admiral Kimmel is a good leader and I expect he will put up a brave and courageous fight"

"What if the attack is not a surprise at all?" worried Ugaki.

"Then we will simply have to fight our way to the target, and we should be prepared for that possibility, as well."

December 2, 1941, Honolulu, Naval Intelligence, Office of Commander Joe Rochefort, Chief of the Navy Decoding unit in Hawaii

Colonel William F. Friedman directed the Signal Intelligence Service (SIS) and Commander Joseph J. Rochefort ran the code-breaking unit in Honolulu as part of the Communications Intelligence Unit of the Fourteen Naval District in Pearl Harbor, otherwise known as "Station Hypo". Code-breaking had come a long way since the 1920s, when Herbert O. Yardley's team deciphered the Japanese diplomatic code for the U.S. envoys to the Washington Naval Conference. Secretary of State Henry Stimson closed the code-breaking operation with the famous phrase, "gentlemen don't read each other's mail." Code-breakers could now only smile at that naivety.

Rochefort, a thin, caustic man, led his small band of analysts while roaming around his chilly offices (nothing more than a basement in the Fourteen Naval District and known as "the Dungeon") in a red smoking jacket over his uniform and tattered bedroom slippers and, like most code-breakers, was addicted to crossword puzzles. He'd been breaking codes since the 1920s, and in the fall of 1940, helped break the Japanese naval code. Indifferent to personal comfort, he lived off sandwiches and coffee consumed right in the office and slept most nights on a cot a few feet from where he worked. Occasionally, his co-workers would throw him out, commanding him to take a bath before he returned. His caustic attitude toward all his superiors except Nimitz, whom he considered his only boss, was legend. Only his code-breaking abilities kept him from being fired by Admiral King, who could not abide by the man. Indeed, virtually all the code-breakers in his office, working behind locked door, possessed highly idiosyncratic personalities, but were people of high intelligence and utterly devoted to their jobs.

Code-breaking was not an exact science. Rochefort estimated he could break some 10% to 15% of the coded message. The rest was pure analysis and guesswork, combining information on individuals ships, places of past operations, and even the familiar touch or "fist" of a particular operator that might give away the source of the transmission. Combining fragments of information, the Hypo team came up with surprisingly accurate forecasts and predictions. Even when the Japanese used Western names of places, the Japanese sequence of syllables often sounded different from the original, taking some time to recognize the place. Fortunately for the Hypo people, the Japanese did not change codes very often, fervently believing their top naval code could never be broken-and especially by the Americans.

As the war progressed, the Hypo team capabilities increased with experience, giving Admiral Nimitz good information of where enemy ships were located and what their intentions were.

The problem from a code-breakers standpoint was maintaining the secrecy of their work and, at the same time, getting it to the commanders who had the power to act on the information the code-breakers uncovered. Secrecy, Rochefort knew, was self-defeating, because if you can't tell anyone about it, how can it be used? So it became a great balancing act, as they were to see in the Battle of Midway. It often presented a dilemma. Should the information be acted upon if it would reveal to the enemy Hypo's capability to decode?

The entire Honolulu operation was code named "Magic", and in non-capitalized form, "magic" represented the specific decrypted intercepts which it produced. The Magic operation, classified higher than 'top secret', had a very limited number of people who even knew about it. Certain individuals in the War Department and Navy Department had access to Magic, and only on a "need to know" basis. Neither the White House nor the State Department was given access, out of fear of leaks by political appointees.

The firm belief of the Japanese that their top naval code could never be broken made it easier to maintain the secrecy of Hypo's work.

"Shit!" Joe Rochefort exclaimed. "The bastards have changed their naval code. It'll take us over a week to break it enough to figure out what they are doing. Something is going on. It's the first time the Japs have changed their code twice in thirty days!"

"So, we don't know where their carriers are?" one of the coding clerks asked.

Rochefort shook his head. "Not the foggiest. I assume at least three of them are with the Jap Fleet going into southern Asia. Frankly, I am uneasy with the lack of radio traffic from the Jap ships. Something is going on, but I'll be damned if I can figure out what. I think their fleet is out to sea."

"Maybe they'll attack the Philippines?" the clerk asked.

Rochefort shrugged. "Could be. Our fleet in the Asia Pacific area is very weak. Well, we have our work cut out for us. Let's get to it and break their code."

Same Day, Pacific Ocean, Aboard the Flagship *Akagi*

The Japanese strike force crossed the international date line and Admiral Nagumo opened his sealed orders and along with a message from Yamamoto: "The fate of the empire depends on this war. Do your duty."

If there was any lingering question that war was coming, it was answered by a quick burst radio message from Yamamoto, "Climb Mount Niitaka!"

December 3, 1941, Honolulu, Hawaii, Office of Naval Intelligence

"We just got word that the Jap consulate here is burning and destroying all their important papers," the chief of the office said.

"Reliable?" asked his aide.

"Should be." The chief responded. "One of our operatives of Japanese ancestry had a beer at a bar with a cook from the Jap consulate that he cultivated a friendship with, and that's what the cook told him."

The aide shook his head. "Damn, sounds very war-like!"

The chief nodded. "Yeah, I informed the Commander-in-Chief of the Navy, Admiral Stark, and he said he would inform Kimmel and all the commanders in the Pacific area."

December 3, 1941, Washington, D.C., the White House

Roosevelt's naval aide, Captain John R. Beardall, also picked up the warning of Jap destruction of documents and felt it was important enough to bring to the attention of the president.

Roosevelt read the warning and put it down. He looked at his naval aide. "When do you think it will happen?"

The naval aide shrugged. "Don't know, but I would guess it can happen most any time."

The president handed the document back to his aide. "Pass this on immediately to the Joint Chiefs."

December 4, 1941, Tokyo, Naval Headquarters and Later, Aboard the Flagship *Nagato*

Yamamoto paid a surprise visit to his wife and four children in their Tokyo home, spending the night there. He'd eaten dinner with them, but it was clear that the admiral was preoccupied and there was little family talk. Since that was his usual demeanor at home, no one thought much of it.

Now, he had arrived at Naval Headquarters this morning for a party to celebrate the Imperial rescript. All the Navy brass hats were there drinking ceremonial sake sent over by the emperor from his own supply and considered by its drinkers as an extreme honor. The party ended shortly before it was time for lunch, so Yamamoto left and searched for and found a flower shop where he bought a dozen red roses.

He marched over to the geisha house in the Umenoshima neighborhood and picked up his favorite geisha, Chiyoko, for a late lunch.

The meeting was not particularly joyful. Yamamoto fretted throughout the entire lunch making conversation difficult for Chiyoko.

As the lunch was ending, Chiyoko tiring of Yamamoto's silence, asked, "What time is it?"

He looked at her angrily. "I don't know, after all I am not a clock!"

The lunch and their tryst ended on that sour note.

Yamamoto arrived back at the flagship several hours later, in a foul way.

Ugaki could see Yamamoto was in no mood for pleasantries. "You'll be happy to know that our spies in Honolulu and our submarines outside the harbor have confirmed that all the battleships were in the harbor, lined up like sitting ducks."

Yamamoto nodded. "That's good. What about the aircraft carriers?"

Ugaki shrugged. "They are not in port."

"Shit," Yamamoto muttered.

"Well, at least we got Germany on our side," Ugaki consoled.

Yamamoto laughed harshly. "Yeah, a lot that will do us in the Pacific Ocean!"

"It was the Army got us into the Tripartite Pact in the first place," Ugaki said.

"I know," Yamamoto spit out, "and they got us in the war with China. They are a bunch of half-wits, lunatics, and idiots! The sad thing is they pushed aside our civilian leaders and are now running the country."

Yamamoto had the strong sense that he would not survive this war; that he would probably go down with his flagship somewhere in southeast Asia waters. It saddened him that he had left the love of his life, Chiyuki, while he was in such bad humor. He'd spent many nights with her on his Tokyo visits and she would often travel by train to where his ship was anchored and spend a glorious day and night with him, also taking him clean socks and underwear and sometimes, bringing gifts for the wives of his aides.

December 5, 1941, Washington, D.C., Office of Naval Intelligence

The ensign handed to the captain the coded message Tokyo just sent to its consulate in Honolulu. "Captain, sir, we just decoded this communication we intercepted from their Foreign Office and the Japs in Tokyo are asking the consulate people to map out a grid layout of the harbor at Pearl and plot the position on that grid of each ship in its anchorage. The team needs your evaluation to send this on to the Army and Navy stationed at Pearl."

The captain read the decoded message. "We can't keep inundating the military at Pearl with all this crap! This is not emergency. I'll pass it on through routine channels. We can still read the Jap government's coded messages but not the Jap Navy's codes that Joe Rochefort advises has just been changed."

"But sir," the ensign protested, "our intelligence group thought it was important enough to get to Pearl as soon as possible."

The captain frowned. "I'm the one to make that decision, ensign. Understand? You are dismissed!"

Same Time, Later that Evening, Office of Naval Intelligence

A new clerk, wanting to impress her bosses, volunteered to work late on Friday night. Everyone at the decoding facility, except the duty officer, had gone home early for the weekend.

The clerk found several Japanese cables detailing American ship movements, most around the Hawaiian Islands. She brought over to the duty officer.

"Lieutenant, I think someone in authority should see these now," handing the cables to the naval officer.

The officer scanned the cables and slapped them on the desk. "Nothing important. We'll have someone deal with them on Monday. Why don't you go home?"

Disappointed at being waved away, she closed her desk drawers and left for her apartment in Honolulu.

Same Date, Tokyo, Office of the Minister of Foreign Affairs

Minister of Foreign Affairs, Shigenori Togo, under orders from Prime Minister Tojo, cabled the Japanese Ambassador to Germany, Hiroshi Oshima, that we may be at war at any time now and instructed the ambassador to advise Hitler and Foreign Minister Ribbentrop of this. Togo then summoned the German Ambassador Ott to his office.

"Ambassador Ott, would Germany come to our aid in event of war?"

Ott replied without hesitation, "We will give you all possible help."

Same Date, Tokyo Bay, Aboard the Nagato

Ugaki burst into Yamamoto's office aboard the *Nagato*. "Good news, Admiral, Nagumo has signaled that the fleet has successfully refueled from the tankers, notwithstanding the rough seas."

Yamamoto smiled. "I was sure they could, but that Nagumo is such a worry wart, insisting they'd never make it to Hawaii because of the fuel requirements. It's too bad we did not replace him with an admiral who is more aggressive."

"You know the shit-storm that we would have created," warned Ugaki, "if we jumped over his seniority position in the Imperial Navy and put in a more capable junior officer!"

"I know, I know," said a resigned Yamamoto, his arms spread out in frustration. "It's a hell of a way to run a war!"

CHAPTER EIGHT

Tora! Tora! Tora!
The Surprise at Pearl Harbor

December 6, 1941, Washington, D.C., the White House

AT HULL'S SUGGESTION, ROOSEVELT hurried home to Washington from his winter retreat in Warm Springs, Georgia, where he regularly sought relief for his polio-afflicted legs.

Secretary of State Hull and Admiral Stark greeted the president on his return. They were ushered into the oval Office by his secretary Grace Tully, who promptly left, closing the doors softly but firmly behind her.

"How's the negotiations going with the Japs?" the president asked.

"Not good. They added Kurusu Saburo to the team. In the past, he's always been friendly to us, but now he's obviously under constraints. They weren't too happy with my demand for Japan to withdraw from the Axis Tripartite Pact. I warned them Hitler's appetite is insatiable and if he is victorious in Europe, he would come looking to bring pressure on the Japanese for territory in southeast Asia. I also demanded that they get out of China and French Indochina and they refused that demand, too. But that's not the big news."

Roosevelt looked at him questioningly.

Hull handed Roosevelt Foreign Minister Togo cables to Ambassador Oshima in Berlin Japan that had been decoded. The president scanned them.

"So, they are asking the Germans to support them in a war, which he is convinced is coming rather soon, heh? Looks like these negotiations are nothing but a Jap stall tactic. It doesn't look good," the president grumbled.

"With your approval," Admiral Stark said, "I plan to cable MacArthur that the Japanese expeditionary fleet was heading his way and might attack in southeast Asia or the Philippines at any time now."

The president puff on his cigarette in the long holder, thinking. "Okay, send it, but also warn MacArthur that we must not fire the first shot unless it absolutely cannot be avoided."

Picking up the cable again, the president smiled. "Well, if do go to war, I hope Hitler does me the favor of entering it on the side of Japan."

Admiral Stark looked a little perplexed. "Excuse me, sir?"

Roosevelt laughed. "Hell, I could never get that isolationist Congress to declare war on Germany, even if Japan attacks us. I hope Hitler solves that problem for us!"

Later the Same Day, Washington, D.C., the White House, the Oval Office

Hull called Roosevelt on his direct-access phone. Hull wasted no time with preliminaries. "Tojo had just made a very explosive speech calling on Japan to take immediate steps to end American and British exploitation in all the Far East. Tojo's speech convinced me that a Japanese attack was imminent."

"Certainly no surprise there," Roosevelt noted.

Inwardly, the president admitted no small measure of frustration, *finding myself, as president, a spectator on the sidelines; I don't like having to watch others shape the course of both history and the fate of the United States. My admirals report that a significant part of the Japanese carrier fleet could not be located and is probably heading south from Japan. If the Japanese attack the East Indies or Thailand British forces would resist, and I would have to provide them with some form of armed support, depending on what was happening in the Atlantic. If, on the other hand, the Japanese attack the Philippines, then clearly, a state of war will exist between the United States and the Empire of Japan.*

✸✸✸

Roosevelt was speaking to Harry Hopkins when his direct-access telephone line rang.

"Mr. President, George Marshall here. We have intercepted and decoded a cable from the Japanese government to its ambassador to the United States. Ambassador Nomura has been instructed to break off negotiations and destroy sensitive documents. I believe an attack is imminent. I'll cable our forces in the Pacific to go on the highest alert. General MacArthur has told his military commanders that the Philippines are absolutely secure against air attack."

Roosevelt snorted. "I hope, for once, one of his typically bombastic statements turns out to be true, but I sincerely doubt it." His tone hardened. "Tokyo's message to its ambassador portends war, I'm certain of it."

Roosevelt hung up the telephone and looked at Hopkins.

"Too bad we can't strike the first blow and avoid a surprise," Hopkins ventured.

The president shook his head. "No, we can't do that, we're a democracy and a peaceful people."

War with Japan is the last thing I wanted until American forces could dispose of Germany, Roosevelt ruminated. But for the moment, it is out of my hands and I'll just have to sit back and play the cards I get dealt. I'll send a cable, through Ambassador Grew, to Hirohito, suggesting we work together to avert war. It's was a shot in the dark, I know. I doubt whether the Jap emperor would even answer.

Marshall's cable warning to Admiral Kimmel at Pearl Harbor, however, was not marked urgent in the Washington Naval Communications Office and arrived on Kimmel's desk too late to do anyone any good.

December 6, 1941, Aboard the *Nagato*, Anchored in Tokyo Bay

"The fate of the Empire depends on this expedition. I expect each of you to give your all to the point of exhaustion and even death in doing your duty," was Ugaki's message, on behalf of Yamamoto, to the task force approaching Hawaii. "Y-Day is December 8, Japan time, or December 7, Hawaii time, at which point we shall be at war with the United States, Britain, and Holland."

But Yamamoto exhibited no excitement at the coming surprise attack, spending most of his time meditating—and waiting. Tokyo advised him that there would be only a limited number of torpedoes fitted with the new fins that will be available for the attack. The armada would not be as powerful as it could have been, dampening his spirits.

Ugaki reacted differently, as he thought, in his excitement, *Hawaii is just like a rat in a trap. Enjoy your dream of peace just one more day! Our torpedoes and bombs will get you. It's not unfair to attack a sleeping and careless enemy!*

Late that night, Yamamoto received a report that a Japanese fighter had shot down a British seaplane just off the coast of Thailand when it ventured too close to the Japanese invasion fleet

While it was the first shot fired in Pacific war, Yamamoto ordered that no aggressive actions be taken; absolutely no attacks before Pearl Harbor. *It was good,* he thought, *that the British battleship Prince of Wales and the battle cruiser Repulse, did not move out of the harbor at Singapore to challenge us after that incident. The war could have started there and then, warning the Americans at Pearl Harbor and fouling up our carefully-laid plans.*

Ugaki brought Yamamoto the latest reports from Honolulu: all the battleships are in their anchorages but the bad news—there were no carriers in Pearl.

Yamamoto nodded. "Too bad about the carriers, but the attack will still commence; at least we can inflict serious damage on those big boys!"

December 6, 1941, Tokyo, Office of Prime Minister Tojo

Foreign Minister Togo rushed in with the cable from Roosevelt to the emperor.

"Does the message offer any concessions?" asked the prime minister.

"None at all."

"Very well," Tojo said, "let us work out a polite refusal before taking it to the emperor."

December 6, 1941, 6 P.M. Hawaiian Time, in the Northern Pacific, a Few Hundred Miles North of Oahu

Admiral Nagumo watched, in the last light of day, his formidable armada of six large carriers, two fast battleships, heavy and light cruisers, eight destroyers, three oilers and a supply ship. His flagship, the carrier *Akagi (Red Castle)*, led the way followed by the newest and largest carriers, the *Shokaku (Soaring Crane)* and *Zuikaku (Happy Crane)*, and two smaller but modern carriers, the *Hiryu (Flying Dragon)* and *Soryu (Green Dragon)*. Altogether, he had 360 warplanes at his disposal. He was ready, his flyers were ready. Now the whole operation is in the lap of the gods.

Japanese Aircraft Carrier Soryu

He recalled the last day in port when Admiral Yamamoto visited the Akagi to wish him, Nagumo, and his flight leaders and other key personnel, good luck. Fuchida told Nagumo that it was an act;

that Yamamoto was grim and had already warned Fuchida that Japan was facing the strongest foe in their history. Nagumo took that warning to heart while Yamamoto, slapping him on the back, assured him, "I think your operation will be hugely successful."

Then all the staff officers except Yamamoto drank several toasts to the emperor. Yamamoto limited himself to some fruit juice.

The trip of the fleet to this point had been difficult in the heavy seas of the North Atlantic, not to mention many days of heavy fog. With radio silence enforced, all communication had to be by flags or flashing lights using semaphore to keep the ships in formation and not have them crashing into each other. This was a constant worry for Nagumo, adding to the tension. It took thirteen days to reach the force's attack position, very slow because of the need for refueling and maintaining a slow cruising speed of fourteen knots in a persistent fog and the plodding tankers.

Japanese intelligence kept up a steady stream of phony radio transmissions to fool eavesdroppers into thinking that much of the fleet was still anchored in the Inland Sea of Japan. Nagumo smiled. *We made no secret of some the fleet moving toward southern Asia.*

Even the vaunted code-breakers in Hawaii, facing total radio silence by Nagumo's ships, had lost track of the carriers and assumed that at least three of the carriers were with the southern Asia task force.

But one of the biggest concerns for Yamamoto and Nagumo—and uncontrollable—is the danger of being discovered by happenstance before the attack began, such as by a passing ship. Nagumo ruminated, *there should be none in these waters at this time of year, but who knows?*

One of his captains wanted to know what to do if he ran into a Soviet merchant ship out of Vladivostok. "Sink it," Nagumo ordered, "sink anything flying any flag."

Genda and Fuchida had worked out a system of signals as their planes approached their targets. Fuchida, in the lead, instructed his pilots that he would fire his flare pistol once if the American were caught napping, in which case the torpedo planes would charge in first and take out the outer-docked battleships. But if he found the Americans on guard, he would fire twice, and then the dive bombers and horizonal bombers would charge in first drawing fire upwards so that the torpedo bombers could enter the scene at a low level.

Nagumo knew that not everyone was in favor of this surprise attack. He'd heard from the captain of the Kaga that his Chief Aviation Officer , Commander Naohiro Sata, openly criticized the entire operation because what Japan needs is oil and that was to the south, not at Pearl Harbor. He thought the attack was the height of stupidity.

Well, thought Nagumo who had some of the same feelings, *we shall soon see, shan't we?*

Nagumo was tired of Genda lobbying him to be flexible; to launch repeated attacks and hit the enemy until he remained helpless. He confronted Genda, "One attack only and then we are out of here!"

Genda is not responsible for the entirety of this attack force, but I am, Nagumo ruminated. *They can't tell me where the American carriers and cruisers are, yet they want me to hang around a leave ourselves vulnerable. My orders are to get this fleet back home, and that is just what I intend to do!*

Genda, for his part, was tired of Nagumo's negativism. *I begged him, do the unexpected, go all out! But he was not listening and kept repeating his mantra of "one attack only, one attack only." Well, I'm preparing for repeated attacks, and pray that the good results on Oahu will convince Nagumo to go for it. Perhaps the success of our efforts will pry open that closed door of his mind.*

December 6, 1941, 8PM, Washington, D.C., Office of Naval Intelligence

The U.S. Navy communications intercept station at Fort Ward on Bainbridge Island, Washington, passed on for decoding to the Naval Intelligence decoding center in Washington, D.C., a message from the Tokyo government to the Japanese Embassy.

The coding clerk handed the papers to his superior. "We've finished decoding the thirteen parts of the message from Tokyo to Jap embassy here in Washington. We haven't got the fourteenth part yet, but you'd better read these—pronto!"

The duty officer could not find Admiral Stark in his quarters on Observatory Circle, or General Marshall at his home, so he contacted one of his own bosses, Lieutenant Commander Alvin Kramer, who raced over to the Intelligence office, read the messages and determined that the president had better see it immediately. In the absence of Admiral Stark, he decided that after delivery to the White House, he'd deliver a copy to Navy Secretary Knox.

December 6, 1941, 9PM, Washington, D.C., the White House, Upstairs Study

Roosevelt finished reading the thirteen-part message sent to the Japanese Embassy. He handed it to Harry Hopkins. "You'd better read this. It looks like we are going to war with the Japs."

"Where?" Hopkins asked.

Roosevelt smiled. "That, my dear Harry, is the jackpot question!"

"Probably the Philippines. We ought to alert General MacArthur," Hopkins advised.

The president shrugged. "Or Guam; or Samoa. Somewhere in the Western Pacific I imagine."

"It's too bad we can't strike the first blow," Hopkins groused.

Roosevelt shook his head. "No, we can't fire the first shot. All we can do is wait."

December 7, 0030, Hawaiian Time, Oahu, Hawaii, Home of Admiral Kimmel

Kimmel tossed and turned. He was not going to sleep well tonight—and he knew it. *Where the hell was the damn Jap fleet??*

Kimmel knew that he did not have enough long-range reconnaissance aircraft to cover all the waters surrounding the

Hawaiian Islands, so he concentrated most of them in the area south of Oahu, since he knew the north and northwest Pacific was no place for ships in the turbulent winter storms. *Still, with the war warning from Washington, I'd have been a lot more comfortable with a 360-degree search of the ocean around Pearl Harbor. Short had twelve B-17s, but six were out of commission. He could borrow the six B-17s but that would only increase the search area by eight degrees. He felt it simply wasn't worth it, being that it is highly unlikely that Pearl would be attacked. Well, at least the aircraft carriers Enterprise and Lexington are on a mission to deliver more warplanes to our western possessions at Midway and Wake Island.*

December 7, 1 A.M. Hawaiian Time, Aboard the *Nagato*, in Tokyo Bay

Yamamoto sat still in the war room, eyes closed in a seemingly meditative state, unlike his assistants, Ugaki among them, that were highly excited, awaiting for word of the attack

Ugaki wondered. *Was his boss sleeping? This is hard to believe while on the cusp of this great attack we had planned!* But Ugaki did not have the nerve to try and find out by waking him. His mind pictured this glorious day in Japan's history. *What pride I have in our forces that are as ready for war as any nation could be. The two years of intense planning will guarantee our victory at Hawaii and by the time the Americans make some sort of recovery, we will have southeast Asia and all their oil! Yamamoto does not like the Tripartite Pact with Germany and Italy. But the fact is that those two countries are winning the war in Europe, Russia, and Africa. Forcing the Americans into a two-front war will be to our great advantage and help us destroy British and American power in the Pacific and establish Japan's Greater East Asia Co-Prosperity Sphere—provided we can accomplish this in two years.* Ugaki was aware of the separate Army and Navy studies of six months ago, ordered by the emperor, on how long Japan could wage war. The conclusions were similar. Both studies agreed Japan could wage war successfully for eighteen months, and after that Japan must negotiate a peace or she would gradually lose everything. These chilling conclusions were overridden by Prime Minister Tojo, who assured the emperor that figures could lie, and much could happen to assure victory.

December 7, 1941, 3 A.M. Hawaiian Time, in the Northern Pacific, a Few Hundred Miles North of Oahu

The attack was on. Admiral Nagumo had the Z flag, used by Admiral Togo in his great victory in 1904, and ran it up the Akagi mast for all the ships in his force to see. The ground crews were already awakened and engaged in preparing the planes—arming and fueling them—for launch. Planes were then pushed onto the elevators and brought up on deck to be parked precisely in predetermined places, tethered down with its wings unfolded. Nagumo, not a flyer himself, always felt that carriers were extremely vulnerable. His Chief of Staff Rear Admiral Ryunosuke Kusaka, confident they'd find at least eight battleships moored in the harbor at Pearl, eased Nagumo's mind somewhat.

Leading the left-hand column of ships was the *Akagi* followed by the *Kaga* and then the *Hiryu*. In the right-hand column, was the *Soryu* followed by the brand-new carriers, *Shokaku* and *Zuikaku*.

Commander Fuchida frowned at the disturbing news. At 0050 this morning, Imperial General Headquarters advised Admiral Nagumo that there were no carriers at Pearl Harbor. The carriers had been chosen as the top priority targets for their attack. All American carriers and all heavy cruisers apparently had put out to sea and we have no idea where they are. *Well, he thought, at least we have the full count of battleships moored in the harbor. They were secondary to the carriers, but nevertheless, important targets. But I'd trade all eight battleships for two carriers!*

Admiral Nagumo decided we had no other choice but to go ahead with the attack. *I certainly agreed with that decision, Fuchida thought. Maybe, just maybe, some of the carriers will have returned to the harbor in the meantime. I can't worry about that now. Now, I must brief my flyers.*

The cooks fed the awakened flyers a hearty breakfast of fish and rice and provided glasses of sake with which to drink toasts to the emperor and to the success of their mission. Many flyers took some time to write their last letters, inserting hair and clipped fingernails into the envelopes. Some had a bellyband, a *senim bari*, worn as a good-luck charm—what they called a thousand-stitch belt sewn by a thousand friends and family representing a thousand prayers to ward off enemy bullets and to provide good luck and heroic results. To achieve the thousand-stitch belt, mothers and sweethearts, on street corners, called out to other women to sew a crimson stitch into the 1000-stitch belt to create this talisman believed to protect the wearer against enemy bullets. Millions went off the war with these thousand-stitch belt wrapped around their middle.

Fuchida looked over the assembled pilots on the *Akagi* aircraft carrier. "The first wave of attack," he advised, "will consist of 189 aircraft—Nakajima torpedo planes and Mitsubishi Zero fighters. Some of the Nakajimas will be carrying the Mark 91 torpedoes and they will go for the outside-anchored battleships. Other Nakajimas will be carrying 800-kilogram armor-piercing bombs, actually modified battleship shells, and their mission is the low-level bombing of the *inside*-anchored ships that our torpedoes cannot reach. Some of the Mitsubishi Zeros will remain in the skies above the fleet to protect it; others will accompany the attack force to protect you from American fighters sent up to intercept you over Pearl Harbor. The second wave, 171 planes from the carriers *Shokaku* and the *Zuikaku*, will be directed against the airfields on Oahu and mopping up any ships that we may have missed in the first wave. You should know that your attack will be complimented by a submarine attack to add more punch to our efforts. They will go after any ship that manages to escape out of the harbor during the attack and they will form a picket line around Hawaii to intercept any American carriers returning to Pearl Harbor. Also, five midget subs will make their way into the harbor, each with two torpedoes to do what damage they can. We have some encouraging news. One of Honolulu's radio stations has stayed on the air all night playing music. It's obvious the Pearl Harbor base has no idea of what is coming this morning. And that radio station provides a perfect beacon to home in on for our flyers!

"Good luck to you, good hunting and Banzai!"

The pilots stood as one. "Banzai! Banzai! Banzai!"

Commander Genda, sitting in the back of the room did not like that midget sub plan. Genda ruminated, *Admiral Yamamoto insisted on it and rejected my arguments that the midget subs would not add much but might very well compromise our plan of surprise if they were discovered.*

Akagi Flight Deck with the Other Japanese Carriers in the background

December 7, 1941, 5 AM, Hawaiian Time, Aboard the *Akagi*, Just North of Oahu

The cruisers *Chikuma* and *Tone* were about to launch two Zero float planes for a reconnaissance of Pearl Harbor.

Nagumo watched from the bridge as the planes were lined up and the air crews appeared on deck after the gathering in the briefing room. He knew it would be a rough takeoff because the seas were high, and the salt spray drenched the men on the deck. The admiral was troubled because the latest reports had the American carriers out to sea with none at Pearl Harbor. *Is it worth it now? Should I call off the attack and head home?*

Commander Fuchida, already in his flying suit, reported to Nagumo. Fuchida would lead the attack on Pearl.

Fuchida could see Nagumo was troubled. "What's the matter, Admiral?"

Nagumo shrugged. "With no aircraft carriers in the harbor, I wonder, is the attack worth it?"

Fuchida looked at Nagumo steely-eyed. "Admiral, there are eight battleships anchored side-by-side at Pearl Harbor. We can sink all of them. Isn't that worth at least three aircraft carriers? We haven't come all this way and expended all this effort to back down, have we?" asked Fuchida somewhat rhetorically.

Nagumo stared out into the early morning gloom, silent, contemplative.

Suddenly, Nagumo jumped up and grabbed his hand. "I know you can do the job."

Fuchida smiled, nodded, and then hurried to the flight deck before the admiral could change his mind.

For takeoff, the fleet headed east at 24 knots into the 30-knot wind to assure there was sufficient speed over the flight deck to provide enough lift-off for the bomb-laden planes to clear the deck and get into the air.

The Air Officer twirled his green lantern and at that signal, the planes, one by one, began to take off from the still-dark *Akagi* flight deck.

✸✸✸

Meanwhile, aboard the *Nagato* in Tokyo Bay, Ugaki received word on the wireless that the attack was underway. He approached Yamamoto who appeared to be in a deep trance.

"Admiral, the attack has started," Ugaki said in a soft voice.

Yamamoto hardly moved. One eye opened slightly, and he nodded, then returned to his meditative state.

December 7, 1941, 6 AM, Hawaiian Time, Pearl harbor, Naval Headquarters at Makalapa

"Lift the torpedo net at the entrance to the harbor, we have a mine-sweeper coming in," ordered the duty officer.

"Aye, aye, Lieutenant," replied the two-striper, nailed for Sunday duty himself. "Shall I put the net back in place after she enters?"

"Nah, there should be a few more ships coming in this morning, so there's no sense in hauling back it across the entrance."

The radio operator burst into the room. "Sir, the destroyer *Ward* just radioed in that it has spotted a small submarine attempting to enter the harbor. The destroyer dropped four depth-charges on the sub."

"Did he identify the nationality of the vessel?" the lieutenant asked.

"No sir. I imagine he would have if he knew. With subs, it's almost impossible unless they are forced to the surface."

The lieutenant nodded and picked up the phone. "Connect me with the Captain Earle, it's important. He's probably at home."

Captain John Earle, Admiral Kimmel's Chief of Staff he just rolled out of bed when the phone rang. He picked up the receiver.

"Captain Earle here."

"Sir, this is the duty officer at headquarters. The destroyer *Ward* just radioed in a report that they spotted a submarine near the entrance to Pearl and we have none of our own there right now, so he depth-charged it and asked to report it in."

Earle shook his head. "Lieutenant, we get so many false sightings, we simply can't order general quarters and go off half-cocked each time. I want the destroyer to verify this first."

"But sir, how is the *Ward* going to verify? The sub's either sunk or submerged!"

"That's his problem. Just relay the message to *Ward's* captain."

Same Time, Washington, D.C., Japanese Embassy

The decoder handed the secret pilot message to the Ambassador Kichisaburo Nomura. He looked at it and turned to fellow diplomat

Saburo Kurusu. "The foreign minister has instructed me to deliver the substance of fourteenth part of the message to Secretary Hull before 1P.M. But it is still being decoded and then it has to be typed and I am under orders not to use employee typists!"

"What are you going to do?" Kurusu asked.

"One of my attachés will try to type it, but he's no typist. His hunt and peck approach will take some time. But I don't see how I can deliver it by one o'clock."

Kurusu shrugged. "We can only do the best we can."

December 7, 1941, 7:30 AM, Hawaiian Time; Noon, Eastern Time, Washington, D.C., Army Communications Center

The last part of the Japanese message was deciphered and given to General Marshall after he had returned from his Sunday horseback ride.

General Marshall ordered the Army Communications Center to transmit the message to overseas bases in the Pacific including Pearl Harbor, with the Philippines being "most urgent." Pearl could not be raised by wireless because of atmospheric conditions, and the Army colonel had no direct Army teletype service to Honolulu because RCA had been installing a new system. The lieutenant colonel in charge that day elected not to use the very fast communication facilities of the rival Navy Communications service; instead, he ordered the message sent by Western Union, which did not even have a direct line to Honolulu. Such was the state of the inter-service rivalry at this time. The decoded Jap message, tantamount to a declaration of war, did not reach Honolulu until after the attack on Pearl Harbor. Commanders in the Panama Canal, the Philippines, and San Francisco had been warned early, but neither Admiral Kimmel or General Short in Hawaii had been.

Same Time, Oahu, Scofield Barracks, Army Infantry Headquarters

"The radar outpost at Opana at Kahuku Point has telephoned in, reporting that a large number of blips heading our way," the switchboard operator advised the only officer on duty this Sunday morning.

"I didn't know that unit was even operational," the second lieutenant responded.

"Shall I connect you?"

"No, just tell them we are expecting a squadron of flying fortresses coming in from the mainland. It's probably them, so they shouldn't worry about it."

✴✴✴

There were indeed approaching. A few minutes later, twelve B-17s approached Oahu, but they were not the blips the radar operators saw.

The B-17s were flying in from California's Hamilton airfield in Marin County, on their way to the Philippines—and scheduled to be refueled at Hickam Airbase on Oahu.

Notwithstanding the enjoyment of listening to Hawaiian music coming from a Honolulu radio station, the lead pilot, Major Truman Landon, was not happy with his situation because he was warned by General Hap Arnold that he may be flying into a war zone, though admittedly, it was unlikely the fighting would be in Hawaii. To save fuel so they could reach Hawaii, the planes had to have skeleton crews with no gunners or a bombardier. So the fact that they carried machine guns full of grease and inoperable and had no ammunition or bombs really didn't matter. They had no one to do the fighting and nothing to fight with—in other words, they were defenseless.

As they approached Oahu, Sergeant Lee Embree, a passenger, reported to the Landon that there was a lot of burning going on at the island.

"Wonder what that's all about?" Landon asked.

"Fighter aircraft approaching, sir," one of the crew yelled.

"Escorts?" Landon queried.

"I don't think so, sir. They got Jap markings."

"Bastards are firing at us, sir."

"Great," the pilot muttered. "We stumbled into a war with no ammunition, no gunners, no fuel, and our guns encased in grease."

"Break formation and scatter," the lead pilot ordered. "Find your way to one of the fields as best you can!"

"They must think we're armed," Sergeant Embree yelled. "They're taking potshots at us, but from a good distance."

"We're almost out of fuel. I'm going to land at Ewa Airbase and hope for the best," the pilot said almost prayerfully as the plane set down gently on the runway with about five gallons left in the tank.

All the planes except one made safe landings, albeit some had a few bullet holes in their fuselages. The one plane burned on landing at Hickam, but the crew got out safely. One B-17, out of gas, safely made an emergency landing on a golf course.

December 7, 1941, 7:58AM, Hawaiian Time, Above Oahu, Hawaii, and Pearl Harbor (December 8 in Tokyo)

Commander Fuchida, piloting the lead Navy bomber, approached Pearl Harbor. Flying this rugged Navy dive bomber, a large Aichi Type 99 carrier plane he knew was constructed to survive the rigors of diving at steep angles and high speeds and pulling up at the last minute, after releasing their bombs, managing well the tremendous gravity stress to which both the plane and the pilot were subjected. It was important for the pilot to have confidence in his machine and Fuchida did have that, in abundance. Indeed, most of his flyers were expert veterans who fought in China and probably accumulated over 700 hours of flying time, more than twice that of American pilots.

Through the light clouds, he could see the battleships lined up around Ford Island. He counted quickly; there were eight of them, but no carriers. With no perceivable opposition, no antiaircraft fire, no enemy planes rising to meet them, he smiled. He looked at his watch; just two more minutes. He could see that the attack was a complete surprise. He fired up the one flare signal for the torpedo planes, to lead the raid with torpedoes and, for the first time, Fuchida broke radio silence, shouting, "*To, To, To, To, To*," the code for CHARGE, or, in Japanese, the first syllable of *TOTSUGEKI!*

To the fleet Fuchida radioed *TORA, TORA, TORA!* That told Admiral Nomura in code that complete surprise had been achieved. The *Kido Butai*, "the Mobile Force," proved itself beyond their wildest expectations.

✹✹✹

"Admiral," the communications clerk aboard the *Nagato* anchored in Tokyo Bay, shouted.

Yamamoto's eyes flew open, ending his meditation. "Keep listening!"

The communications clerk nodded.

A few minutes later, the communications clerk looked up. "Radio signal sir. TORA, TORA, TORA!"

Ugaki, beside himself with excitement, shouted out "TORA, TORA, TORA! We achieved total surprise!"

Yamamoto smiled, now well out of his trance. In the operations room both admirals listened intently to the wireless reports of the pilots, now no longer on radio silence.

"I got a battleship! It's sinking!"

"I bombed Hickam Airbase and destroyed many planes all conveniently lined up wing-to-wing!"

Ugaki handed Yamamoto a slip of paper setting forth the intercepted American messages at Pearl. "Attacked by Jap bombers." "General Quarters! This is not a drill, repeat, this is not a drill! This is the real thing!"

They waited for the reports from the retuning pilots.

"Two battleships sunk, four badly damaged."

"Several cruisers sunk."

"Three hundred planes destroyed on the ground."

Yamamoto listened in deep concentration. Suddenly he began issuing orders. "Have the cruiser *Tone* detached immediately and sent south to see if we can locate any of their aircraft carriers!"

Same Time, Hawaii, at Pearl Harbor

Kimmel, preparing for his Sunday golf game with General Short, heard it before he saw it—the muffled explosions, the rattling of the windows.

His yeoman aide ran up to him. "Message from signal tower, sir, 'This is no drill.'"

Kimmel raced outside to his neighbor's lanai, which commanded a clear view of the battleship row at Pearl. He could see the swarms of planes, the flames, and smoke in the harbor. He watched as a tremendous explosion lifted the battleship *Arizona* out of the water and then the big battleship just sank to the harbor bottom.

"Oh shit." He picked up the phone and called his headquarters. "Alert all the ships in Pearl to release all the ammo, man the guns, and get the hell out of the harbor if they can. Sound general quarters for the entire base and all our airfields This is no drill. We are at war! Alert General Short."

The admiral raced outside just as his driver pulled up to pick him up for golf.

"Get me down to my office in the submarine base at Pearl as fast as you can."

"In your golf outfit sir?"

"No time to change. I have a spare uniform down at the base. Just get going and get me there pronto."

Shit, there are 96 ships anchored in Pearl Harbor, he ruminated, *and most of them are sitting ducks to this Japanese onslaught with half the fleet onshore or in their hammocks, sleeping off those Saturday night binges on this Sunday morning. And I bet the Japs knew it!*

✽✽✽

"What's the count?" Kimmel demanded as he watched the debacle from the window of his office at the submarine base.

"All the battleships were sunk or disabled, sir. *Oklahoma* just capsized. Didn't think battleship could go keel up like that."

"If it floats, it can capsize," Kimmel grunted. "Did we get any planes up in the air?"

"Very few, sir. The Japs destroyed most of the aircraft before they could take off Some tried, but very few made it. It was a complete surprise!"

Kimmel took a deep breath. "You don't have to tell me!"

"Sir, General Short is on line one."

"Walt, Kim here, how are things at your end?"

"Bad, we got caught with our pants down. We lost most of our planes that were closely parked wingtip-to-wingtip and unarmed," and then added angrily, "just as Washington ordered, to prevent, they claimed, sabotage by the local Japs. As a result, we were unable to get our planes in the air to intercept the bastards; our planes on the ground were sitting ducks. The Japs were able easily to knock out a lot of my B-17s and almost half of my Wildcat fighters."

"Where in hell, Walt, did these bastards come from? It's implausible for them to be from land-based planes at any Jap possession in the Pacific because they're all too far away for any of the Jap planes to reach Hawaii, much less return to their home base. Were they launched from carriers? If so, from the north? From the south? Why hadn't we detected them?"

"Those Washington idiots and their suggestions about sabotage—watch, now they'll blame us for their foul-up!" Kimmel growled. "The Japs even got two of my fleet boats at Kaneohe Marine Airbase. And here I am looking out the window at my office watching our ships get mauled and there's not a damn thing I can do about it."

"I feel the same way, Kim. Their fighters are shooting up our barracks, hangers and other targets of opportunity. They're also strafing citizens in downtown Honolulu! But we've got our antiaircraft guns in action now and we've shot down a few Japs."

"Yeah, a few of our ships not at the bottom of the harbor are firing back with all they can muster."

"Incidentally, I am sending a few Army units down to the beaches to dig in as a defense if the Japs try to invade Oahu," Short advised.

"Thank heavens I sent our two carriers out of Pearl on missions to Midway and Guam," Kimmel said.

"You only have two carriers?"

"Actually," Kimmel advised, "I have three. The *Saratoga* is in San Diego being refitted. Our brilliant leaders stripped us of many of our warships and sent them to the Atlantic."

"I hope the Japs don't know how shorthanded we are," Short noted.

Kimmel managed a smile. "The president relieved of command JO, my predecessor here at Pearl, because after taking the fleet to Hawaii for maneuvers, he was ordered to keep it there. JO complained that leaving the fleet anchored in Pearl was too dangerous and made us very vulnerable. The West Coast was just too far away to support adequately a big force in Hawaii."

"JO?"

"James O. Richardson, a big gun blackshoe admiral, former captain of the cruiser *Augusta*, and commander of the Battle Force here in the Pacific. He was made commander of this naval base— until he opened his big mouth and stated the obvious. He was my immediate predecessor here."

Admiral Stark told the fleet they would be stationed here as a deterrent to the Japs moving into the East Indies. After JO asked what his fleet in Hawaii could do if the Japs did make such a move, Stark admitted he did not know. But JO went further, he told the president that the senior officers in the Navy do not have the trust and confidence in the civilian leadership in this country, essential for the successful prosecution of a war in the Pacific That leaving the ships in Pearl was a God-damned mousetrap."

Short grimaced. "Jesus, in the military, you can't just say, 'Look, the emperor isn't wearing any clothes.'"

"No, you can't, and JO paid the price. He crossed the line between military and political matters. But Walt, now you'd better be prepared. The shit is really going to hit the fan for us on this one."

"Kim, no doubt we'll take the fall for Washington's foul ups," Short grumbled.

"For sure, for sure." Kimmel said softly. He hung up and returned to the window to watch the agonizing scene of terrible violence being played out before him.

Kimmel mused, *JO refused to put up the torpedo nets because he felt torpedoes were not a danger in these shallow waters. It really pissed off Secretary of the Navy Knox, so when I came on I had them put up, and they only came down to permit ships to enter the harbor, and that's what happened just before the Jap attack. I suppose I'll get blamed for that, too.*

Then Kimmel jumped as the office window exploded. A 50-caliber machine gun bullet crashed through the glass cutting his shirt and imbedding a small shard of glass in his chest. A dark red splotch appeared on his shirt.

His communications officer leaped to the Kimmel's assistance, but the admiral waved him off

"I'm okay. The wound is small. It would be better, Commander, if it had killed me," Kimmel snapped.

Same Day, 9AM, Hawaiian Time, Pearl Harbor

The second wave arrived over Pearl Harbor with eighty dive bombers, fifty-four high level bombers and thirty-six fighters. The difference this time, the Americans were ready, and shot down six fighters and fourteen dive bombers, but enough Japanese planes got through to inflict further damage at the harbor and airfields.

Six of the planes, confused by the flat-deck appearance of the target ship *Utah*, and thinking she was a carrier, wasted many bombs on her.

At the end of the day, Kimmel and Short totaled up the damage. Six battleships sunk and two damaged, three destroyers and two cruisers damaged, and more than three thousand had been killed or wounded. Of the 169 Navy planes in Hawaii, 92 were destroyed, 39 damaged. 96 Army Airforce planes were destroyed. There was a bright spot. The carriers were not in port!

Two American pilots had raced by car to the small auxiliary airstrip at Haleiwa, and missed by the Japanese attackers, jumped into two P-40s, managed to get them in the air, and greeted the incoming second wave of Japanese bombers, shooting down several and breaking up the Japanese air formations.

Same Day, Noon, Hawaiian Time, Aboard the Carrier *Akagi*, the Bridge

Fuchida and the excited pilots reported in, describing the devastation they inflicted on Pearl Harbor and the military airfields.

The first question Admiral Nagumo asked. "Did you find any carriers at Pearl?"

"There were no carriers in the harbor, I am sure of that. But we must go back and finish the job," Fuchida urged. "We must hit the fuel storage tanks and wipe out Oahu's vast reserves. With Hawaii's oil stocks, it would force the war back to the American continent."

All the pilots agreed and pushed for another strike.

Rear Admiral Kusaka, his chief of staff asked Fuchida, "Suppose we do launch another strike, what would be our objectives?"

Fuchida thought a moment. "The repair facilities to prevent them from raising those ships in the shallow waters and salvaging them very quickly. We should also hit the heavy-oil tanks and deprive them of a local source of fuel and make them depend on fuel 2,000 miles away."

Kusaka disagreed. "Not worth it. We still do not know where the American carriers and the rest of the fleet are. They are not at Pearl Harbor. We are in no condition, fuel-wise, for an extended surface battle with those enemy carriers and cruisers. Our destroyers are critically low on fuel and our tankers are more than a day's steaming away. And our orders are to return to Japan with the fleet intact. I would withdraw as soon as all our planes have been recovered."

Nagumo nodded. "I agree, the first two waves of attacks inflicted a tremendous amount of damage and I do not think additional attacks now would increase the damages to the American fleet that much more. Our anticipated results have been achieved. But by staying here, we be well within range of their land-based warplanes and possibly the American carriers, whose whereabouts are presently unknown to us. This leaves our force seriously exposed to counterattacks. Besides, the element of surprise is gone and the American defenders at Pearl were getting much more efficient at shooting down our planes. It's not worth the risk. And don't forget, initiating another strike now would leave our planes returning in the dark and all the landing risks that entails. Besides, what if the American planes caught us as we were launching our planes for another strike? My orders are to strike and get the hell out of here. There is no contingency for another strike and I have no such orders. so my decision, for the safety of the fleet is that I am ordering us to withdraw."

Genda was not surprised. He knew there would be no more than one double strike against Pearl. They'd argued about it often enough on the way here. Fuchida's arguments, he knew, would fall on deaf ears. In his mind, Nagumo was a miscast misfit. *Things would have been different if either Admirals Yamamoto or Onishi was here leading the task force!*

Genda pleaded with Admiral Nagumo, "At least stay in the area for another day or two and search for the American carriers."

Nagumo gave him a baleful stare. "We gambled, and we were lucky—we did not lose a single ship. We stayed in America's backyard long enough. Now, we are going home!"

The decision made, at 1:30PM, Nagumo had the signal flag hoisted on the mast of *Akagi* ordering the Task Force to withdraw on a north-northwest course and head home with all due speed.

✳✳✳

If Genda was not surprised, Kimmel sure was. He'd expected a third attack and girded what was left of his forces to meet it. After all, there was still many undamaged ships in the harbor, and the repair facilities and tank farms all were untouched.

By late evening, Kimmel ordered his forces to stand down, thankful the Japs had not completed the job.

Attack on Pearl Harbor

CHAPTER NINE

The Aftermath: The Rise of Admiral Nimitz

December 7, 1941, 1:40 PM, Eastern Time, Somewhere Just West of Hawaii

THE *ENTERPRISE*, HAVING DELIVERED warplanes to the Marshall Islands outpost, was a day late getting into Pearl because heavy trade winds delayed the refueling process. They were a half-a-day's journey from Pearl Harbor when a telephone call came through that the Japs were bombing Pearl Harbor. Admiral Bull Halsey's flag secretary, Lieutenant Douglas Moulton delivered the message to the Admiral.

"Fire up those boilers, we are going Jap hunting," Halsey ordered. "The Japs had to be using carriers. No land-based Nippon planes could possibly reach Hawaii from any of their bases."

"Where do we look?" the Moulton asked.

"Got to be north or northwest of Hawaii. We haven't seen anything here south of Pearl. So let's head north and see if we can intercept the Jap fleet! And recall the planes we just sent on to Pearl. We may need them. The naval authority Mahan once said bad ships and good men make a better navy than good ships and bad men. And I truly believe it!"

"Should we wait for some cruisers and battleships to escort us?" Mouton asked.

"Hell no, we don't need help from those uptight blackshoe sailors. Our brownshoe guys are in the fighting Navy. Besides, if we wait for those guys, the Japs will get away! Now, if our pilots can just hit a ship with their bombs, we'll be okay." He was not pleased with the miserable performance of his pilots who, in practice, couldn't seem to hit the target ship with their bombs, unlike their Japanese counterparts whom Yamamoto had drilled ruthlessly hard and demanded excellence and accuracy from his flyers.

Moulton smiled inwardly at Halsey's reference to the brownshoers and the blackshoers. The brownshoers were the Navy officer flyers who earned their wings. They were an independent group, who wore more informal khaki uniforms instead of the Navy officer's black. The blackshoers were typically surface sailors on the battleships, cruisers, and destroyers. Halsey and some other high echelon naval people took aviation training to earn their wings so that they could command aircraft carriers, but many of the brownshoers distained these latecomers. The talented brownshoers who'd earned their wings in the 1920s and led air squadrons, were now approaching the flag rank level, and did not trust the blackshoe commanders for air operations, though it was the blackshoe admirals that controlled the promotion board and duty assignments. Moulton knew Halsey agreed with the brownshoers—that they were the future of the fighting Navy. Commander John Towers, a brownshoe leader, was already urging Nimitz to use the carrier task force aggressively against the Japs rather than simply providing air cover for landings. But Nimitz knew that the carriers must fit into the grand scheme of amphibious landings supported by a carefully planned and choreographed logistics.

Admiral Chester Nimitz

December 7, 1941, 1:40 PM, Eastern Time, the White House, the Oval Office

Roosevelt and Hopkins, dressed in old clothes, wholly appropriate for a relaxed Sunday afternoon, chatted about lend-lease while ignoring the valet who cleared away the lunch dishes. Roosevelt's direct-line telephone rang interrupting Hopkins in mid-sentence.

Hopkins watched the president's face turn red with anger. "No!" he shouted, then groaned. Hopkins leaned forward as the president listened silently. Rarely had he seen the president so upset.

Frowning, the president hung up the receiver. "That was the secretary of the navy. The Japanese have bombed Pearl Harbor."

Hopkins's eyes widened in shock. "There must be some mistake, he must have meant the Philippines! Surely, the Japs would not attack Hawaii."

"Sadly, the report's true. It's just the kind of thing the Japs would do—a sneak attack. I'm not surprised we're at war, but I really didn't expect it to begin at Pearl Harbor."

"What's the damage?" a concerned Hopkins asked.

Roosevelt shrugged. "No reports in yet. I just hope our warships managed to leave the harbor in time. I doubt it, though, because it was early Sunday morning and the posts were most likely manned by a skeleton duty staff." The president shook his head. "It doesn't look good, not good at all."

"Did you know," Hopkins asked, "that for the Japanese, 1941 is the year of the snake?"

The president removed the cigarette holder from between his lips. "Snake, eh? How God-damn appropriate! You know, cousin Teddy Roosevelt warned me, when I became secretary of the navy under Woodrow Wilson, that trouble may come, and if it does, in his words, 'it will come suddenly.' How prescient he was!"

Roosevelt picked up the phone, which connected to the White House switchboard. "Connect me with Governor Poindexter in Honolulu and make it sooner than later."

For a while, the president stared absently at the silent phone, then he relaxed. "In one sense, I suppose I'm relieved the waiting is over. The Japanese have taken the decision out of the hands of Congress and ended the debate on whether we should go to war. For that, at least, we should be thankful." He shook his head. "Just think of all the cries of 'warmonger' from Congress if I had expressed publicly my fears of a Jap sneak attack and…"

The phone rang. The president stiffened, grabbed the receiver and listened intently. "Poindexter," he whispered to Hopkins. Then his face grew dark. He looked at Hopkins as he cradled the phone under his ear. "My God," the president exclaimed, "there are more Japanese planes coming in over Hawaii at this very minute!" Roosevelt hung up after Poindexter said he was leaving for the shelter.

The phone rang again. The president listened and then ordered, "Cordell, I want you to receive the Japanese envoys and pretend we haven't decoded the message the Jap government sent to them. Then get rid of them and come on over to the White House."

Same Day, 2:15 PM, Eastern Time, Washington, D.C., State Department, Office of the Secretary

Finally decoding the message sent by their own government, Ambassador Kichisaburo Nomura and Saburo Kurusu, the Japanese envoy sent to assist the ambassador in the negotiations with the Americans, rushed into the State Department Building heading for Cordell Hull's office as fast as they could go without appearing unseemly. Their instructions were to advise the Americans that negotiations were broken off and that a state of war now existed between the Empire of Japan and the United States. The message was intended to be delivered just minutes before the attack on Pearl Harbor, but it was now well after the attack had commenced. Hull had read the decoded secret Japanese message almost an hour before the Japanese diplomats had.

The Japanese diplomats sat in the reception area, cooling their heels and exchanging nervous glances. At first Hull felt inclined not to see them, but finally decided to take the president's advice and invite them into his office. Hull came out and motioned them to enter. They bowed politely while Hull returned only the faintest of nods and refused to shake hands.

Nomura, looked at Hull questioningly, then handed the secretary of state the Japanese Government note. Hull already knew its contents; ironically, American code-breakers in intelligence had decoded the same message hours before the Ambassador himself knew its contents. He did not invite the envoys to sit; they stood stiffly while he pretended to read the note for the first time.

Hull looked up. "Are you presenting this note on behalf of your government?"

"I am," Nomura responded.

Hull glared at the envoy. "We have been at these negotiations for how long? The last nine months?"

Nomura nodded.

"In all that time, I have never uttered an untruth to you. But I must say," Hull raised his voice, "that in all of my five years of public service I have never seen a document that had so many falsehoods and deceptions—on a scale so large that I never dreamed that any government, including yours, was capable of uttering them. How you had the nerve to come here *after* your planes launched a sneak attack on innocent Americans at Pearl Harbor is beyond my understanding."

Well, I-I-I want to say..." Nomura stammered, trying to find the right words.

Hull put up his hand, stopping Nomura in mid-sentence.

"No, I don't want to hear it," Hull spit out. "Please leave immediately." He pointed to the door. "Scoundrels and piss-ants," Hull muttered just loud enough for the Japanese diplomats to hear as they made their way out.

Hull waved the paper, shaking his head. "The Jap bastards only now advise me that a state of war exists between the Empire of Japan and the United States."

Hull handed the document over to his aide. "Run this over to the president immediately!"

The aide took the document and hightailed it out of the room and ran through town in a straight line to the White House.

Same Day, 9 PM London Time, Chequers Country Estate of Churchill, near Ellesborough, England

Prime Minister Winston Churchill enjoyed the weekend at Chequers, his country estate about 40 miles west of Central London, with his guests, Averell Harriman, the American lend-lease coordinator and U.S. Ambassador John Winant. Churchill rued that the weekend was ending, and he would soon find himself back in the rat race at 10 Downing Street.

"Excuse me, sir," the butler had burst in the room, "but you ought to listen to the BBC station on your radio. The Japanese have just bombed the Americans at Pearl Harbor."

Churchill immediately switched on the radio, already tuned the BBC station. All three of them listened intently as the breathless announcer described the Japanese "sneak attack."

Churchill immediately called in his aide. "Set me up immediately on the BBC to announce Britain's declaration of war against Japan!"

Harriman put his hand on the prime minister's shoulder. "Winston, you can't declare war simply on the basis of one radio broadcast."

Churchill paused. "I suppose you are right." He turned to his aide. "I'll get it directly from the horse's mouth. Get President Roosevelt on the telephone."

He turned to his guests. "This reminds me of what Sir Edward Grey said to me concerning America's entry into the First World War, 'Once the fire is lit,' he said, 'there is no limit to the power it can generate.'" He smiled. "Gentlemen, tonight I expect to go to bed and sleep the sleep of the saved and thankful."

Same Day and Time, Washington, D.C., the White House, the Oval Office

"Mr. President," Grace Tully said, sticking her head in the open door, "Prime Minister Churchill is on the phone."

Roosevelt picked up. "Mr. Prime Minister, good of you to call!"

"I just heard a radio report, Mr. President, that the Japanese have attacked Hawaii."

The president sighed, "It's true, I'm afraid. A large fleet of planes bombed Pearl Harbor. It looks as if we are all in the same boat now.

"The Japs," Roosevelt observed, "accomplished what I could not. The sneak attack hardened the hearts of the American people, including even our isolationists and made them outraged at the Japs and ready to fight."

"What about Hitler?" Asked Churchill.

"Unless Hitler does something stupid like declaring war on the United States or attacking our ships or troops, Congress will never approve a war against Germany or any other two-front war."

Churchill chuckled. "He's not that smart."

The Same Day, 10AM, Hawaiian Time, Pearl Harbor Submarine Base, Office of Admiral Kimmel

The aide rushed in to Kimmel's office. "Urgent message from Admiral Stark at the Navy Department, Admiral."

Kimmel took the paper and read it. EXCECUTE UNRESTRICTED AIR AND SUBMARINE WARFARE AGAINST JAPAN. *Just a little late, Admiral,* Kimmel thought, *we could have used that warning two hours ago.*

Kimmel read Admiral Bloch's report that he'd just been on the phone with Secretary of the Navy Knox." Kimmel shook his head. *Another Washington bureaucrat who is too little, too late.*

Looks like the battleships Arizona and the Oklahoma are total losses, but Pennsylvania and Tennessee are damaged only superficially, and we can raise the California out of the mud without too much trouble. We're fortunate because the Japs failed to hit any of my repair facilities. And there's no damage to our oil reserves. Well, I guess this attack settled the question of aircraft carriers versus battleships with the big wagons clearly coming out second best. The 'big gun ships' Fleet doctrine will have to be rewritten—and fast!

The Same Day, 3:00 PM Eastern Time, Washington, D.C., Home of Admiral Chester Nimitz

Chester Nimitz enjoyed relaxing at home with his family on Sunday. He had a fondness for brisk morning walks and, after taking one on this Sunday December 7th, he joined his family. In the afternoon, he sat by the radio with Mrs. Nimitz and youngest daughter Mary, preparing to enjoy the concert of the New York Philharmonic,

Artur Rodzinski conducting. Daydreaming, he played with his partial ring finger, part of which he lost to a diesel engine in 1923. He now had something in common with his next foe and nemesis, Admiral "eight-fingers" Yamamoto.

The concert's opening notes began and almost immediately, they were interrupted by a news flash that the Japanese had bombed Pearl Harbor.

Nimitz jumped up like he was shot. Grabbing his overcoat, he headed for his automobile. Then it hit him as an afterthought. Turning, in mid-step, he looked back at his wife. "Catherine, I won't be back until God knows when."

She just waved as he disappeared out the side door into the garage.

The Same Day, 3:00 PM, Washington, D.C., the White House, the Cabinet Room

Either out of town or spread out over the Washington area on this day of leisure, the members of the cabinet began straggling in. General George Marshall and Secretaries Frank Knox, and Henry Stimson went straight to the Oval Office then moved to the adjacent Cabinet Room, where the president's naval aide, Admiral John Beardall, joined them. The group sat around a huge mahogany table under the watchful eye of Woodrow Wilson, whose portrait hung over the large fireplace, while they continually received typed reports coming in every few minutes. Pa Watson rushed them to the president, sitting at the head of the table. Admiral Stark had remained behind at the Navy Department to monitor developments and report by phone to Roosevelt.

Roosevelt looked grim as he read a series of communications from Stark. "Our losses, I'm afraid, have been staggering. They caught much of the fleet at anchor in the harbor. Several battleships have been sunk."

"It's unbelievable," Stimson roared. "How in the name of hell could Pearl Harbor be sustaining such high losses? Aren't they fighting back? How was the fleet so unprepared? For crying out loud, we knew something was coming for several days."

"Believe me," growled Navy Secretary Knox, "I'm going to get to the bottom of this. There's no excuse for being caught with our pants down. Heads are going to roll at Pearl! The first thing I'm going to do is fire Admiral Kimmel and make Chester Nimitz Commander-in-Chief of the Pacific Forces! I'm going to replace Navy Chief Harold Stark with Ernie King."

The president nodded. "I know both, they are good men. That Nimitz is well versed in ships and men. Tell him to get the hell out there and not to return until the war is won!"

Roosevelt took a drag on his cigarette, leaned back in his chair, and rubbed his chin, his expression one of infinite sadness for the Navy that was his pride and joy. An accomplished skipper of his own boat, Roosevelt had been secretary of the navy under Woodrow Wilson in the "Great War." He stopped to collect himself. "It seems…" he hesitated, searching for the right words, "our sailors were caught unawares. The Japs unleashed their bombs on ships that were not in fighting shape." He shook his head. "They just stayed tied up in port and did not move while most of their sailors were galivanting around Honolulu."

The president sat silently, staring into space for a few moments. The others in the room knew not intrude. Then he lit a cigarette and girded himself for what had to be done next. He lost his hesitation—his voice became firm and authoritative—he was once again the commander-in-chief. "Gentlemen, we have a lot of questions and, for the moment, few answers. Our priority, however, is to get our armed forces and industries on a war footing and worry later about who is at fault."

Cordell Hull arrived and reported on his meeting with the Japanese envoys.

The president smiled for the first time that afternoon. "You gave them hell; I didn't know you had it in you to be so unpatrician. Excellent, Cordell, excellent."

Slowly, other Cabinet members who were in the Washington area began drifting in.

"What about Hitler, Mr. President?" Morgenthau asked. "You had earlier decided to settle with him first. I hope the attack hasn't changed your priorities. Are we going to declare war on Germany?"

"Good question, Henry. I certainly would like to stay focused on Germany, but that may be difficult, given the mood of the country and the isolationists in Congress. We will declare war on Japan, but as far as Germany goes, I simply don't have the votes to go to war against Hitler, unless he does something stupid. Cross your fingers that he does!"

"We're all agreed," General Marshall put in, "except, of course, for MacArthur, that if we ignore Germany, it will only get stronger with the increasing resources it'll take from its conquered territories. If we go against Germany now, I am sure we can finish off Japan later, after the Nazis are defeated. I'm not so sure it would work in reverse."

"George," the president said, "we'll get focused. Meanwhile. Let's play the priority issue by ear."

Pa Watson rushed in with another update from Stark. Roosevelt read it and shook his head. "It's from MacArthur. The Japs have bombed the Philippines and he thinks an invasion is imminent." Roosevelt frowned. "They have knocked out thirty-five of our bombers."

"My God," Marshall exclaimed. "For some time already, he's been lining up those new B-17s wingtip to wingtip to prevent sabotage. I've warned against doing that, but you know him. You'd think, though, that once alerted, he'd have moved them."

Roosevelt read the update and shook his head. "You won't believe this. MacArthur speculates that because the air attack was carried out so brilliantly, the missions must have been flown by white mercenaries since Japanese fleet do not have the skills to accomplish such a feat.

"But Admiral Stark says that lady luck, who seemed to be all in the Japanese corner on this attack, decided to give us a break because none of our three aircraft carriers in the Pacific were in Pearl at the time of the attack. The Saratoga was being refitted on the West Coast, the *Enterprise* was at Guam, and the *Lexington*, bless her heart, was at Midway."

138

Same Day, a Few Minutes Before Midnight, Washington, D.C., the White House, the Oval Office

All the visitors to the White House had left. Only White House resident Harry Hopkins remained behind. Roosevelt watched the indefatigable Grace Tully, seated in front of the large presidential desk, her pencil at the ready, preparing to take dictation. As yet, however, he'd not uttered a word. He took several deep drags on a cigarette. It had a calming effect Harry Hopkins, seated nearby in a leather club chair, also lit up.

Roosevelt wanted badly to go after Hitler by declaring war on Germany, but he knew there was not enough congressional support and to fail would have been political disaster. Even worse would be a favorable vote in a deeply split Congress. An America divided could very well threaten its war effort. As for war with Japan, Congress had no choice. Japanese Prime Minister Tojo had achieved what Roosevelt could not-delivering the votes for a declaration of war against the Empire of the Rising Sun. He'd heard from even the worst reactionaries—Lindbergh, Senator Burton Wheeler, and Herbert Hoover—all of whom urged that the country go to war with the Japs.

He picked up a brief telegram from Joe Kennedy. "Name the battlefront," it proclaimed. "I'm yours to command."

He scrunched the telegram and tossed it in the wastebasket. "It'll be a cold day in hell before I answer that Hitler lover," the president muttered.

"Excuse me, Mr. President, did you say something?"

"No, Grace, just a tired old man talking to himself. Are you ready to take down my address to Congress tomorrow?"

She nodded. "Anxiously awaiting your words, Mr. President."

Roosevelt cleared his throat and put out his cigarette. "Yesterday, December Seventh comma 1941 dash a date that will live in history..." He stopped and made a face. "Scratch that, Grace, I'll start again."

Tully nodded, crossing out those first words.

"Yesterday, December Seventh dash nineteen forty-one dash a date that will live in *infamy* dash the United States of America was suddenly and deliberately attacked by the naval and air forces of Japan."

Roosevelt went on to condemn the sneak attack and the treachery of the Japanese negotiators; he reviewed the extensive loss of life, ships and planes in Hawaii and the Philippines, and the assaults on Wake Island, Midway, and the British possession of Hong Kong. He tried to be hard-hitting but brief. Concluding, Roosevelt dictated to Tully, "I ask that the Congress declare that since the unprovoked and dastardly attack by Japan on Sunday comma December Seventh comma nineteen forty-one comma a state of war has existed between the United States and the Japanese Empire."

Roosevelt turned to Hopkins. "Harry, I need a strong ending. Got any ideas?"

Hopkins thought for a while. "How about this? 'With confidence in our armed forces—with the unbounding determination of our people-we will gain the inevitable triumph-so help us God.'"

The president's face lit up. "Excellent, Harry. Take that down, Grace, word for word."

Tully smiled. "I already have, Mr. President."

December 8, 1941, the Next Morning Aboard the Nagato, in Tokyo Bay, the Operations Room

Ugaki shook his head. "You just sent Nagumo a congratulatory message? You should have fired him for cowardice!"

Yamamoto shrugged his shoulders. "He's the one in command in the field. We must rely on him. The commander of the task force must assess the risk and act accordingly."

"Rely on him?" Ugaki shouted. "Order him to turn around and attack again."

Yamamoto sighed. "You know very well I do not countermand the orders of the commander in the field. It would dishonor him."

Ugaki angrily knitted his brow. "This is one time you should! He should be dishonored. His lack of daring and failure to follow up on American weakness is a disgrace. He seems content with apparently not achieving much in life."

Yamamoto did not really disagree with Ugaki. *But Nagumo was a brave sailor, if not a daring one, and the error, if any, was my leaving him in command of the task force. I can't believe he did not attack again. With all our available fighters to protect the fleet, American land-based planes posed no serious threat. And so what if the American carriers found us? Numerically, we are far stronger and would have wiped them out.*

On return to his cabin, Yamamoto looked over the thousands of congratulatory cables coming in after a government broadcast by Tojo proclaiming the great and decisive victory for the Imperial Navy at Pearl Harbor, and a "New Order and a Great East Asia Coprosperity Sphere that will bring peace and stability to the area."

That broadcast was followed by the announcement and reading of the emperor's rescript officially declaring war on the United States and Great Britain, with the message, "this aggression, if left unchecked, would endanger the very existence of our nation." Gloom, it seemed, disappeared in Japan and left the public ecstatic. Even the emperor celebrated by dressing for the day in in his naval uniform.

Yamamoto should have been elated at the adulation, but he wasn't. Instead, thinking about it, he felt depressed for several reasons. *First, I am angry at Nagumo for not finishing the job at Pearl Harbor, for leaving the fuel storage tanks there untouched— but I have held my tongue, To order him to stay and press his advantage, he knew, would humiliate Nagumo. Second, we failed to find and sink their carriers, and that can come back to haunt us. Third, I fear that the diplomats stupidly let us jump the gun, attacking before the American were notified that war had been declared. I hope not because that would be a drastic mistake that will make the Americans, even the isolationists, enraged and cause them to act beyond reason. They are already calling it "Japan's sneak attack." That makes me suspect that the diplomats were late in notifying the Americans. I do not want this attack to be considered a "cowardly blow." For me, it is a matter of personal and national honor. Finally, I despair that Army and the Navy will ever have any coordination, for each has been going its own way for so long and reporting not to the prime minister or any unified command, but to the emperor alone. Neither knows what the other is up to and I doubt that will change. That can be our undoing.*

Yamamoto wrote to a friend in response to a cable of congratulations, "A military man can hardly be proud of having smitten a 'sleeping enemy.' But for the enemy, it was more a matter of shame for being asleep. I would rather have your appraisal after seeing what the enemy does. I expect that, angered and outraged, he will soon be launching a counterattack. The Japanese public is cheering wildly now, but it makes me fear that the first blow on Tokyo will make all these mindless cheering masses wilt on the spot."

He sat back in his chair and sighed. *Maybe we should have left the sleeping giant alone like I wanted and suggested!*

Yamamoto tried to examine his own failings in the attack. He always demanded punctuality and he'd heard that some of his staff referred to him as the "On-time Admiral". Some complained that his schedule for the attack on Pearl Harbor was too tight, especially when coordinating with the diplomats. He had demanded the attack begin no sooner than 8AM Hawaiian time. *But it was necessary, he ruminated. It had to be a close schedule. The Americans had to be given the declaration of war before the attack. But if too much time elapsed between the end of diplomacy and the start of the war, the Americans would have been able to prepare and that would be a disaster. It was a great plan. The diplomats just had to be sure to hold up their end.*

Yamamoto entered the communication room. "Send Admiral Nagumo a coded message as follows: 'On the way home, the task force, if circumstances permit, raid Midway and try to put the submarine base there out of action once and for all.'"

Nagumo read Yamamoto's message and interpreted the "if circumstance permit" to give him, Nagumo, wide discretion in the matter. Nagumo found the weather to be getting worse, so he decided to make a beeline for home and ignore Midway. His grounds? "Bad weather."

The high waves Nagumo encountered made take-off problematical and he was satisfied he met the terms of the language of Yamamoto's order "as far as the situation permits," to return to the home base.

But Yamamoto fumed at Nagumo's timidity.

One thing kept nagging on Yamamoto, who still did not know that the diplomats were too late in notifying the Americans. *Why were the Americans so unprepared? The Americans had not put up much of a defense. I hope this is not a "sneak attack." That would instill in them a fury that would be hard to quench and fill them with such a thirst for revenge, that any negotiations short of total surrender by us would be impossible. I'll have to find out from our diplomats if they informed the American before the attack. And how great, really, was the victory? Our aviators tend to exaggerate greatly.* He was a pilot and knew that things looked vastly difference high up in a fast-moving plane. *Yamamoto sighed. It's going to be a long war!*

Indeed, he, Yamamoto, could become the hated treacherous aggressor that planned the sneak attack and, in twisted Allied propaganda, the person who, in his arrogance, planned to dictate the terms in the White House.

Congratulations kept pouring in from all over Japan. *As far as I am concerned, the victory at Pearl was like a small bridge slam barely made. It still stuck in his craw that the timid Nagumo didn't stay around for another attack and wreck the port facilities and oil storage tanks and perhaps, catch the carrier Enterprise returning to port. Instead, Nagumo chose to nervously retreat from the scene.*

But Yamamoto sighed. He knew that many long battles lay ahead and that in the long run, victory over the Americans would be impossible.

Same Day, Washington D.C., the White House

Roosevelt snorted, reading Japanese note. "Typical Japanese. They sent us a document declaring war against the United States, a day after they attack us and actually go to war!"

General Marshall nodded. "First a sneak attack, then a declaration of war. The Japs do that all the time. It's no surprise."

"In a sense," the president noted. "they did us a favor. As I told Winston, that sneak attack should rile up the American people like no other act could. I doubt if there will now be any dissenters on going to war against Japan. Congress passed the declaration of war on the Japs with only one dissenting vote, Congresswoman Jeanette Rankin from Montana."

General Marshall shook his head. "She also voted no in 1917, when President Wilson asked Congress to declare war on Germany. When the hell is Montana going to retire the old girl?"

"Think we'll go to war with the Germans now?" Marshall asked.

"I'd love that, but I don't have the votes in Congress. We'll just have to see what Mr. Hitler does. Maybe he will accommodate us," Roosevelt replied.

Same Day, Pearl Harbor, Submarine Base, Office of Admiral Kimmel

Bull Halsey, swept into Admiral Kimmel's office and sat down.

"Couldn't find the bastards. I ran north as soon as I heard, but the Japs had already hightailed it out of there. None of our reconnaissance planes could find the sons of bitches."

Kimmel shrugged. "Probably just as well. Counting the number of planes in the attack, they must have come with a shit-load of carriers. You'd have found a hornet's nest if you had caught up with them."

"But we'd sink a few," growled Halsey.

Kimmel frowned. "You're one of the best we have. We don't need a dead hero, we need a live Bill Halsey to lead our counterattack against the Japs when the time is right. For now, we need patience to gather our forces and decide what to do next. But someone else is going to have to worry about that. Secretary Knox relieved me of command—I'm the sacrificial lamb!"

Halsey frowned. "Who's taking your place?"

"Chester Nimitz."

CHAPTER TEN

Early War in the Pacific: Late 1941-Early 1942

December 10, 1941, Tokyo Bay, Aboard the Nagato

UGAKI REPORTED TO YAMAMOTO. "I just heard that our forces have captured Guam without much resistance."

Yamamoto nodded. "That's nice to hear, but you and I know that Guam wasn't much of a test of our prowess. Stiff tests will be coming up sooner than we realize. But let's keep it going while the going is good."

December 12, 1941, Early Morning, Japanese Airfield in Southeast Asia

On the orders of Admiral Yamamoto, thirty-two long-range G4M "Betty" twin-engine bombers warmed up and, armed with torpedoes, stood ready to take off to hunt down and destroy two British ships, the battleship *Prince of Wales*, and the heavy cruiser, *Repulse*, reported to have arrived at Singapore.

December 12, 1941, Later that Day, Sea of Japan, near Indochina, Aboard the *Nagato*

The aide rushed in with a message from the 22nd Air Flotilla and handed it to Yamamoto.

PRINCE OF WALES AND THE *REPULSE* HIT BY OUR TORPEDO BOMBERS. WE CAN AFFIRM DEFINITELY THAT BOTH SHIP WERE DESTROYED AND SUNK.

Yamamoto, looking at Ugaki, smiled broadly. "That should finally put to rest the argument of air power versus surface ship power! You lose our bet that we couldn't sink the *Prince of Wales* battleship."

Ugaki nodded. "It's a bet I don't mind losing. Congratulations!"

Yamamoto nodded. "And I say to my fellow battleship admirals, The fiercest serpent can be overcome by a swarm of ants."

December 12, 1941, Late Afternoon, Washington, D.C., the White House, the Oval Office

"So, Hitler and Mussolini handed to you on a silver platter what you could not accomplish on your own—you lucky dog," a smiling Harry Hopkins observed.

Roosevelt nodded happily. "Exactly. As I told Churchill and General Marshall, I could have never gotten Congress to declare war on the Germany and Italy. Not even the sinking of our ships could persuade them. So, what does Hitler do? *He* declares war on us at the very time he has his hands full with Russia! He's a madman."

"And so is Mussolini," Hopkins added.

"And so is Mussolini," Roosevelt repeated agreeably. "Not only that," the president guffawed, "The bombastic Il Duce beat Hitler to the punch by declaring war on us first ahead of his Axis boss!"

"Did you hear from Congress on a declaration of war against Germany and Italy?"

Roosevelt nodded. "About a half hour ago. It passed unanimously in both houses. Even Congresswoman Rankin went along!"

"That should make Churchill very happy," Hopkins observed.

Roosevelt laughed. "'Ecstatic', is the more accurate word! Like he just won World War Two."

147

December 14, 1941, Tokyo Bay, Aboard the *Nagato*, Cabin of the Chief of Staff

Admiral Ugaki read the dispatches announcing that Italy and Germany had declared war on the United States. He smiled and pulled out his diary and considered this latest news for a while. Then he picked up his pen and wrote, *Now, it really has turned into the Second World War. Everything rests on the shoulders of our empire in so far as leadership of the new world order is concerned. The Rome-Berlin-Tokyo Axis will become the center of the world.*

Ugaki dismissed Yamamoto's misgivings about allying with the Germans and Italians. *With the German gains against the Soviets in Europe*, Ugaki thought, *they'll soon overrun Moscow. This will give us time to consolidate our gains before we prepare for the coming war with Russia.*

The excellent results from our naval aviators has the congratulations pouring in. But I just tell these people not to make a mountain out of a molehill because while things did go well, this is just the prelude, the drama is not yet on.

Ugaki's good mood dissipated as he continued to write in his diary.

The Imperial Army, as usual, is trying to take credit for all the naval air victories in the Philippines and elsewhere. They are trivial cheats that will be disclosed to all people shortly. And our own failure to knock out the American carriers and destroy the submarine base and other facilities is very frustrating.

Ugaki looked at the Imperial rescript that Yamamoto had handed him earlier. The emperor had written, *The air forces of the Combined Fleet have displayed their brilliant merits by destroying the fleet of the British Navy, the Repulse and the Prince of Wales, in the South China Sea. We highly appreciate the achievement.*

He smiled. It was always a great honor to get recognition from His Imperial Majesty personally.

✵ ✵ ✵

Yamamoto considered the emperor his commander-in-chief, while to most other Japanese, he was also a god-like figure. Under the emperor, all Japan's military were fighting for him and in the firm belief that they were forced into this war by the intransigence of the Americans and the British. Yamamoto did not believe it. *But now that the reality of war was upon us, I am determined to prosecute it as effectively as I can. Having left the Navy ministry and becoming Commander-in-Chief of the Combined Fleet, I gave up all political processes and was now merely a cog in the Japanese military machine. But I don't have to accept all the outlandish claims of victory put out by the Japanese military including some of the excessive claims put out by our naval headquarters. That's what separates me from Ugaki, my chief of staff.*

Our war plan envisioned a defensive perimeter running through the Marshall Islands and occupying strategic points in the Gilbert and Ellice Islands, extending the ring to protect the Carlines, where we set up an excellent naval base at Truk. In the south, we must prepare for an American counteroffensive and build up our forces in the Marianas, New Guinea, and the Bismarck Archipelago. We will make that defensive perimeter unbreakable with a strong defensive ring!

But that Nagumo! I told him to stop at Midway and raid the base there. He just ignored me, claiming bad weather. That's bullshit. He's fearful of the American carriers he could not find so he heads for the safety of Truk. Hell, even if the Americans find him, Nagumo has far more firepower, including three times the number of carriers! It would have been our good luck, but our admiral ran with his tail between his legs. It makes me just boil!

The honorable thing for my country to do was to declare war before attacking Pearl Harbor. Now I find out that we informed the Americans fifty-five minutes after the attack. We have given them the thirst for revenge and the fighting spirit that no other act could have accomplished. What utter foolishness and stupidity! Eventually, the Americans will overwhelm us with predominant air power and carriers. Will they play out the revenge factor? We'll have to wait and see.

December 14, 1941, Washington, D. C., Naval Headquarters, Office of Admiral Nimitz

H. Arthur Lamar, Nimitz's aide and flag lieutenant, answered the admiral's phone line.

"Let me speak to Chester," the disembodied voice demanded.

Lamar frowned and said, with no small bit of irritation in his voice. "This is *Admiral* Nimitz's office, sir!"

There was a slight pause, then a chuckle. "Swell, sonny, and this is *the President of the United Sta*tes. Now put him on, I have something to tell him!"

December 14, 1941, Washington, D. C., Home of Admiral Chester Nimitz

After receiving orders to take command of the Pacific Fleet at Pearl Harbor on the personal phone call from Roosevelt himself, he broke the news to his wife.

Catherine showed no surprise. "Chester, you always wanted to command the Pacific Fleet. I am so proud of you. That is the height of glory."

Nimitz smiled and shrugged. "Dear, the Pacific Fleet is at the bottom of the sea. I've just got to tell you but remember that nobody here at this base must know that."

Catherine nodded. "You always liked a challenge, didn't you? Well, here's a doozy."

Nimitz shook his head. "Admiral Kimmel and General Short were sacrificed on the altar of expediency. It was no more their fault than anyone else's. Nobody expected the Japs to attack Hawaii. They are good military men. But you know politics. Someone had to take the blame and who better to blame than the commanders where the sneak attack occurred? They even replaced my boss, Admiral Stark, with Admiral King as commander-in-chief of naval forces." Nimitz chuckled. "The first thing King did was change his acronym of CINCUS, which means naval commander-in-chief, United States

Navy, and sounds like 'sink us', to COMINCH, Commander-in-Chief, U.S. Fleet."

King didn't think much of the move to replace Kimmel either. After all, Admiral Stark did not pass on several important intercepts that would have alerted him to the threat of attack—messages that went to the Asiatic Fleet, but not to Hawaii! I think Kimmel has a legitimate complaint on that score, but still, Kimmel and General Short should have been more alert. Their own decoders warned them, and the Chief of Naval Operations warned them, that a surprise aggressive move by Japan in any direction is a possibility. Of course, no one in the American camp was aware that the Japs had perfected their torpedoes to work so well in the shallow waters of Pearl Harbor. There were a series of misunderstandings and wrong guesses both on the part of Washington and the Hawaiian command."

"Well, you should be proud King selected you to lead our naval forces in the Pacific It's a big challenge for you and I know you are up to it," his wife encouraged.

Nimitz grimaced. "Bigger than you think, dear. The Japs have landed in the Philippines and we can't stop them; and now they are about to take Singapore and the Netherlands East Indies. Thailand has already surrendered to Japanese.

"I'm afraid I'll be there for the duration of the war, and the islands being under threat of attack, I doubt you will be able to join me. I won't be back until heavens knows when."

She patted him on the shoulder. "I am sure you will do your best and end this war quickly."

Nimitz looked at her and smiled. "From your mouth to God's ears!"

Nimitz knew he'd been quite lucky. Earlier in his career, when the president wanted to appoint him to command the Pacific Fleet at Pearl Harbor, he declined it because he was too junior and would jump ahead of many deserving admirals. Instead, Roosevelt appointed Kimmel, who is now taking most of the blame, unfairly, for the Pearl Harbor attack. It could have been him, Nimitz, in that hot seat!

December 16, 1941, Princeton, New Jersey, Home of Dr. Albert Einstein

Vannevar Bush, former dean of engineering at MIT, and now director of the Office of Scientific Research and Development, headed coordinating the efforts of some six thousand leading American scientists to apply science to warfare and was intimately involved in the Manhattan Project, the nation's effort to produce an atomic bomb. He shared in his scientists' frustrations when, in early December, they had hit a stonewall trying to solve a key technological problem, namely, the separation of uranium 235 from its chemically identical isotopes. One thing was clear—his people needed help on gaseous diffusion, the process whereby uranium could be passed through many barriers pierced with miniscule holes. The problem had to be solved now, and if anyone could do it, it was that man at Princeton. So, Bush had asked Frank Aydelotte, one of the scientists on the project, to approach Albert Einstein, even though project overseers in Washington had deliberately excluded the great Jewish scientist from the Manhattan Project, viewing him as a possible security risk. But a solution was too important to stand on such ceremony.

In fact, it was Einstein, in 1939, who penned a letter to Roosevelt warning him that the Germans were developing a bomb that could wipe out cities—an atomic bomb. But the president's "experts" said such a bomb was not possible. But Dr. Alexander Sachs, a director and vice president of Lehman Brothers, who delivered the letter, and was a friend of both Roosevelt and Einstein, convinced the president otherwise and so began the enormous, but deadly, scientific race morphing itself into the Manhattan Project.

Aydelotte had presented the problem to Einstein in person in early December. Ten days later, Einstein had called Bush and advised him that he had the solution. Aydelotte rushed back to Einstein's Princeton home. Secrecy concerns did not permit such discussions over the telephone.

Einstein poured tea for Aydelotte and offered him some pastries. His preoccupied visitor politely refused.

"An interesting problem you brought to me." The venerable scientist's eyes sparkled. "If there are other aspects of this problem that you want me to address or you require any part of the solution amplified, I will be only too happy to help. Let me know and I will drop everything and do all in my power to assist you."

"We appreciate your willingness to help, sir. Your contribution will be important to the war effort."

Einstein smiled, still with the twinkle in his eyes. "But you cannot tell me the progress you are making because you consider me a security risk?"

Aydelotte shifted uncomfortably in the chair. "Not a security risk, I assure you, Dr. Einstein. It's a problem of clearance and the need to know. There are very few people who know all the parts of our efforts; most know only so much as to carry out their part of the assignment. Washington has taken secrecy to a new level in connection with this research."

Einstein nodded. "I assumed as much when so many of my colleagues in nuclear physics disappeared into the maw of the government. I assume they will never be heard from until the end of the war."

Aydelotte shrugged. "I'm afraid I can't comment on that, sir."

Einstein thought it ridiculous for them to consider him naïve enough not to know they were working on a nuclear bomb. "I understand and assure you I take no umbrage."

Einstein reached for a folder in his lap. "Here, Dr. Aydelotte— the solution to your problem. Let me say I am deeply satisfied to be able to help in any endeavor useful to the national effort."

"Your efforts are greatly appreciated, and I thank you on behalf of Vannevar Bush and the nation."

Einstein led his visitor to the door. "Again, if there is anything else, I will be very happy to assist."

December 22, 1941, 10PM, Eastern Time, Washington, D.C., The White House, Roosevelt's Bedroom

Roosevelt, propped up in his bed, welcomed the late arriving Winston Churchill.

"I hope I'm not keeping you up past your bedtime, Frank," Churchill said.

The president smiled. "Hardly, Winnie. I do my best work in this bed after midnight! But I must say I am surprised you came, with all those German U-boats plying the Atlantic."

Churchill pulled out a cigar. "The captain of our largest battleship, *HMS Duke of York*, assured me he'd keep me safe."

Roosevelt shrugged. "As an old Navy man, I'd be wary of such assurances. You know, some of my admirals tell me the battleship is passé, it's the aircraft carriers they are clamoring for. And after Pearl Harbor, I can understand why."

Churchill lit up. "Franklin, now that Hitler has declared war on you, I hope your thinking hasn't changed about fighting the battle of Europe first."

"Some of my admirals and General MacArthur," the president said, "are pressing me to send more ships and troops to the Pacific But as of now, my interest is first and foremost Germany. To me, it's a simple proposition. Defeating Japan does not defeat Germany and if we concentrate our American efforts in the Pacific in 1942 and 1943, Germany might just be able to dominate Europe and Africa. And we don't want that, do we?"

Churchill chuckled. "Well, I certainly don't, so you're preaching to the choir!"

"It's Germany first," Roosevelt asserted, "unless something a hell of a lot more important crops up. Of course, in a war, no one ever knows. We still must counter the Jap attacks in southeast Asia and the Pacific. We can't let them get too close to Hawaii. So, I have decided to transfer some aircraft carriers to the Pacific since Germany does not have those type of assets to threaten us—only U-Boats, which are better handled by destroyers." Roosevelt, former secretary of the navy, loved to display his naval warfare knowledge.

Destroyers are only a football field long and thirty-nine feet wide, which are small, by comparison to the battleships and cruisers, but lethal to subs, with their 30 to 35-knot speed, search and destroy capabilities, and depth charging abilities. Basically, they are a power plant inside a thin steel-plate hull. Known as "tin cans" because of that thin 3/8-inch hulls, they could be sunk by a single shell from a cruiser or battleship. But they could also dish it out with their ten torpedoes, each with a high explosive charge that could sink a larger ship. Bristling with antiaircraft batteries, the destroyers could play havoc with enemy aircraft, and were often placed in a position as the first line of air defense for our carriers.

Same Date, San Francisco, Naval Headquarters

Lieutenant Lamar, Nimitz's aide, handed him a briefcase. "Sir, this contains a detailed briefing of the situation at Pearl. Admiral King wanted to have this before you got to Hawaii."

Nimitz sat down and went through the photos of the devastation at Pearl.

December 23, 1941, Tokyo Bay, Aboard the Nagato

On the return of the attack force to Japanese waters, Emperor Hirohito bestowed on Fuchida, the rare honor of an audience, given his rank as junior officer. Yamamoto received a personal letter of praise from the emperor together with a set a sake cups. This same Yamamoto became to the Americans the evil genius behind the treacherous attacks; the man who not only planned the attack on Pearl Harbor, but by his widely reported remarks, he arrogantly planned to dictate terms in the White House.

After giving a congratulatory speech to the fleet returning from the Pearl Harbor attack and warning them that the real fighting is yet to come, he pulled Fuchida aside.

"Tell me," Yamamoto began his questioning, "the precise timing of the attack."

"Actually," Fuchida responded, "we launched five minutes early, encountering no opposition on the way."

"I suppose I shouldn't complain about a mere five minutes, but America is publicizing it as a 'sneak attack,' with the new slogan all over that land being 'Remember Pearl Harbor.' That my dear captain, is going to come back to haunt us."

"I—I didn't know that," Fuchida stammered.

Yamamoto shook his head. "Not to worry, it wasn't your fault because *our diplomats* did not inform the Americans that a state of war existed until an *hour after* the attack. I expect the Americans will come at us in a fury in retaliation for Pearl Harbor."

Yamamoto ordered the bombing and invasion of Wake Island and lost his best bombardier to surprisingly accurate American antiaircraft fire. Japan also lost two destroyers in the action. He was shocked that the occupation force sent to take Wake Island was repulsed by the small number of American defenders. Some of the Japanese pilots protested the assignment, saying Wake wasn't valuable enough to risk our pilots and staff and also to give the Americans a valuable preview of our strategy and tactics.

But Yamamoto, if surprised by the invasion's failure, was not swayed and continued the bombing of these island outposts.

Yamamoto welcomed into port the *Yamato*, the first of the two new, great battleships—faster, better armored and bigger gunned than any other ship in the world. *It couldn't come too soon!* he thought.

December 24, 1941, Washington, the White House, the Oval Office

"I don't disagree with your Germany First policy," General Marshall assured the president, "but we do have Japanese troops advancing in from Burma to West New Guinea, confronting our ABDA forces."

The president looked perplexed. "ABDA forces?"

"It's the combined American, British, Dutch and Australia troops confronting them."

"What are the chances of for a successful defense in that area?" the president asked.

"Slim to non-existent. We chose British General Sir Archibald Wavell to command those forces. He probably doesn't realize he's being sacrificed on the altar of the principle, 'unity of command.'"

The president smiled. "Not very nice, but expedient."

December 25, 1941, Pearl Harbor Naval Base at Makalapa

Nimitz's arrived over the Hawaiian island of Molokai where, for security reasons, his plane was met by several fighters and escorted to the Naval Air Station at Pearl Harbor.

The first thing Nimitz did when he reached the naval headquarters at Makalapa, on the periphery of Pearl Harbor and Hickam Airbase, was meet with the staff of the replaced Admiral Kimmel.

"As far as I am concerned," Nimitz told them, "neither you nor your then boss Admiral Kimmel are to blame for what happened. Admiral Kimmel did not have the fleet or fire power to stop the Japanese and if he had had the warning, which he did not, and tried to intercept the Jap force, the American fleet would have been sunk in water too deep to salvage. As it is six of the eight battleship will be returned to duty. Of the 101 ships at Pearl Harbor, only twenty percent were affected, and most of those, not for long. Not a single submarine at the base was damaged.

"As far as your assignments, I have utter confidence in your abilities, and I need you to stay on now as *my staff* and keep doing the jobs you have been doing. If you have any questions, please feel free to ask them."

One of the commanders stood up. "Admiral, did you see the devastation in the harbor? Do you think we'll recover?"

Nimitz smiled. "It's a good question. Yes, I saw the wreckage at Pearl. But you know, the Japanese made the three worst serious mistakes an attacking force could make. God was with us."

Nimitz could see the surprise in his audience. He continued.

"Mistake one: Attacking on a Sunday morning when nine out of ten crewmen were on shore on leave. If they attacked on a week day we would have lost 38,000 men instead of 3,800!

"Mistake two: The pilots were so excited seeing all those big battleships lined up in a row, they got carried away with sinking them and forgot about our dry docks and repair ships. Not a single bomb fell on those facilities! Had they destroyed them, we'd have had to tow every damn ship that was salvageable back to the Mainland for repair. Now, the ships are in the shallow water of the harbor and a tug can pull them over to the dry docks and repair them and have them at sea in less than time it would have taken simply to tow them back to the Mainland. We are already working on those ships.

"Mistake three: Every drop of our fuel in Pacific is in above-ground storage tanks within five miles of Pearl. One plane, strafing those tanks, could have destroyed our fuel supply.

"The loss of these facilities would have delayed our counter offensive far longer than simply those sunk ships.

"That is why I say that God was taking care of America."

The captain of one of the submarines asked. "What are our marching orders, sir?" "Admiral King," Nimitz replied, "wants us to first secure the seaways between Midway, Hawaii, and the North American mainland. Then, as soon as we can, we should extend and protect the lifeline between North America and Australia by holding the Hawaii-Samoa line, including Fiji. You submarine boys, who are relatively unscathed from the sneak attack, are going to play a very important part in our defense, and soon hopefully, in our offensive."

"But what about the Philippines?" the captain continued.

Nimitz left the podium without answering.

His chief of staff buttonholed him privately. "I thought that was a good question, sir."

Nimitz nodded. "It was but I did not want to give a public answer. Every other concern will be ruthlessly subordinated, including the Philippines, Hong Kong, Malaya and Singapore. The ramshackle collection of old ships in the Asiatic Fleet probably don't stand a chance against the Jap Navy. And we can forget those old canards that Jap planes were poorly engineered knockoff and their pilots inept. I admire how good they were at keeping their aviation advances secret. They basically wiped out our airpower in the western Pacific We now discover that they have two fine medium bombers with a long range and could carry 1,700 pounds in bombs or torpedoes and their Mitsubishi Zeros, 'Zekes', as we call them, are superb single seat fighters that can outclimb, out-turn, and out maneuver any other fighter we or our allies are now flying. It completely outclasses our fighters. Our old Buffalo warplanes are hopeless in a dogfight So, we have our work cut out for us. However, I just don't want to make that public and tell the Japanese."

"So, what's our responsibility?"

Nimitz pointed a map of the Pacific Ocean. "MacArthur will control the Southwest Pacific theater, including Australia, the Philippines, and New Guinea."

"From the Philippines? That's a good trick!"

Nimitz shook his head. "Nah, he's been ordered to Australia and that's where his headquarters will be. We'll have control of the rest of the Pacific The Philippines are lost—for now—the Japs bombed Manila even though MacArthur declared it an 'open city.' And I just got word a few minutes ago that the British have surrendered in Hong Kong."

Nimitz was just the man needed at Pearl Harbor to lead the Pacific Fleet. He had the capacity to do the necessary detailed planning with clear thinking, supreme confidence and the optimism that the American would ultimately win this war. He knew he'd have to start out on the defensive, protect Midway, with limited offensive weapons, and a carrier task force group with a superb man to lead the charge, Admiral William "Wild Bill" Halsey—for now.

December 28, 1941, Hashirajima Bay, Aboard the *Nagato*

Ugaki sat facing Yamamoto in his leader's cabin.

"Right now," Yamamoto said, "we have a significant numerical advantage over the American ships, but we won't have for long. We must entice them into a decisive sea battle where we will go after of them with overwhelming force, grouping all six of our fast carriers into a single powerful attack group of fighters, bombers, and torpedo planes, all striking at once with overwhelming strength. The new tactics can assure us of victory in that battle."

Ugaki nodded. "Sounds brilliant. Let's do it."

Yamamoto shrugged. "We can't, for the time being, because our leaders in Tokyo are thoroughly satisfied with the destruction of so many American battleships and have become completely complacent. Our naval headquarters has ordered Nagumo to take the fleet south to support what they call the 'MO Operation', the invasions of Rabaul and other islands in the Bismarck Archipelago. They might even end up in the Indian Ocean! They are forcing the Imperial Navy to support the Army in the southwest Pacific and the attempt to capture Port Moresby. I agree with Captain Fuchida who led the Pearl Harbor raid that we should go after the Americans and their fleet, and forget for now, those lesser foes, in order to prevent the American fleet, if left to its own devices, from strengthening itself considerably."

"In the meantime," complained Ugaki, "we sit here safe with our formidable battleships in Hashirajima Bay."

Yamamoto nodded. "I hear some of our airmen scathingly refer to the *Yamato*, the *Nagato*, and the other battleships anchored here as the 'Hashirajima Fleet'."

"If you are so pessimistic about the ultimate outcome of a war with America, why are you planning this attack?" asked Ugaki.

"Do I have a choice? The emperor appears determined to go ahead. I am simply making the best of a bad situation."

"I've just received a report that our forces have captured Wake Island," Ugaki informed.

"It's about time!" Yamamoto grumbled. "It was so lightly defended we should have taken it the first time we tried. Instead, we lost two warships and several experienced pilots, who are irreplaceable."

December 29, 1941, Tokyo, Office of Prime Minister Tojo

Tojo enjoyed the adulation of the public after the Pearl Harbor attack. But not all shared this view. General Ishiwara Kanji, who commanded the Japanese troops in Manchukuo, stormed into Tojo's office.

"You are," Kanji shouted, "a complete simpleton for committing us to a war with America. It will be disastrous because we simply cannot compete with the Americans in material terms. You ought to resign or shoot yourself."

General Kanji was soon relieved of command and reassigned to a local Army base at Maizuru, on the seacoast near Kyoto.

January 1943, Tokyo, Cabinet Room of Prime Minister Tojo

Tojo presided over the Cabinet meeting.

Tojo began, "I am pleased to report that now there is a permanent solution to our petroleum shortage with our occupation and total control of the islands in the Netherlands East Indies. Not only that, but we are flush with lead, cobalt and tungsten from Burma; rubber and tin from Thailand and French Indochina, bauxite from Malaya, and light metals and ferroalloys from Korea."

"And foodstuff particularly rice, do we have enough to satisfy our people?" asked a cabinet member.

"Absolutely, with the rice we ship back to Japan from East Asia," replied Tojo.

"I have just come back from a tour of our East Asia positions," one cabinet member advised, "and I must say these populations are getting restive and not too happy with what they claim are beatings and atrocities by our soldiers and the use of their wives and daughters as 'comfort women' for our troops—or to put it bluntly, to act as prostitutes."

"Our claims of racial superiority do not go over too well with them," added another cabinet member.

Tojo glared at both cabinet members. "First of all, we are racially superior and these people in East Asia are going to have to accept that. Second, don't they know there's a war on and we must do whatever is necessary to come out victorious? The other complaints are simply the grumblings of a conquered people that have no choice but to submit. Occupation of these countries in southeast Asia," Tojo continued, "have given us the ability to create a defensive perimeter on the islands in the western and southern Pacific on which we can fight the Americans to a standstill.

January 2, 1942, Pearl Harbor, Naval Headquarters at Makalapa, Office of Admiral Nimitz

Nimitz met with the top officer in his command, including Admiral Halsey, whose ship, the carrier *Enterprise*, was in port.

161

"The carriers, *Yorktown* and *Hornet*, are on their way from the Atlantic. They are officially being transferred to the Pacific Fleet," Nimitz announced.

"It's about time," Halsey grumbled. "The Germans and Italians have no carriers to speak of. No reason for our fleet to be there in the first place."

"We only have four carriers to cover this wide Pacific Ocean," Nimitz noted.

"What do the Japs have?" One of the commanders asked.

"Let's see." Nimitz paused. "They have six big, fast carriers, and four smaller ones, for a total of ten."

"Yamamoto must like those odds," Halsey said, as he grimaced.

"That's not all the bad news," Nimitz reported. "We lost Manila; the Japs have occupied it. Our forces have retreated to the offshore islands of Bataan and Corregidor. MacArthur's headquarters are now in a tunnel in Corregidor."

Nimitz then waved a paper in the air. "I just got this secure cable from our boss, Admiral King, chewing ass about the 'half-hearted' deployment of our carriers since the attack on Pearl."

"What does he expect?" groused Nimitz's chief of staff

Nimitz shrugged. "Simply to send our carriers into enemy waters at top speed and surprise the hell of them. Bomb their land-based planes on the ground, kill their pilots in their beds, destroy their fuel dumps, torpedo their ships at anchor, level their hangers and repair shops, and crater their airstrips."

"He doesn't want much, does he?" muttered one captain. "I thought sending carriers within the range of enemy land-based twin-engined bombers was a tactical loser. They can counterstrike us a hell of a way off, well beyond the range of our carrier planes. If we lose those carriers, Hawaii will be very vulnerable. We already almost lost the *Saratoga* when a Jap sub torpedoed her. She had to return to the West Coast for repairs!"

"And besides, how do we surprise them now, with the war on"? Chief of Staff asked.

Nimitz rubbed his chin. "I know, but I cannot ignore my boss. I'm not so sure what is the most prudent course."

Halsey jumped up. "Well, damn it, I am all for it! I'm ready to take the *Enterprise* into the Jap backyard and raise a little hell like in the Gilberts and the Marshalls. Shit, there's no war without risks. Hell, the Japs inherited those islands from the Germans as reparations in World War One but didn't do a damn thing to help us except to cheer from the sidelines."

"But those Jap bombers have much longer legs than your carrier planes, Bill," Nimitz warned.

"Don't you think I know that?" Halsey rejoined. "But we'll be out of there before they can counterstrike, while those fucking armchair admirals safely in Washington play with themselves!"

Nimitz looked at Halsey. "Most of your pilots are green and never have been in combat."

Halsey nodded. "They have to learn sometime. But I promise, they'll practice and practice and learn while we are sailing. I'll see to it that they lift their game. Admiral, there's a war on and that's what we do in a war! I agree with Admiral King, we got to strike the enemy somewhere—and soon."

"Anything we do now will have little impact on the Japanese juggernaut, especially in the South Pacific, but you know," Nimitz mused, "I think we can surprise them on a few of their islands. But you're not going in alone. I'm sending in the *Lexington*, too."

"Just don't send me out on the thirteenth," the superstitious Halsey warned.

January 8, 1942, Aboard the *Nagato*, at Sea off the Coast of Japan

Ugaki shook his head.

"What's the matter?" Yamamoto asked.

"The war's a month old now," Ugaki answered, "and our armed forces, now appear invincible with the devastation at Pearl Harbor, the great victories in the Philippines, Malaya, Dutch East Indies, and just about anywhere we've sent our troops. Yet I am very uneasy. However tremendous our military exploits are, whatever they achieved at the sacrifice of lives, it will be in vain unless our statesmen can pull themselves together and fashion a coherent policy for the country. Look at Roosevelt and Churchill. They have already established a unified command for the Allied powers."

Yamamoto sighed. "I wholly agree. Despite all Tokyo's brave words, I still think the enemy may have the ability to bomb Tokyo. And that will be disastrous for morale."

Ugaki slammed his fist into the palm of his hand. "I am going to recommend we improve the air raid warning and protective systems in our major cities."

Yamamoto snorted. "They won't listen—until it's too late."

"Maybe you should tell them," Ugaki said. "After all, you are now officially a national hero."

Yamamoto sighed. "It's intolerably embarrassing to be given the credit and made the star of the campaign for the achievement of those under me who actually participated in the battle. Quite frankly, I am ashamed to wear these medals. With all the bombast and self-congratulations, they are creating a euphoria that is both infantile and shortsighted because, let's face it, we have not encountered the enemy at his best, and at some time later, we definitely will. There's no need to bang the big drum; just keep telling the people the truth. Once we start lying, the war is as good as lost! The capabilities of the United States certainly have not been destroyed and, let's face it, they have ten times the latent military-industrial strength we have. So, we must find a way to deliver an early devastating blow before they are all geared up, so they will want to settle this war with us on terms we can accept."

"Our forces have just about completed this first stage of our operations," Ugaki noted. "What's next? Australia? Hawaii? India? Or destroying the Soviet Union?"

"Hunker down and defend ourselves," Yamamoto answered. "While the war is gong splendidly now, there will be a time soon when industrial America will recover her strength and fight back with enormous power. We can't spread ourselves too thin by letting these victories go to our head."

Ugaki frowned. "You are too much of a pessimist! Our Navy is invincible, and our Army is unstoppable. We have achieved all victories and suffered no defeats. I am confident we will surely win."

Yamamoto shook his head. "The Naval General Staff in Tokyo is sending five large carriers, four fast battleships, three cruisers and nine destroyers into the Indian Ocean! And for what? To confront some decrepit ships of the Allied Asiatic Fleet? Ridiculous! You and the people in Tokyo don't realize that by pressing the attack in southeast Asia and the Indian Ocean with our finest ships, we are handing the Americans a respite and the time to recover and fight back. Would you believe our Navy bosses in Tokyo are also pressing the Imperial Army to invade Australia with five divisions? And Captain Sadatoshi Tomioka of the General Navy Staff is pushing it. What folly!"

"Are they going to invade Australia?" Ugaki asked.

"Of course not! Cooler heads prevailed. The Army had a fit, arguing that Australia was twice the size of the area Japanese troops were occupying in China. Five divisions would nowhere be enough, the Army warned. One Army colonel even threatened to resign if the plan was approved. Besides, the troops were needed to occupy the Soviet Far East after Hitler's spring and summer offensive defeats the Russians. They ended the Australia invasion plan.

"The Army General Staff still has its eyes on the Soviets coming down from Siberia. I tried to convince them that the only workable plan right now is to advance into the Central Pacific and thereby cut off any chance of an American strike force conducting an air raid on Tokyo."

Ugaki rubbed his chin. "And just where in the Central Pacific would we be going to strike?"

Yamamoto smiled. "I was thinking of Midway Island for the decisive battle that has been eluding us. There, we can finish off the American Pacific Fleet. I think we could draw the American Navy to those islands and wipe them out for once and for all. We've got way more carriers and don't forget our newest weapon, the *Yamato*. We must find a way to lure the American carriers into the open sea.

I'm willing to bet that threating to take that Midway will do it. And then, we'll spring the trap! Of course, we'll have to wait until Admiral Nagumo returns from the Indian Ocean with all our carriers."

Ugaki nodded. "I like it. If we take Midway, we can strike at Hawaii again, perhaps even invade, and at the same time occupy vital points in the Aleutian Islands. Our inner defense will be substantially enlarged, protecting the Japanese main islands from attack."

Yamamoto knew, better than anyone, the necessity of a decisive battle with the American fleet to wipe out its remaining carrier force before Japan could hope to force the Americans into a favorable peace settlement—that is, favorable to Japan. It put a lot of pressure on Yamamoto. He was glad he had a chance to go ashore before they left, supposedly to visit the wounded sailors, but also to relieve some of the pressure, by visiting a well-known and excellent brothel near the Naval Base in Tokyo Bay.

January 11, 1942, Pacific Ocean, West of Hawaii, Aboard the *Enterprise*

The *Enterprise* had left Pearl Harbor, setting a zigzag course to avoid Japanese submarines. The *Lexington* accompanied her, sailing 150 miles astern.

Halsey knew this would be a dangerous and difficult mission, requiring particularly difficult night refueling, as he watched the screening vessels of cruisers and destroyers spread out over the horizon to protect the task force. *But I'm going to get it right*, he thought determinedly.

January 15, 1942, Tokyo Bay, Aboard the *Yamato*

Japan's new super battleship passed all her sea trials and sailed proudly into Tokyo Bay. In size alone, she was an amazing sight, displacing almost 73,000 tons with speeds of over 31 miles per hour, not to mention the largest caliber guns ever fitted on a warship— nine eighteen-inch monsters, quite capable of flinging thirty-two hundred-pound projectiles with high-explosive or armor-piercing shells 26 miles! Her gun turrets weighed as much as a normal destroyer. Her sister ship, the *Musashi*, just as large and lethal, was almost ready, now undergoing her sea trials.

But now, Admiral Yamamoto claimed this mammoth vessel *Yamato* as his flagship, releasing the much older *Nagato* for sea duty.

The day at the new quarters started out auspicious enough, when one of the Japanese submarines radioed that they had sunk an American carrier, at least that's what it sounded like to the sub's captain. He thinks it was the *Lexington*.

January 16, 1942, Pearl Harbor, Naval Headquarters at Makalapa, Office of Admiral Nimitz

The chief of staff rapped on the door and came in. "Just heard from the *Saratoga*. It took a single torpedo hit from a Jap sub west of Hawaii. It's in no danger but will require repairs."

Nimitz shook his head. "How the hell did a Jap sub find her?"

The chief of staff shrugged. "Her captain said they were zigzagging and just zigged into the Jap's path. I guess it's the luck of the draw."

"Send her back to the San Diego shipyards for repair, we have no room here," Nimitz ordered. "That should keep her out of action for at least two months. We didn't need that!"

January 31, 1942, Pacific Ocean, Just North of Kwajalein, Aboard the *Enterprise*

1830 hours finally arrived and a cruiser force, led by Admiral Raymond Spruance, peeled off from the task force in preparation for bombarding the islands of Wotje and Taroa early the next morning. But first, Halsey read aloud to his commanders the coded messages from Nimitz that just arrived. DRIVE HOME THE ATTACK. EXPLOIT AND EXPAND OPERATIONS WITH ALL OF TASK FORCE, REPEAT AIR ATTACKS AND SHIP BOMBARDMENTS AS DEVELOPMENTS AND LOGISTICS MAKE FEASIBLE. IF PRACTICABLE, EXTEND OFFENSIVE BEYOND ONE DAY.

At 0300 hours reveille sounded and the awakened pilots sat down for a good breakfast of juice, eggs, bacon and toast. They were quiet and introspective. Few had ever been in a battle before. Many were running on coffee and adrenaline. How will I do? How many would come back? Would I be one of them? Can I beat the new Jap Zero fighter?

Suddenly, the loudspeaker boomed. "Pilots man your planes!" Gear and parachutes in hand, the pilots raced up to the deck, where the deckhands guided each of them to their aircraft. The airmen climbed on the wings of their aircraft while a deckhand made sure each of them had their gear and parachutes in place.

At the start engines order, the planes roared to life as the propellers spun, stopped, coughed, and finally caught with a roar of triumph.

When given the all-clear, the pilot released his brakes and his craft lurched forward on the deck into the headwind that would lift him off the carrier and not into the Pacific Ocean. Once in the air, the planes formed up and headed for the islands of Kwajalein and Roj to hit the airfield and the ships at anchor.

At about 1500 hours, the planes returned, reporting that the Japs were taken by total surprise. There was almost no opposition. Some Jap planes were caught on the ground and destroyed and several ships in the harbor were sunk.

"Admiral," one of the pilots suggested, "they still have some Betty long-range bombers we couldn't get. Don't you think it's time we get the hell out of here?"

Halsey smiled. "My boy, I've been thinking precisely the same thing myself. Let's haul-ass out of here!"

Steaming back to Hawaii at full speed, some Jap long-range bombers did catch up to them but did only slight damage from the bombs that were near misses. One bomber, hit by the ship's antiaircraft fire, tried to crash into the *Enterprise* but managed only one wing grazing the carrier and clipping one of the planes off the deck. This is what Halsey later referred to as "the first kamikaze attack in the war." He also became known as—but not to his face— "haul-ass Halsey."

The *Enterprise* met up with the *Lexington*, returning from an attack on Jaluit. The *Lexington* had no casualties, but her pickings were slim because of lousy weather—the victims were two Jap four-engine flying boats—and that was it.

February 15, 1942, Somewhere in the Japanese Sea, Aboard the *Yamato*

"I received a dispatch from the Imperial Army," Yamamoto announced to his chief of staff and other officers gathered in the ready room. "The Army has taken Singapore, just as they planned. The British had all their large fixed guns pointing out to sea and our troops attacked them by coming through the jungle and falling on Singapore from the rear overwhelming the defenders. Ha! The British guns were useless because they could not conceive an attack from land. The British, Australian, and New Zealander soldiers had to surrender. We now have most of the Philippines, all of Thailand, Malaya, and Northern Indochina."

"That's great news," Ugaki piped in. "Congratulations. Our Army and Navy are invincible."

Yamamoto frowned. "Let's save the celebrations for later— if there is anything to left to celebrate. The Americans have not yet started their counter-offensive. Their audacious attack on the Marshalls was only a pin prick. But it should serve as a warning, the Americans are not about to roll over."

"You really think they'll attack, with so many big ships sunk?" one officer asked.

Yamamoto stared at the bulkhead for a few moments. "Of course, they will. It's not a matter of 'if', but 'when'!"

Ugaki smiled. "Well, we may as well enjoy our early triumphs while we can!"

Same Date, London, 10 Downing Street, Prime Minister Winston Churchill's Office

General Hastings "Pug" Ismay, chief of staff to the secretary of defense stood there stiffly, as Prime Minister Churchill gave him a withering look after the General brought him the news that Singapore had surrendered to the Japanese.

"Surrendered did you say? What you had called 'Fortress Singapore' has surrendered?"

"Yes, sir, Prime Minister."

Churchill slammed his fist on the desk. "Pug, I am outraged, after all your assurances that the city could be successfully defended."

"Sorry, sir, but we had not expected an attack from the rear, only from the sea and our permanent fortified guns and positions only face the sea."

"Pug, have you not got a single general in the British Army that can win battles? Do we have any with enough brains to put up a decent defense? Who can figure out that the enemy might attack from any direction? Why must we continually lose battles this way?"

"Well, sir…"

"No," Churchill interrupted, "don't bother answering.

"But do tell me this, General. How can we have the Fortress Singapore, with its splendid moat half a mile wide, and not think to fortify against an attack from land in the rear?"

"It was an utter surprise, sir."

Churchill uttered a harsh laugh. "I should say so, General, I should certainly say so! My point exactly!"

February 16, 1942, Pearl Harbor, Naval Headquarters at Makalapa, Office of Admiral Nimitz

Bill Halsey reported in to Nimitz, his carrier, the *Enterprise*, having just docked in port.

170

"Bill," Nimitz began, "Jap Admiral Yamamoto may be brilliant, but he has some glaring weaknesses."

"Oh yeah, go tell Kimmel that!"

"Seriously," Nimitz continued, "the man has no idea about submarine warfare. He keeps his subs safe near home base to protect his big ships. They are used purely for defensive purposes."

Halsey shook his head. "Aren't you forgetting something. A Jap sub put a fish into the *Saratoga!*"

Nimitz slapped the fist of one hand into the open palm of the other. "That's just my point, Bill! It was one lone Jap submarine that just happened to be in the right place at the right time. Can you imagine what havoc they could inflict if they were serious about sending their entire fleet into our waters? Also, they haven't been going after our supply vessels, only warships. And that's a big mistake. They could have choked off our war materiel if they started sinking our merchant marine ships. They could have cut off Hawaii from the mainland and crippled our Pacific war efforts for many months. All they had to do is sink our relatively defenseless supply ships.

"We, on the other hand, have sent our sub fleet out to attack their merchant ships around and near their home waters, and already we've got some impressive tonnage sinkings. In the long run, I think Yamamoto's strategy will hurt them badly."

"It's our damn torpedoes," Halsey said. "They aren't worth shit. Half of them don't explode on impact. But the Jap torpedoes run true and they can fire them accurately from a much greater distance! The Jap 'Long-Lance' torpedoes are fast, large and can inflict a lot of damage on our ships. You should hear our submarine and destroyer skippers on this topic. They put themselves in harm's way, score a great hit, and no explosion. Now, they become the target!"

"I know," acknowledged Nimitz, "I have our ordinance people working overtime on this problem."

"We have another problem, Admiral," Halsey added. "One of our Marine Generals says reports filtering back from the Philippines reveal that soldiers there are calling the Jap troops unbeatable. The Japs are alleged to have a preternatural sense and ability, they can see in the darkness, they are fearless and superb snipers and willing to fight to the death rather than give up a position."

"That's bullshit," Nimitz spat out. "We have to train our men to recognize these assertions for what they are—just racial myths. They're no braver or better than our own Marines—and our guys better believe that! We'll need to incorporate that into their training."

March 1, 1942, Pearl Harbor, Naval Headquarters at Makalapa, Office of Admiral Nimitz

"The Allied ABDA Fleet in the Java Sea just got their teeth kicked in by the Japs," Nimitz announced to the staff "We lost all our ships in that sortie, five cruisers, and nine destroyers, mostly Dutch ships, but some American, British and Australian also."

"What did the Japs lose?" a staff member asked.

Nimitz sighed. "As far as I can tell from the reports, it was a night battle, for which the Japs were specially trained, and they didn't lose a single ship. We knew that Asian fleet in the South Pacific and Indian Ocean was old and decrepit. They just couldn't not stand up to the modern cruisers and destroyers the Japanese threw at them, much less do it in a night battle."

Japanese battleship, Haruna

March 7, 1942, At Sea Aboard the Battleship *Yamato*

Yamamoto, aware of the many shameful episodes of rape and civilian massacre by the Imperial Army in occupying areas of southeast Asia, picked up pen and, in carefully crafted calligraphy for which he was noted, wrote a letter to one of the generals warning him that there is real anger against the Japanese troops in Hong Kong, French Indochina, Singapore and elsewhere. They could very well cause disruption behind our lines. Yamamoto suggested that the generals do a better job in controlling their troops.

He and Ugaki had just celebrated the great Japanese naval victory in the Java Sea. Now, they had to get down to business and face the far more formidable American Pacific Fleet.

Yamamoto went over the plans of the young staff officers who had considered attacking Hawaii but could not figure out how to neutralize the land-based air force brought in there in the past few weeks. So, they recommended an attack on Midway and Yamamoto studied their plan carefully.

Interesting, he thought. *They propose we take the islands of Midway, Johnston and Palmyra, then send our air strength there and mobilize for an invasion of Hawaii. At the same time, the American Navy would not dare ignore us, particularly at Midway, and we could use this to lure them into a decisive battle. Good thinking! We could also conduct diversionary raids in the Aleutians at Dutch Harbor to draw off some of their naval forces and then occupy the Aleutian Islands of Kiska and Attu. Yamamoto smiled. Wouldn't that give the American Navy a kick in the pants!*

Same Date, Pearl Harbor, Naval Headquarters at Makalapa, Pacific Fleet, Office of Admiral Nimitz

The three battleships, *Tennessee*, *Pennsylvania*, and *Maryland*, raised from the Pearl Harbor bottom reached the West coast under their own power and were repaired, modernized, equipped with the latest radar. They now arrived back in Pearl ready for battle, along with the new battleship, *Colorado*.

"I expect," Nimitz told his chief of staff "that by August, we'll get three more battleships from the Atlantic Fleet: the *Idaho*, *Mississippi*, and *New Mexico*." Nimitz smiled. "By then, we'll be far more powerful than we were before the Pearl Harbor attack."

"Can we then go on the offensive, sir?" asked his chief of staff.

"We still have a problem," Nimitz explained. "Fuel!"

"Fuel? Don't we have enough, sir?"

Nimitz shook his head. "Quantity is not the problem, delivery is. Our big ships are fuel guzzlers and we don't have enough tankers to feed all the battleships and carriers."

"Didn't we get tankers from the Atlantic Fleet?"

Nimitz shook his head. "They need them to sustain the flow of oil to Great Britain. Oh, we'll get more, just as soon as our shipyards build them. But for now, we have enough to sustain the battleships or the aircraft carriers in battle mode. I chose to give the fuel primarily to the carriers."

Same Date, Washington D.C., Office of Admiral King

"So, Admiral, I propose a raid on Tokyo by medium bombers flying off our aircraft carriers," offered Captain Francis Low, King's operations officer.

"Medium bombers taking off from one of our carriers?" King asked skeptically.

"Sir, I've worked with Lieutenant Colonel Jimmy Doolittle, who had his pilots practice short takeoff He assures me it can be done. And Admiral Halsey said he's willing to give it a try."

King shrugged. "Well, it is audacious, and those pilots will need a lot of luck. You know there is no way on God's earth they can return to the carriers and land those big planes."

"We know, sir. That is why the plan is to fly these planes to China and land there."

King nodded. "If it's good with Nimitz and Halsey, it's good with me."

CHAPTER ELEVEN

King to Nimitz: Just be Aggressive; and Nimitz was

March 15, 1942, San Francisco, Meeting Room in the Fairmont Hotel

ADMIRALS ERNEST KING AND Chester Nimitz met halfway, well, almost halfway. King flew in from Washington and Nimitz, from Honolulu.

"Ernie, we've got to use our carriers as a single strong strike force in order to seize the initiative for the offensive operations for which you have been pushing."

King frowned. "Chester, I just hesitate to commit our carriers *en masse*. I think I'd rather keep them separated for safer hit-and-run operations."

"Damn it, Ernie, that means keeping each carrier tethered to these older, slower battleships. I got to tell you, they are millstones around our neck. Four carriers together, without the battleships, will give us one powerful force."

King sighed. "It's a gamble, Chester."

Nimitz shrugged. "War is always a gamble. It's just that I feel our odds are better striking with our carriers in force and not individually."

"Okay, Chester, you're the theater commander. You do what you feel you must. Just be aggressive!"

Nimitz smiled. *Finally*, he thought, *we are moving away from the battleship mentality.*

April 19, 1942, Aboard the *Yamato*

"The Americans bombed Tokyo and five other cities! I can't believe it," Yamamoto growled. "I told Tojo not to promise Tokyo would never be bombed."

He glared at Ugaki. "And so much for your suggestion that we try to take Ceylon. No, we must concentrate on clearing out the Central Pacific and their bombers operating there."

Ugaki frowned. "But they have no land-based bombers that can reach us from the Pacific and we know they did not come from China."

Yamamoto hypothesized. "Aircraft carriers; they used aircraft carriers and somehow were able to launch medium-range bombers from them. Now I am totally convinced that we must lure the American Pacific Fleet into a decisive battle in the Central Pacific and eliminate them for once and for all to get rid of this danger to Japan's cities. And our threat to occupy Midway will be the bait to lure out the American Fleet."

Ugaki's eyes widened. "And the naval leaders in Tokyo. . .?"

Yamamoto smiled. "They were so shocked at the bombing. If the Americans can do it once, they can do it again. The powers in Tokyo agreed immediately that the priority should be to expand our Pacific defense perimeter and to eliminate of the American carrier fleet. I told them the 'children's hour' is over; now brace for the adult's hour."

"At least there was not much damage inflicted," Ugaki observed.

"That's not the point," Yamamoto muttered. "It's a disgrace that enemy planes could fly over the imperial capital at will and defile it and yet not a single plane was shot down! I am ashamed that American carriers could get so close to our sacred homeland."

"Roosevelt," Ugaki stated, "claims the planes came from Shangri-La. Where is that?"

Yamamoto shook his head. "Fool, Shangri-La is a fictional land described in the English novel, *Lost Horizon*. Its author, James

Hilton, describes **Shangri-La** as a mystical place, somewhere in the mountains near Tibet. The American president is playing with us. No, those bombers had to come from American aircraft carriers."

"Big bombers taking off from carriers?"

Yamamoto shrugged. "Quite obviously, they figured out how to do it. We've got to eliminate those floating enemy bases!"

Yamamoto stood up. "I am ashamed that I permitted this bombing to happen. I will retire now to my state room and contemplate. Do not disturb me. I leave it up to you, Ugaki, to have our forces search out and find those carriers who defiled our homeland and sink them!"

His meditation did not reach its usual restful state; his thoughts disturbed his inner peace. *The new weapons system that was just evolving, the carriers—nobody is sure how to use them or integrate them with our other fighting ships. The advances in this technology is almost frightening. Yesterday's imperatives become today's discarded tactics! We must keep massing our carriers together and strike as one large hammer. This way we can attack with dive bombers, torpedo planes, and level bombers. That will be my approach until someone proves me wrong—go with the well-balanced heavy air attack. Our problem is we don't have enough of the right aircrafts. Stupidly, production is split between the Army and the Navy, while the Navy air wing supports the Army efforts in southeast Asia and its own efforts in the Pacific So why does the Army need so many planes? The Navy has to borrow from Peter to pay Paul and, as a result, many of our carriers do not have enough warplanes to make a difference. For the Pearl Harbor attack, we "borrowed' so many planes that some of our smaller carriers do not have a complement of warplanes or are using aircraft ill-suited for carrier operations. Our industries are having production problems and I expect they will only produce fifty or sixty carrier attack aircraft this year. Pathetic! At this rate, with demands of a full-scale war, we'll never keep up with our losses!*

April 12, 1941, Hashirajima Bay, Aboard the Yamato

Returning from Tokyo, Yamamoto met with his senior staff including Ugaki, his chief of staff.

"Too many of our ships are being lost to bombers and submarines," Yamamoto observed to the assembled throng. "We are here now to plan an invasion of Midway, which will eliminate a major submarine base and a large air field used as a staging area for American land-based bombers. I have the clearance of the Naval General Staff to proceed. By attacking Midway we can stop both means for sinking our ships. But more important, it is a lure to get the American Fleet out of Pearl Harbor so that we can engage in the decisive battle to eliminate them once and for all.

"The Imperial Army, as usual, was dead set against the venture, saying we have enough on our plate in southeast Asia and China."

"But you were still able to get your way?" Ugaki asked.

Yamamoto smiled. "I threatened to resign from the Imperial Navy if they did not permit the Midway operation. That convinced Imperial General Headquarters to approve the campaign, which they are calling 'Operation MI'. We have a lot of work and planning to do, so let's get to it."

May 1, 1942, Island of Tulagi

Expecting a big fight and supported by the aircraft carrier *Shoho*, Japanese troops waded ashore to no opposition, no enemy troops. It surprised the hell out of them, but they quickly adapted and were immediately followed in by Japanese engineers who quickly built an early-warning seaplane base within sight of Guadalcanal across the straits. A half dozen Mitsubishi FIM2 float planes arrived from Rabaul, distinct in their biplane design. Japanese troops, after experiencing nothing but triumphs since the war with the Americans began, found also victory here easy. There was no reason to expect anything different on Guadalcanal.

May 5, 1942, Hashirajima Bay, Aboard the *Yamato*

Yamamoto called Ugaki into his ready room. "Today, I received imperial orders for the invasion of Midway and certain Aleutian Islands. We can now finish what we started at Pearl Harbor and force the discouraged Americans into a negotiated peace or have them dash themselves against an impregnable defensive perimeter that bars their way into the western Pacific "

Ugaki smiled. "Excellent. It coincides with the surrender of the Americans at Corregidor, which means the fleet can now move freely in and out of the harbor in Manila. We also took Tulagi without opposition! We built a seaplane base there, but two American carriers wiped out the planes we brought in."

"We shall occupy Guadalcanal," Yamamoto insisted, "and build an airfield on that island to control the entire area and prevent raids like this. The carriers would not dare to come close once we have land-based planes on Guadalcanal. It will be our land-based carrier—unsinkable!"

"Our invasion force is in the Coral Sea," Ugaki advised, "approaching Port Moresby on New Guinea."

Same Date, an Island off New Guinea in the Coral Sea

The all-volunteer coastwatchers set themselves up secretly on Japanese-held islands to report on Jap shipping and planes passing through or over the Coral Sea. Like the code-breakers, they were never referred to publicly. Their lives depended on secrecy. Japanese patrols searched and searched for the coastwatchers, who were constantly on the move to avoid capture. Some were plantation owners uprooted by the Japanese, still others were Australian Royal Navy personnel, volunteers sent into harm's way.

These venturesome men went by the code name "Ferdinand." Ferdinand, in an American children's book, was a non-aggressive bull who enjoyed lounging around and smelling the flowers. This was not unlike the coastwatchers, who were charged with avoiding combat at all costs and to simply sit and watch, and gather information, and radio it out.

Of course, it wasn't so simple. Each coastwatcher had a portable radio with which they reported to a receiver of the coastwatcher network located on the northern coast of Australia that, in turn, forwarded the messages to the appropriate military service.

This one coastwatcher, spanning the Coral Sea with field glasses, couldn't believe what he was seeing. Japanese ships, transports and warships, as far as the eye could see. He picked up his radio transmitter and reported the sighting. He then had to move out quickly because he knew the Japanese troops would try to triangulate on his position and rapidly show up in the area. If caught, of course, his life was forfeit, but only after torture.

What passed for a portable radio back then was anything but. Moving to a new location was a production, something that could not be accomplished by one man. He needed the help of volunteers and natives. Using natives always presented a danger of being turned into the Japanese for a reward. Usually though, the coastwatcher did not have a choice. His equipment included a transmitter, a receiver, an antenna, a speaker and a large supply of spare parts. Also, the radio batteries had to be recharged often and that required a gasoline generator. As I said, it was not a one-man operation, nor was it simple.

On this occasion, the coastwatcher had much to report, counting at least three large carriers, probably the *Shoho*, the *Shokaku*, and the *Zuikaku*, heading into the Coral Sea to protect what obviously was an invasion force.

Same Date, Near the Coral Sea, Aboard the American Carrier *Yorktown*; at Naval Headquarters in Pearl Harbor; and Aboard the Japanese Carrier *Shoho*

Admiral Frank Jack Fletcher examined the maps in the chartroom. His flagship, the carrier *Yorktown*, along with cruisers and destroyers, sailed into the Coral Sea to intercept the Jap carriers. Coming in from another direction was another group of ships led by the American carrier, *Lexington*. Admiral Nimitz, Fletcher knew, was probably on pins and needles waiting for news of the engagement brewing in the Coral Sea with a task force that really was not sufficient for the job—but he had to do with what he had, not what he wished for. If they could surprise the Japs, that would go a long way toward evening the odds. That's what he—and Nimitz—counted on. That was the way it was in war.

Nimitz could kick himself for permitting Colonel Doolittle's raid on Tokyo. Oh, it was daring, all right, and a great morale booster, but with Halsey somewhere near Japan providing the ships for the raiding Army bombers, Halsey was now out of the equation for the coming battle brewing in the Coral Sea. The aggressive Halsey was who Nimitz needed to command that task force, not the conservative Fletcher, who would rather spend days, floating around, waiting to refuel than taking the fight to the enemy.

Our naval force must try to block the Jap invasion force without too many losses that would leave us helpless for further Jap incursions. I need to somehow thwart the Japs in the Pacific until 1943, when our building program will start to give us the advantage. Damn it, I needed Halsey, my most skilled and aggressive commander at the Coral Sea, not screwing around near the Sea of Japan. I should have never authorized that raid and left the fleet so vulnerable. Well, like or not, it's up to Admiral Fletcher!

✳✳✳

As the Japanese invasion force, heading for Port Moresby, entered the Coral Sea, Captain Izawa Ishinosuke, commanding the Japanese carrier *Shoho*, couldn't shake that uneasy feeling of not knowing just where the American carriers were. He ordered out scout planes in a southern search pattern looking for them. *They had to be there somewhere!*

✳✳✳

The Americans were indeed there but the thankful rain squalls and a thick layer of cumulus clouds provided adequate cover from prying reconnaissance planes—but Fletcher did not know for how long. As morning broke in the eastern sky, the commander of the *Lexington* sent out search planes in a radius of 175 miles.

The Americans had the advantage of radar on their ships while the Japs had none, but the Japan's two big carriers, the *Shokaku* and the *Zuikaku*, were veterans of several engagements and knew how to work together.

May 7, 1941, Coral Sea, Aboard the *Shoho*

Admiral Shima watched as the carrier turned into the wind and increased its effective speed to 30 knots as his warplanes took off in the opening move of long-planned invasion of the Solomon Islands and Port Moresby.

Shima waited for the usual good news of a successful strike. Instead, suddenly appearing in the skies above him were a swarm of American dive bombers and torpedo planes attacking his ship while his planes were off somewhere near Port Moresby.

Six bombs and three torpedoes were what it took to sink the *Shoho*. The *Yorktown* planes sank her in less than twenty minutes.

Four American planes from the *Lexington* found the *Shokaku*, scoring a bomb hit, but the many torpedoes launched either missed or failed to detonate, the common—and frustrating—flaw of the American torpedoes.

Two torpedo bombers located the *Zuikaku* but released their torpedoes from too far away and the carrier easily evaded their wakes. Zeros, flying cover for the carrier shot down several of the cumbersome Devastator torpedo bombers while they damaged many others.

Other American planes sank a Japanese destroyer, a transport, and two patrol boats.

✳✳✳

Land-based Japanese bombers found the *Lexington* and the *Yorktown*. They sank the *Lexington*, a destroyer and a tanker, and damaged the *Yorktown*.

✳ ✳ ✳

Nimitz received the reports of the sea battle on the Coral Sea.

His chief of staff shook his head. "I guess we came off second best with more ship losses."

Nimitz looked up from the report he had been reading. "Not really, if you think about it. The *Shoho* is gone, and the *Shokaku* was put out of commission into the foreseeable future. The *Zuikaku* lost so many planes it is essentially punchless and I suspect will not be a factor for quite a while. But most important, and that was our main objective, we forced the Japs to call off the invasion of Port Moresby and bought some time. For now, Port Moresby no longer represents a threat to northern Australian cities and military bases.

"Incidentally, Joe Rochefort, our master code-breaker and his whole Hypo team, the ones who gave us a heads up on the Coral Sea venture, are now telling us that there is something else very big brewing in Tokyo. Something involving Midway and the Aleutians."

Nimitz turned to his chief of staff. "Keep an eye on this one and keep me advised. Work closely with Rochefort—a very valuable asset for us."

CHAPTER TWELVE

The Tide Starts to Turn in the Pacific; Battle of Midway: Just Who is Ambushing Whom?

May 9, 1942, Aboard the *Yamato*, Anchored in the Inland Sea, just off the Japanese Mainland

ADMIRAL YAMAMOTO STOMPED AROUND the chart room. The officers, including Admiral Ugaki, gave him room, standing silently. Finally, Yamamoto faced them, hands on his hips.

"Can you believe it? With the planes from three of our carriers and the support of land-based planes, we still lost the *Shoho*, and the *Shokaku* was put out of commission. The *Zuikaku* lost so many planes that we had to return her to Japan to assemble a whole new air group to replace the lost pilots and planes—so she's not available either. All these carriers won't be there for the decisive battle at Midway."

"But sir," Ugaki ventured, "the Americans lost more ships than we did, including two carriers."

"I don't believe that for one minute," Yamamoto retorted. "You know how those pilots exaggerate. We have only one confirmed sinking—the *Lexington*. The *Yorktown*, I do not think, was sunk. Order our warships to chase down the wounded *Yorktown* and sink her. We don't want her coming back and biting us in the ass!

"But a more important result of the battle is that our fleet is literally running away from Port Moresby. For now, there will be no invasion. With no carriers available, our brave admirals fear that we do not have enough air support to try that now. What we lost in that battle was many experienced and veteran pilots and crews—170 of them—who are irreplaceable. And since we will not have the *Shokaku* and the *Zuikaku* and all their planes and crews for our Midway attack, you still think we won that battle?"

"Well sir,' one of the officers chimed in, "Tokyo is proclaiming it as a great victory."

Yamamoto rolled his eyes. "They claim everything is a great victory. But we know better, don't we? My question to you is how you let these American carriers lurk around here undetected? We are now facing a mobile enemy whose pilots do not shy away from combat. Their dive bombers are good, scoring at least three direct hits on the *Shokaku*. We are extremely lucky their torpedoes performed so abysmally. Gentlemen—let's face it—you have been too smug. Our carriers obviously are not, as you thought, immune from bombs, torpedoes, and damage. We have a war on our hands and those Americans will not back down. One of our Air Staff Officers summed up the feeling I have: that we lacked the fighting spirit to engage the enemy."

With that, Yamamoto stalked out of the room, slamming the heavy steel door behind him. *I have the feeling,* he mused, *that we have shot our bolt, and this may be the farthest we'll ever advance unless we can trap them at Midway and sink their carriers in a decisive battle. We must, if we are to prevent any more bombing of Tokyo like the Doolittle raid. Perhaps with a four to three carrier edge, we'll win the battle of Midway. If we are successful in destroying the bulk of the American fleet at Midway, I will press our nation's leaders to negotiate a peaceful settlement.*

Yamamoto obviously was unwilling to interpret the results of the battle of the Coral Sea for what it was—an ill omen, suggesting much greater risks for the Midway plan than they allowed themselves to believe.

185

Ugaki, facing the closed door of Yamamoto's cabin, sighed. *Since there is an opponent in this war, one cannot always progress as one wishes. When we expect an enemy raid, why can't we employ our forces in a more unified way? I wonder whether we are underestimating our adversary?*

What had happened at Coral Sea was something conservative admirals on both sides feared would happen to vulnerable battling carriers. Each would send its planes up for simultaneous attacks, resulting in mutual annihilation of both sides' carriers.

Coral Sea was the first naval battle where the opposing ships never saw each other.

Same Date, Hashirajima, on the Inland Sea, Aboard the Flagship of Admiral Nagumo, the *Akagi*.

Captain Shingo Ishikawa of the Navy Staff at naval headquarters in Tokyo called on Admiral Nagumo on his flagship.

"Some of us on the Navy Staff are not too happy with this Midway operation," Ishikawa began. "Even if we take Midway, it is too far from our supply lines and too close to the American naval bases. Our supply ships will be cannon fodder for the American submarines. If we succeed, it will do nothing but make headlines. If we fail, we'll all be in the soup. It's pointless, but I can't convince Yamamoto of that. Why don't you try to dissuade him?"

Nagumo looked at him. "I know what you mean, and I don't necessarily disagree with you."

"Then you'll talk to him?" Ishikawa pressed.

Nagumo shook his head. "I'm afraid not. Remember—I did not follow up on the attack at Midway after we bombed Pearl Harbor and Yamamoto criticized me to all the staff officers. He called me 'no good.' Can you imagine? He said, 'after all the bravado, I came slinking home without attacking Midway.' If I oppose Midway this time, I'll almost certainly be labeled a coward and fired. So I'd rather go and get killed at Midway—just to show him."

May 12, 1941, Pearl Harbor, Office of Naval Intelligence, AKA, the Hypo Station

Joe Rochefort and his Hypo Station team worked overtime decoding the latest Japanese messages. The Japs made some changes in the code, so it took a little while longer to break enough of the code to get the gist of what Yamamoto was planning.

Considering the difficulties of code-breaking into a language like Japanese, the code-breakers had to be satisfied with interpreting just enough of the message to have a good idea what the Japs were up to and planning. This one was important enough for Rochefort to get off his duff and rush this down to Admiral Nimitz's office to deliver the news personally, including a point by point Japanese operating plan and the exact battle order of the Japanese Striking Force. Also, the fact that the Striking Force no longer included the large carrier *Zuikaku*.

May 13, 1942, Pearl Harbor, Conference Room in Naval Headquarters at Makalapa

The admiral from Fleet Intelligence uncovered the easel.

"Gentlemen, thanks to some great intelligence, we have the complete plans, which the Japs call 'Operation MI'. It is a scheme, developed by our old adversary, Admiral Yamamoto, to occupy Midway Island and several islands in the Aleutians. I am sure you can understand why we cannot divulge, even in this room, exactly how we obtained this information. So far as we know, we have all the details of the enemy's size, his intentions, and his strategy. Our advance knowledge is worth at least one fast carrier task force and we plan to take full advantage of it. As you may know, Midway is appropriately named, being almost at the geographical center of the Pacific Ocean. The atoll, part of a chain of volcanic islands, consists of two islands, Eastern Island and the larger, Sand Island. Sand Island, which has an airstrip, is undoubtedly, their main target. We even know which Jap operator from which ship did the transmitting. Though they change their call signs often, we get to recognize a radio operator's touch on the key and that tells us a lot.

"The Japs have committed four large carriers, three lighter ones, eleven battlewagons, fifteen cruisers, forty-four destroyers, fifteen submarines, and a host of supporting vessels. CINCPAC will meet this gigantic effort with three big carriers, eight cruisers, eighteen destroyers, and nine submarines. As I said, this time, it is we that have the element of surprise and we will, I promise, use it to our full advantage."

"What about Yamamoto?" a commander in the audience asked.

"Oh, he's coming along," explained the admiral, "but hanging safely back about three hundred miles east on the *Yamato* along with a few other battleships and cruisers."

"Too bad," the commander replied, "I'd love to get that bastard in my sights!"

Another commander asked, "How do we know they are not planning to invade the West Coast?"

The admiral smiled. "Come on, now. With just 5,000 troops in their convoy? No, we are sure the attack will occur at Midway Island. But you are not alone in your doubts. Intelligence Ops in Washington still stubbornly insists it's all a Japanese ruse but Admiral King, Nimitz's boss, finally came around and agreed the Japs are aiming for Midway."

May 20, 1942, Hashirajima, in the Inland Sea, Aboard the *Yamato*, in the Large Dining Room

The massive 69,000-ton *Yamato*, Yamamoto's flagship, overshadowed every other warship in the bay.

It was on this great ship that Yamamoto held a grand party for several hundred naval officers, including Admirals Nagumo and Kusaka, who would command the Midway Force.

Yamamoto's steward pulled him aside. "A disaster, sir. The cook has made a terrible mistake."

Yamamoto frowned. "So, tell me already!"

"The cook broiled the *tai* fish in miso, a salted bean paste, instead of plain salt. He's made a mess of things."

"Just ignore it," Yamamoto ordered. "By the time we finish all the toasts, they'll be so drunk they won't know the difference!"

After many toasts with warm sake drunk out of cups presented to Yamamoto by the emperor, confidence was at a high, especially with all the victories in southeast Asia, and at Pearl Harbor.

One captain rose and offered a toast. "To Cordell Hull, whom the newspaper reports quoted him as saying that trying to rally a war-weary people is like trying to drive an unwilling horse into a bull fighting arena."

They all laughed heartily and happily downed the sake.

✳✳✳

The following day, Admiral Ugaki, held a briefing for the commanders of this task force.

Admiral Nagumo was the first to speak. "What are your orders," he asked, "if we sight the American fleet on the way to Midway? Should we attack immediately or take Midway first."

Ugaki smiled. "Admiral Nagumo, you are in command and on the front line, so you can assess the situation better than I or Admiral Yamamoto can. Use your best judgment!"

Admiral Kusaka stood. "No, this operation is too complicated for us to accept responsibility. Our ship, the carrier *Akagi*, has a poor antenna, unlike the battleship *Yamato*."

Ugaki shrugged. "It's immaterial, we'll all be on radio silence to maintain the surprise. But I will say this. The prime and broader objective is to draw out the remaining American fleet and destroy it in a decisive battle. The more limited objective is to seize Midway as an advance air base to facilitate the early detection of enemy forces flying or sailing westward from the American mainland or from Hawaii."

Kusaka shook his head. "The plan is way too complex and would have to unfold with exquisite timing while we are on strict radio silence. To me, it's a recipe for disaster. Our battleships are stationed too far away to be of any help."

Admiral Kondo objected. "Taking Midway is crazy because it is too far away for us to effectively supply occupying troops there. American submarines would make mincemeat out of our supply ships. We are taking on too much. What if the American planes attack our carriers while our planes are away attacking Midway?"

"Well," Ugaki responded, "you don't have to worry about that because you are commanding the naval force attacking Attu and Kiska in the Aleutian Islands. It will give us a great listening post off the American coast and provide a good diversion for our Midway attack. We will handle the protection of the fleet while our planes attack Midway to destroy its aircraft on the ground and clear the beaches for our invasion forces."

"We should scrap the Midway plan and push westward through the Solomons to New Caledonia, where at least we can get support from our powerful land-based planes," Kondo grumbled. "Here, we face not only the American carrier planes, but also the land-based planes on Midway."

Ugaki looked at him. "You worry too much, Admiral. We will have many options once we wipe out the American carrier fleet and the planes at Midway. There is no reason for fear if surprise is achieved."

Kondo was still worried. "What if they discover our plans?"

"They won't," responded Ugaki, "if we maintain radio silence."

Kondo turned to Admiral Nagumo, the leader of this force. "You tell him it's a crazy plan!"

Admiral Nagumo just shrugged. "We were eminently successful at Pearl Harbor, we were eminently successful in the Indian Ocean, there is no reason to think we won't be eminently successful here. Our carriers are almost invincible, especially with six of them massed against the Americans."

Frustrated, Kondo asked, "What good will the battleship do, 300 miles from the action?"

"Not much," Nagumo replied, "but we are so strong, we can smash the enemy fleet singlehandedly, without help from the battleships."

Kusaka just did not like the whole operation. He kept going over it in his mind. *Indeed,* he thought, *Yamamoto fears the Americans will catch up, but we are plunging into this battle without adequate planning. We are splitting our fleet with this second attack simultaneously on the Aleutian Islands. Admiral Kondo feels the same way, I guess that's why they sent him up to the Aleutians. Yamamoto doesn't even trust Admiral Nagumo, yet he couldn't bring himself to change the leadership! The damn plan was impossibly complex and intricate, what with Yamamoto and his battleships hanging back over three hundred miles, his disposition of forces is too widespread so that they do not support each other, and his timing is overly rigid. It won't take much to screw up the entire operation! On the other hand, we've had too little time for training and we haven't yet studied the lessons of recent the Coral Sea battle.*

May 22, 1942, Kure, Japan, near the Naval Base

Before leaving for Midway, with most of the fleet anchored at the Kure Naval Base, many of the seamen were give a three-day pass. Yamamoto took advantage of this brief interlude to bring the love of his life, the geisha Chiyoko, down by train to the southern tip of Honshu. It was not easy. She was, unfortunately, not in good health and suffered a bad cough and pleurisy, requiring a doctor to accompany her and give her shots.

Yamamoto met the train at the station in Shimonoseki and he carried Chiyoko in his loving arms to the car he had waiting. The driver took them to Kure where they checked into one of their favorite places, a Japanese-style inn.

He could see she was very ill, and love-making was out of the question. So he devoted himself to taking care of her at that inn, carrying into the guest room, kicking off his shoes before stepping onto the tatami floor. He set her down gently on a zabuton cushion next to a low table, where fresh tea had just been brewed and appeared ready for serving. Chiyoko examined the large round vase on the table, in which colorful, carefully arranged flowers had been placed. Obviously, the arranger had put much thought into the arrangement which Chiyoko could enjoy. Later, Yamamoto undressed, donned a yukata, a thin Kimono provided by the inn, and gently placed one also over the bare shoulders of Chiyoko as he carried her to the bath where they soaked together in the hot springs, talking quietly and lovingly on all sorts of subjects.

Yamamoto tended to her every need and kept her comfortable. And though very ill, she happily spent this time with her true love.

For two days he tended to her, talking softly about their love and their desires and their future. They talked about his marriage—one of convenience to provide the Yamamoto family with a male heir—and in that he was successful.

Yamamoto gently took her in his arms. "I appreciate that you came to see me," he whispered in her ear, "coming so far in your condition. I know it took a lot of your dwindling energy to make this trip and to help us escape from reality and have time alone together without the intrusion of the outside world."

She smiled. "I hope I have renewed your spirit, my dear sailor."

Yamamoto gave her a gentle hug. "Oh, you have my dearest. Just as you overcame your misfortunes to be with me, I will devote all my energy, when I leave on the twenty-ninth for battle, to my responsibilities to lead our Navy to great victories! But every day, I will be pressing kisses on your photo, my love."

Yorktown in dry dock at Pearl Harbor

May 26, 1942, Pearl Harbor, Naval Headquarters at Makalapa, Office of Admiral Nimitz

"The *Yorktown* has arrived, sir, and she's headed directly into dry dock," Lieutenant Commander Edwin Layton, Nimitz's Intelligence Officer, informed Nimitz.

Nimitz looked up. "Did they give you an estimate of time for repairs?"

"Three weeks, sir."

"Tell them they have three days to get her in shape to join the fleet at Midway!" Nimitz ordered.

"Three days, sir?"

"You heard me. The balance of power in the Pacific may depend on our carriers, including the *Yorktown*. She must be ready to move out to Midway in no more than three days!

"And Admiral Fletcher will command the strike force," Nimitz added.

"Fletcher, sir? Not Admiral Halsey?" Nimitz shook his head. "You heard right, Admiral Fletcher. Unfortunately, our aggressive Admiral Halsey, well versed in air tactics, is in the hospital in a great deal of agony with an aggressive case of dermatitis. So, we must rely on the blackshoe Admiral Fletcher, whether we like it or not, and just hope he can manage those aircraft carriers effectively."

"I've heard," said the chief of staff, "that the skipper of the *Yorktown* fighter squadron is unhappy because Fletcher is not an aviator and had not grown up with carrier-based squadrons and received all the experience and knowledge to command such a carrier task force."

"Well, we'll have to live with it. I can only use what I've got," Nimitz groused. "Besides, he has Admiral Spruance by his side for this one, and he's very good.

"Incidentally, I have recalled," Nimitz advised, "Task Forces 16 and 17 from the South Pacific and they should get to the Midway area barely in time to join Fletcher's and Spruance's groups to lay in wait for the Japs. We must commit our three operating carriers in the

Pacific-the *Enterprise*, the *Hornet*, and the *Yorktown*—to jump their carriers while, hopefully, their carrier planes are away raiding Midway. Now that would be the best of all worlds. The *Yorktown* will be there in time. The repairs can continue as she sails at top speed into harm's way."

"What about the *Saratoga?*"

Nimitz shook his head. "Still in dry dock in San Diego after she took that torpedo from a Jap submarine."

Nimitz looked over Rochefort's report. "How many carriers will the Japs have?"

"According to our intelligence," Layton said, "they'll have four large ones and two small ones. But we will have the element of surprise thanks to our odd-ball, but great, code-breaker Rochefort and his team and, if we time our attack right, we may just catch the Japs with their pants down! What the Japs don't know is we just sent a squadron of B-17 bombers to Midway airfield to greet the them."

"Are we sure it's Midway they are going after, Commander?"

Layton smiled. "Rochefort pulled another rabbit out of his hat." The Japs have been referring to the target as 'AF', so he sent a message in the clear that Midway was short on fresh water. Sure enough, the Japs sent a message to the fleet that 'AF' was having water problems! So, I am confident that the Jap force is headed for Midway, with another force going to the Aleutians."

Nimitz nodded. "Yes, *apparently* they want to take the islands of Kiska and Attu. We'll try to set a trap for the fleet headed for Midway; for now, we'll forget about the Kiska and Attu in Aleutians—they'll not divert us from defending Midway. As for the Aleutians, they'll soon discover the weather is so bad there that there is not much they can do. I think they have some exaggerated view that they can use the Aleutians as a launching site for an invasion or strategic bombing of the American homeland."

Layton smiled. "The Japs will soon discover that the islands are small, mountainous, devoid of any ground cover or building materials. It's useless for any offensive action larger than an occasional whale hunt!"

Nimitz nodded. "I wonder. How do we know those ships are not just heading for their home ports?"

Layton smiled. "As Rochefort put it, based on their position and direction, it would be like doing a tonsillectomy through the rectum!"

"I note that Washington," Nimitz said sarcastically, "reviewed those intercepts and thinks the Japs are heading south toward the island chains, even Australia."

"If we listen to the politicians on the subject of tactics," Layton snorted, "we will all end up as Japanese POWs!"

"Do we know how many Jap carriers are in the force heading for Midway?" asked Nimitz.

Layton nodded. "Four big babies. There's not much we don't know. The Japs laid it all out in their coded messages. We even know who planned it—Admiral Yamamoto!"

Nimitz rubbed his chin. "We'd better concentrate on knocking out the four carriers. Give the task force these orders." Nimitz handed the sheet to Layton.

Layton read it.

"In carrying out the task as assigned, you will be governed by the principle of calculated risk, which you shall interpret to mean the avoidance of exposure to attack by superior enemy forces without good prospect of inflicting, as a result of such exposure, greater damage to the enemy."

June 2, 1942, Somewhere in the Central Pacific, Aboard the *Yamato*, Heading Toward Midway

On his way to a planning session with Ugaki, he could not shake his worries about Chiyoko's illness. *She'd been so sick with pleurisy the doctors had almost given up on her. He wondered whether he was selfish to have her travel to Kure. She insisted it was what she wanted but still, he wasn't so sure—it took a lot out of her.*

He approached Admiral Ugaki's cabin he pushed aside the thoughts of his geisha love, as he knocked and slowly pushed open the door.

"What happened to the seven submarines I sent to intercept the American fleet between Hawaii and Midway?" Yamamoto asked Ugaki.

"They arrived too late. The American fleet had already sailed."

Yamamoto frowned unhappily. "So, we are blind?"

"If you mean not knowing precisely where the Americans are at the moment, the answer is yes," replied Ugaki.

"That's the problem," Yamamoto said. "We don't know where their carriers are. That is why they were able to pull off that daring air raid on Tokyo. We were focused in the southwest Pacific and they hit us on our weak flank."

Ugaki nodded. "It was a lot easier when we attacked at Pearl Harbor because the enemy did not know it was at war. Now, we cannot laugh because they turned the tables after discovering our vulnerabilities trying to defend the homeland. There is simply no foolproof defense against the carriers roaming the Pacific."

"That," Yamamoto responded, "is precisely why we must force the American carriers out of Pearl Harbor to fight and lose the decisive battle."

But Yamamoto, for all his expressions of confidence, could not shake the feeling that the fleet had been discovered by the Americans when he received a report of an "urgent" message by one of the American submarines, intercepted on fleet radio. They could not decode the message, but Yamamoto worried about the urgency part of the transmission. Also, there was a reported heavy increase in radio traffic from Hawaii and the Aleutian Islands area, much from aircraft and submarines, suggesting the American task force may be at sea. It was only a hunch and he was too committed now to turn back.

Some six hundred miles far to the rear steamed Yamamoto's large main force of seven big battleships, including the great *Yamato*, four seaplane carriers, ten cruisers, and many destroyers, Thirty-four ships in all.

Same Date, Japanese Attack Force, Approaching Midway, Aboard *Akagi*

The battle group, called by the Japanese, the *Kido Butai*, the same group that was so successful at Pearl Harbor and in the Indian

Ocean, confidently increased its speed to thirty knots, as they approached Midway, and turned into the wind for the takeoff of the attack planes; Vice Admiral Chuichi Nagumo prepared for another great victory. The offensive move committed almost the entire Imperial Navy led by twenty-eight admirals. The fleet would log more miles and consume more precious fuel in this single operation than they would normally use in a year.

The fog gave some concerns to Nagumo as he headed into battle at Midway on the bridge aboard his flagship, the carrier *Akagi*. He peered out the window, but it was no use. In this thick mist, he couldn't see a damn thing, not even the end of the *Akagi's* 855-foot long deck, the longest in the Imperial Navy. *I suppose this fog also hides us from the enemy, but it's making navigation difficult and keeping us in formation without collisions is very hard to maintain. And we still don't even know where the enemy fleet is. If we can find them, I have no doubt we can destroy them with our superiority in numbers and the battle experience of our pilots. But we must find them!*

Nor was Admiral Ryūnosuke Kusaka, Chief of Staff of under Nagumo, happy. *After the Port Moresby invasion fizzled Yamamoto was finally given his head—after once again threatening to resign. Yamamoto figured that with only an estimated two or three large carriers in the Pacific, the American Navy was clearly outnumbered by the large Japanese carriers. What better time was there to pursue his Midway plan for the 'Decisive Battle?' While the Americans still have inferior numbers, we can pick off their carriers one at a time or, if the situation presents itself, all at once. So, sufficiently intimidated by Yamamoto, Imperial Headquarters decided to let him go ahead.*

Kusaka shook his head. *But he wants too much from us with this dual tactical mission. He wants us to invade and neutralize American land-based air force on Midway and then, as the primary mission, find and destroy the American fleet. But just as soon as we attack Midway all the mobility and secrecy—our best weapons—are gone. If Midway is not overrun within a day, the entire campaign will be upset. It's like a hunter chasing two rabbits at one time. I agree with Yamamoto that an invasion of Hawaii is not feasible until we sink the American carriers.*

But this complicated plan of his may have us biting off more than we can chew. We are stupidly sending fifty-two ships to the Aleutians when we could use them here! And for what? Two lousy islands almost at the North Pole! The grandeur of all this betrays the fundamental flaws in the planning. Look, if we beat them at Midway, then the Aleutians are ours for the taking without sending a large fleet there. If we lose at Midway, then we won't be able to defend any gains we had made in the Aleutians. The prevailing feeling in the Imperial Navy is that the American fleet is beaten and would now have to be coaxed out toward its own annihilation. But frankly, I have grave doubts about the supposed demise of the American Navy!

And with Yamamoto and our battleships positioned so far back, we'll never be able to coordinate our actions like it was a tightly-scripted ballet. Everything here is too complex, and, in battle, Yamamoto should know that nothing usually goes as planned. We have no room to meet unforeseen contingencies. Let's hope our six carriers can answer all those doubts!

Three hundred miles away, in his flagship *Yamato*, Admiral Ugaki fretted. *I do not have much confidence, he thought, in Nagumo's "Sword Theory" of putting all the ships and power together in one massive stroke. At the War College, we learned to disperse the carriers so that the attacks could be launched from different directions and the fleet could not be hit all at once by the attackers. What would happen if we launched our planes to attack Midway and then the Americans attacked us? Our carriers would be sitting ducks. But Nagumo was so enamored with this mass attack idea that I kept quiet. Now, I'm sorry I did. Yamamoto tried to warn Nagumo to spread out his fleet but Nagumo would not listen, and Yamamoto felt strongly about not interfering with the commander of the mission during battle. That's always been his policy. The independence streak of the Japanese Navy can be carried too far, I feel. Me? I would have ordered bastard to spread out his ships. And Yamamoto's fleet, being three hundred miles from the action, cannot give*

Nagumo much support. But Yamamoto felt if we concentrated all our ships at Midway, we might discourage Nimitz from sending his ships out of Pearl Harbor to confront us. I suppose there's some validity to the approach. Who knows?

June 4, 1942, Pearl Harbor, Naval Headquarters at Makalapa, 6AM, Hawaiian Time

The entire CINCPAC staff was assembled in the headquarters' conference room.

An aide burst into the room. "We just heard from Midway, sir. Our Catalina reconnaissance planes sent a message in clear language reporting two Jap carriers and several escorting ships traveling toward Midway at 25 knots. They estimate these ships are 180 miles from the island!" The aide handed the cable to Admiral Nimitz.

Nimitz flashed a broad smile. "The Catalina saw only two carriers, but I am quite sure there must be more in the vicinity."

Nimitz looked at the cable. "According to this cable, Nagumo has already launched his bombers against Midway." Nimitz slapped the conference table with the palm of his hand. "Now is the time to strike, while the bulk of their planes are in the air and attacking Midway; that's when their carriers are most vulnerable. And the Japs launched their planes much further out than is usual."

Nimitz called over his chief of staff. "Tell Fletcher he's on the flank of the Jap fleet and to launch his attack planes! Give him the coordinates."

Same Date, Pacific Ocean, Somewhere Near Midway Island, Aboard the Carrier *Enterprise*

Under orders from Admiral Nimitz, Fletcher had positioned his ships two hundred miles north of Midway at dawn in a bold ambush plan to engage the vast Japanese fleet of two hundred ships. Against his armada, he had twenty-five fighting ships: three carriers, eight cruisers and fourteen destroyers. Fletcher wondered, *with my meager fleet, who's ambushing whom? To be successful we must strike the first blow early and hard, so they can neither launch planes nor recover their planes returning from Midway. We must catch them at that point! Some of our most experienced aviators planned this. I just hope it works, but I have my doubts. He was glad he had three carriers instead of two. It was a miracle that they could put the heavily damaged carrier Yorktown back together in three days to join the Enterprise and Hornet! But he was worried about the Yorktown, whose pilots consisted of a pickup squadron who never worked together and some who never even landed a plane on a carrier.*

On direction from Nimitz, Admiral Fletcher gave the orders to launch his attack planes. He had at his command, torpedo planes, dive bombers, and high-level bombers. The torpedo planes, Douglas TBD Devastators, were anything but. He knew, from his experienced aviators, that the planes were slow and disastrously obsolete, and easy targets for the Zeros and antiaircraft guns—they desperately needed replacing.

Now Nagumo was on the spot. What should he do? Wait to retrieve his planes coming back from Midway for refueling and rearming? Should the Americans attack during the refueling and rearming, the ship could go up like a giant firecracker. But if they could get refueled and rearmed, he'd have a strong attack force.

But Nagumo knew the half-hearted Americans wouldn't cause any trouble at this point because his fleet was too strong and their will too weak. So he ordered his planes armed to strike Midway, and the proud Japanese attack force headed for that island in full confidence. Satisfied that there was no enemy present, he ordered only a cursory search by his reconnaissance aircraft. Thus, in his entire task force, he had only thirty-six dive bombers available to attack the enemy, should that be necessary.

The more aggressive Admiral Yamaguchi, on board his flagship, the carrier *Hiryu*, after the cruiser *Tone's* search plane spotted some American ships, was unhappy with Nagumo's failure to engage in prompt offensive action against an enemy that he, Yamaguchi, considered dangerous. Yamaguchi signaled Nagumo to send out an attack force immediately but Nagumo refused to do because he had no aircraft to send out for fighter protection. Nagumo preferred to wait until his planes returned to launch such an all-out attack.

When his planes returned, on advice of his pilots, he ordered second attack on Midway, which meant arming the planes with bombs again, not torpedoes. They were busy doing this when the cruiser *Tone's* reconnaissance plane reported ten enemy ships within striking distance.

Nagumo had a quick lesson in the American spirit when its war planes showed up. Unfortunately for some American pilots, the first planes to arrive on the scene of the Japanese fleet were the slow, obsolete Devastator torpedo planes which immediately moved into attack mode without waiting for the cover of the dive bombers. Not only that but many of the torpedo crews were raw ensigns, never even have carried a torpedo much less dropped one on a target, practice or otherwise—aiming a torpedo required a highly developed skill. Dive bombing, on the other hand, was much less complicated. When a dive bomber drops its bomb, the force of gravity takes over and the bomb travels in an almost straight line, eliminating the need for complex calculations. The pilot points his diving plane at the target and releases the bombs. It is the most accurate form of attack. Once the Douglas Dauntless dive bomber is committed to the vertical dive with its dive flaps deployed, it is almost impossible for the Zeros to maneuver into an effective firing position to counter it.

But not so for the torpedo planes. The torpedo plane flight leader was warned about this but, in the excitement of the moment of spying the Japanese fleet he attacked anyway—a big tactical mistake with predictable results. He should have known better because training doctrine warned that just before launching a torpedo attack, torpedo planes were extremely vulnerable. To bomb effectively, they must maintain a low straight and level course, which gives them no opportunity for evasive maneuvering. The success of an unsupported torpedo attack upon the enemy main body in good visibility was considered doubtful, especially if there is a protecting screen of destroyers firing their antiaircraft guns. It was planned that the attack would be coordinated, and that the dive bombers and high-level bombers would draw the enemy fire upwards and away from the slow, low-level torpedo planes; there was, however, no such coordination and therefore, no diversion away from this torpedo attack. As a result, all fifteen Devastator planes were shot down by either Zeros or antiaircraft fire. And none scored a single torpedo hit on any Japanese ship.

Nagumo's reconnaissance planes reported finding the American carriers just two hundred miles to the east. Now the *Akagi* torpedo planes, fitted with bombs for airfields, had to be lowered for rearming and conducting the time-consuming task of refitting the planes with torpedoes for sinking ships.

Despite the disastrous results of the torpedo plane attack, it was not without benefit to the Americans. These Devastator pilots had located the Japanese fleet and that enabled the rest of the attack planes to home in on a large part of the Japanese force, and so when the dive bombers arrived on the scene, most of the Zeros were at a low altitude shooting up the American torpedo planes. As the dive bombers prepared to attack, they met resistance from only a few defending Zero fighters. But by now, the American pilots, in these dive bombers, had learned how to counter the more maneuverable but lightly armored Zero, using their plane's diving speed and structural resilience to twist and turn and gain the advantage and thus were able to shoot down a great many of the enemy Zeros. While some planes engaged the Zeros, others bored down, first on the *Hiryu*. All the while, higher in the sky, Flying Fortresses were dropping their bombs.

A dive bomber, diving at a steep angle, requires an abrupt pull-up after dropping its bombs if the pilot does not want to become part of the explosion of the bomb he just released. This puts great strains on both pilot and aircraft. It demands an aircraft of strong construction, with some means to slow its dive. But such a plane was limited to light bomb loads, which could sink a vulnerable carrier, but would not put the larger capital ships, like battleships or heavy cruisers out of commission, even with a direct hit. So attacks used a combination of dive bombers (light bomb loads but very accurate), torpedo planes (lethal torpedoes but slow and vulnerable), and high-level bombers (no accuracy on a maneuvering ship at that altitude).

All three American carriers launched their attack planes. The dive bombers were not vulnerable like the torpedo planes. They came in from high up at great speed, not giving the Japanese gunners much of a look, and dropped their bombs while almost on top of their target, so accuracy their was pretty good.

Nine B-17 Flying Fortress heavy bombers also found the Japanese fleet and attacked but scored no hits.

Same Day, Aboard the *Yamato*, Three Hundred or More Miles from the Naval Battle Near Midway

Yamamoto began the days in jubilant spirits as his happy staff officers reported the successful raids on Midway Island and granted the request for a second strike on Midway to totally destroy American air strength on the island.

But at 7:40 AM, Japanese cruiser *Tone's* search plane reported sighting ten enemy ships, destroying Yamamoto's assumptions that there were no enemy ships in the vicinity and that the Americans would not challenge his strong naval forces.

Nevertheless Yamamoto thought contentedly, *But is what we wanted, to set up the decisive battle to destroy the American Pacific Fleet once and for all. He must find out what enemy ships were in that force.*

A half hour later the reconnaissance plane reported the ships to be five cruisers and five destroyers. Ten minutes later, reconnaissance reported a carrier bringing up the rear!

But the blow fell from the planes from three American carriers. As the day progressed, Yamamoto received reports of the sinking of the *Akagi*, the *Kaga*, and the *Soryu*.

A dejected Yamamoto thought, *Akagi, my first command of a carrier, sunk!*

Sinking Japanese Aircraft Carrier

But this was no time for recriminations. *I still have the Hiryu*, he reminded himself.

Admiral Yamaguchi, aboard the *Hiryu*, planned to go after the enemy carriers and Yamamoto so ordered. *We must salvage this battle!*

But it was not to be. While its planes did successfully sink the *Yorktown*, American carrier planes found the *Hiryu* and sank her, completing the sweep of the Japanese carriers in the battle.

Sinking Yorktown

The battle took forty-eight hours. The toll: the *Yorktown* sunk, but the American planes found many more targets than the Japanese did, resulting in the sinking of *four* of Japan's large carriers, a heavy cruiser and fourteen other ships. The Japanese carriers might have survived the bombs that scored the hits, but with bombs and torpedoes on the deck and exposed during the rearming of the warplanes during the switch, these carriers were virtual powder kegs and it would not take a necessarily large bomb to set off an inferno from which the ship could not recover and that is exactly what happened. In the air, the Japanese fared no better, having lost 250 planes and 2,200 men. Among those that perished were many of the Imperial Navy's ace flyers and knowledgeable mechanics and technicians—irreplaceable experience that took decades to develop.

Yamamoto never participated in the great battle. He was too far away, and the fight was over before Yamamoto's great battleships could get there.

The Americans achieved a great victory in a naval battle where, for the first time in history, there was a gigantic carrier battle and where, the opposing ships never even saw each other. Thus, the day of the mighty battleships and cruisers slugging it out appeared to be over. And the great Japanese Imperial Navy, in just one battle, was decimated almost beyond recovery.

Japan had already reached the high watermark of its conquests and the Midway debacle began the Imperial Navy's slow defensive retreat from the Central Pacific More Japanese sailors died in the Midway battle than ever before. It has lost four of the carriers with which it opened hostilities at Pearl Harbor, basically obliterating the Imperial Navy's ability to wage any new major offensives in the Pacific

But now, the frustrated Admiral Nagumo was determined to save face by using his surface ships to engage the Americans in a night battle, the type of battle for which his sailors trained so hard. Sadly for Nagumo, he could not find the enemy, which had wisely and promptly retired from the scene. Nagumo had no choice but to order a general withdrawal to the northwest.

Yamamoto in his super battleship, together with the rest of his surface ships were, at three hundred or more miles away, in no position to help. It was over before they could possibly get there. Yamamoto called off the invasion of Midway and ordered his remaining ships home.

Several staff officers, rescued after the sinking of the carrier *Akagi*, met with Admiral Kusaka on the cruiser *Tone*. Kusaka, wounded in the sinking of his ship, was still in his battle-stained uniform and limping badly.

A spokesman for the group addressed Kusaka. "We have talked among ourselves and decided we cannot bear the disgrace of defeat. Hence, we are advising you that we have decided to commit hari-kari. All of us will disembowel ourselves."

Kusaka screwed up his face in a fury. "You want to commit suicide because you lost a battle? Bakayaro!" he shouted. He'd just called them the English equivalent of assholes.

"Assemble the entire officer staff in the largest room you can find on this ship," he ordered in an angry voice.

Kusaka waited until staff officers not on watch, assembled.

It hurt to move, but he stood up anyway in front of the officers, now in his unimpressive white hospital gown, intravenous tubes and all.

"I have to laugh," Kusaka began. "You men cheer when the battle is successful and drink yourself into a stupor. When it isn't, you threaten seppuku or hari-kari. Commit suicide? What are you? Babies? You think in a long war you are going win every battle? Well, grow up! Stop acting like hysterical women. You're experienced, battle-hardened veterans. Who do you think is going to replace you if you kill yourself? We cannot afford to lose men like yourselves.

So, stop talking nonsense and prepare yourselves for the next battle. From now on, I will consider any talk of suicide as traitorous."

Kusaka retreated to his hospital bed where he was visited by Nagumo.

"I heard about your rousing speech," Nagumo said.

Kusaka gave him a baleful look. "Are you considering suicide too?"

"It had crossed my mind," Nagumo admitted. "After all I am not just a staff officer but commander of the fleet. It may be appropriate for me, but not the others."

Kusaka sat up in bed, groaning slightly. "Are you crazy," he shouted. "What kind of example do you want to set?" With great effort, Kusaka stood and went face to face with Nagumo. "Lose a battle and turn in all your chips? I'll tell you what I told the staff officers. If we are to win this war we cannot afford to lose our experienced warriors. And it especially applies to you, one of our leading admirals! If anyone should be held responsible, it's me. I should have allowed Genda to send out more search planes. If anyone should commit hari-kari it is me."

Nagumo put his hand on Kusaka's shoulder. "Get your wounds taken care of my dear friend, I got your message. I will carry on for Japan. But listen, we cannot afford to lose you either, so take your own advice."

Yamamoto, agreeing with Kusaka, rejected with fury, all the talk of suicide and, at his first opportunity, addressed the fleet leaders.

"Japan," he began, "could not afford to lose its experienced captains and pilots. Where would our Navy be without all these battle-hardened veterans? It is absolutely primitive to expect a captain to go down with his ship, or for an ace pilot not to survive because he would not use his parachute. The Imperial Navy will not prevail if its commanders and pilots were expected to immolate themselves on the dubious altar of pride. I expect you all to survive to fight another day. You will have another chance to avenge this defeat. You cannot deprive His Majesty of your services at a time when they are so desperately needed!"

Yamamoto ordered his staff not to criticize Nagumo and then he excused himself, retiring to his cabin, sweating profusely. During the battle, he had been stricken with worms in his stomach and suffered from severe abdominal pains. Now was the time for him to take care of himself.

Some officers pointed out to Yamamoto his position created somewhat of a problem for them because the Navy Imperial Headquarters took the position that a pilot should go down with his plane, a tank commander with his tank, and a captain with his ship.

"Whatever you do under my command is my responsibility and mine alone as commander-in-chief. If you fail once and survive I intend to use you again and believe me, you will be a better fighter for it.

"Without your survival, we shall not be able to get through this war. The new interpretation of *bushido*, or 'the way of the warrior,' is totally false. And I have told Tokyo this. They can fire me if they want but I won't change my mind for men *under my command*. I can't speak for the Army and its tank commanders, but as far as Navy pilots are concerned, I expect you to use your parachute rather go down in flames with your plane, and for the captains, you will abandon ship when the ship is about to go under!"

Yamamoto suspected his bosses considered him irreplaceable, and he was correct. Tokyo did nothing regarding his insubordination.

June 6, 1942, Somewhere in the Central Pacific Aboard the *Yamato*

Yamamoto wondered, *How could a fleet as large as I organized be defeated by such a relatively small American force? To lose the four carriers that had played a major role in the Navy's smashing victories all across the Pacific and even in the Indian Ocean is unfathomable. But that is not the worst of it. An even greater blow was the loss of our veteran air crews and skilled maintenance men who went down with their ships. Irreplaceable! Simply irreplaceable! Was the whole plan too ambitious? That's what some of my officers are saying behind my back. They think I don't know what they are muttering. Well, at least we occupy some American territory in the Aleutians—for whatever that's worth. We assumed Midway would be like Pearl Harbor, but it was not. A big mistake because obviously, they were not surprised in the least and were ready for us. That comes from over-confidence because of our early easy victories. But how did they know? That is the question to which we must find the answer. Taking on America, I knew we were overmatched but no one believed me. It was only a matter of time when it would happen, and I fear that time is rapidly approaching.*

Several staff officers approached him, interrupting his ruminations. "What it is you want?" he snapped.

A spokesman stepped forward. "How can we apologize to the emperor for this defeat?"

Yamamoto frowned. "Don't worry, I am the only one who must apologize to His Majesty." He sighed and choked up a little. "Now send out orders to Kondo and Nagumo to withdraw."

"Sir," the communications officer, after barging into the room. "The captain of the *Akagi* carrier radioed that the ship's fires were raging out of control. He requests permission to scuttle her."

Ugaki shot out of his chair. "Damn old women, that's what they are. That was our flagship!"

Yamamoto shook his head. "Calm down Ugaki. Admiral Kuroshima has pointed out that if we don't scuttle her, the Americans would seize and exhibit her in an American museum. Kuroshima," Yamamoto said, with tears in his eyes, "have our destroyers torpedo the ship—sink the *Akagi*."

Ugaki could not let go of it. "The Americans must have been forewarned about Midway. Perhaps one of their submarines had discovered the fleet en route. Could they have broken our code?"

"That I doubt," Yamamoto assured. "We change it often and very few Americans even speak Japanese, which would make it doubly hard for them to decode our messages. Besides, a few people have suggested that it may be my fault by having the fleet dispersed too widely, preventing the different segments from providing mutual support. I did not, they say, concentrate my forces. They may be right."

"I don't know about that," Ugaki countered. "After all, Admiral Nomura certainly suspects our code has been compromised. He warned Japanese Intelligence, but they simply could not believe that the Americans had the mentality or know-how to decode our supercode, as they call it, much less translate from Japanese, even if they had broken the code. Me, I doubt their evaluation of the Americans. Even after our ambassador was warned by a German foreign ministry official in 1941 that German intelligence was almost certain the Americans were able to read our codes, we did nothing."

Yamamoto frowned. "Well, let's hope you are wrong."

When alone with Ugaki, Yamamoto let his hair down a little. "It depresses me so at how many our sailors were lost, thanks to our faulty planning. I don't usually share my poems, my *haiku*, but I will this one, good friend.

'Looking back over the year I feel myself grow tense
At the number of comrades who are no more.'"

Same Date, Pearl Harbor, Naval Headquarters at Makalapa, Office of Admiral Nimitz

Yamamoto was not the only one fretting about the outcome of the Midway naval battle. Admiral Nimitz had telegraphed his congratulations to Admiral Fletcher on "his glorious accomplishments." But then Nimitz received the news that the *Yorktown* was sunk, as was a destroyer, and about 150 American planes were lost.

"They should have saved the *Yorktown!*" Nimitz groused to his aide. "Well, you can bet the Japs are hurt pretty bad."

But later, in a private note to his boss, Admiral King, he wrote, "At the present stage of our carrier building program, we cannot afford to swap losses with this ratio."

In fact, there really was no chance to save the *Yorktown* because Japanese planes from the *Hiryu* located and sent four bombs into the American carrier creating a deadly series of violent explosions as the stricken carrier tilted to one side, forcing those hands left on board to abandon ship. Two Japanese destroyers then torpedoed her, and the valiant carrier gave up and simply slid from sight to her watery grave at the bottom of the Pacific Ocean. But she had company—the four Japanese carriers.

By the time the Japanese warplanes that attacked the *Yorktown* returned to their mother carrier, she was gone, and the pilots were forced to ditch their planes in the ocean. The *Hiryu* had, in the meantime, been sunk by American planes.

And Admiral Isoroku Yamamoto had lost his aura of invincibility.

June 20, 1942, Tokyo Bay, Aboard the *Yamoto*

Yamamoto shook his head as he put down the dispatch from Tokyo. "Can you imagine? Tojo has proclaimed the Midway battle a great victory. The enthusiastic public participated in a government sponsored flag procession and lantern parade! What will the people do when they find out their prime minister is nothing but a liar!"

Ugaki shrugged. "That's the war-time propaganda. You have to expect it."

Yamamoto frowned. "When we must hide our losses from the people, the war is as good as lost. To make matters worse and to prevent news of the defeat from spreading, they are treating our surviving heroes as pariahs and dispersing them to various bases on Kyushu where they are being confined to base and threatened them with arrest if they contact their families. Others were immediately transferred to the South Pacific, with no chance even to meet their families again. What an outrage—being treated like prisoners of war!"

"What about the wounded?" Ugaki asked.

Yamamoto sighed. "Not much better. Those recovering from burns in the hospital were never allowed visitors—no wives, no parents, no girlfriends. They couldn't even visit their fellow wounded! The wounded were carried off the ships in the dead of night and isolated. Is that a way to treat our heroes?"

✳✳✳

Commander Mitsuo Fuchida, hero pilot of the Pearl Harbor attack, had been wounded during the Midway battle while aboard the *Akagi*. He'd been transferred to a hospital ship which sailed to the Yokosuka Naval Base. The Japanese naval authorities would not bring him ashore until the dead of night, and though not seriously injured, he was carried in a covered stretcher though the back entrance to the hospital and placed in a room in complete isolation and cut off from the rest of the Japan, and prohibited from communicating with the outside world, including the nurses and corpsmen.

I am a prisoner of war! Fuchida thought.

June 26, 1942, Tokyo Bay, Aboard the *Yamato*

After a rather sumptuous dinner, Yamamoto and Ugaki sat back in some easy chairs to talk. Ugaki sipped some sake while Yamamoto contented himself with some hot tea.

"Since the Midway disaster," Yamamoto said, "our plans for invasions of Fiji, Samoa, and Port Moresby have been postponed. Now the Army is demanding we send carriers south for raids on Australia."

Ugaki looked puzzled. "But we don't have the carriers for that!" Yamamoto smiled. "You and I know that, but our Army is not convinced. But my idea, and I've said it before, is to build new air bases on islands closer to Australia. One of the islands I am thinking about is Guadalcanal, just across that strait from our seaplane base at Tulagi. We have a small garrison there already. Let's send some engineers and troops to start work on an air base."

CHAPTER THIRTEEN

After America's Victory at Midway, What's Next? Operation Watchtower!

July 1, 1942, Washington D.C., Naval Headquarters, Office of Admiral King

GENERAL GEORGE MARSHALL, CHIEF of Staff of the Army and Air Force, took a seat facing the head of the American Navy, Admiral Ernest King.

Marshall shook his head in disgust. "Well, MacArthur is kicking up his heels again. He accuses the Navy of subordinating the Army's role in the Pacific"

King nodded. "Yeah, I heard about his plans to attack the main Jap base at Rabaul with half of my Pacific Navy fleet. What he will accomplish is to bring my precious carriers thousands of miles from our own bases and real close to the Jap bases, so the Japanese land-based planes can make mincemeat of my ships. MacArthur has absolutely no regard for what might happen to my ships. If he feels subordinate to us Navy people, it's because he is—the Pacific is a very big ocean and troops can't go anywhere without our transports; he can't protect his troops without our warships; he can't invade anywhere or use landing crafts; and he needs the big guns from our battleships and cruisers to sweep the beaches of Japs. So I would tell him to go to hell, but knowing you, I am sure you have a solution that would make King Solomon proud."

Marshall smiled. "Well, I wouldn't go that far, but I think we can split the responsibility by giving Admiral Nimitz the South Pacific Ocean area and MacArthur his current southwest Pacific area responsibility, shifted to the west a little so that at least half the Solomon Islands were clearly under Nimitz's control. If you can put a few Navy ships under his command, then I think we can come to some sort of agreement among the warring parties, MacArthur and Nimitz."

"Just so you understand that a strike against Rabaul in New Guinea is clearly premature until we get some bases closer by a series of advances in the Solomons, which would also safeguard our supply line to Australia. But there is no way in hell, I'll let MacArthur command my carriers. Besides, you know, and I know, that MacArthur, notwithstanding his vociferous objections, doesn't have the manpower to conduct a general offensive in both the Solomons and New Guinea. And even if he did, his troops are not trained to conduct amphibious landings which is precisely what is needed in the Solomons. So, when the time is ripe, MacArthur can attack in the New Guinea area."

And that is precisely what the Joint Chiefs of Staff did a few days later, calling for Admiral Ghormley to command the Tulagi attack using Marine ground troops under Major General Alexander Archer Vandegrift, known to his friends as 'Arch', and General Douglas MacArthur, at the appropriate time, would command the troops on New Guinea in the taking of Rabaul.

July 5, 1942, San Francisco, Room in the Fairmount Hotel

Ordered to meet with his boss, Admiral King, Nimitz flew from Pearl Harbor to San Francisco, a 12-hour plus flight in his own B-24 Consolidated Liberator heavy bomber.

On Nimitz's arrival for the meeting, King looked at his subordinate's strange uniform. "I hear you had a bit of trouble."

Nimitz smiled. "You might say so. We crash landed in San Francisco Bay. Had to crawl out onto the wing. Fortunately the plane was still afloat. I tried to assist in the rescue from the wing of the plane and was told in no uncertain terms by a seaman second class 'to get the hell out of the way so that we can get something done here.'"

King laughed. "Shall we court martial him?"

"No, he was absolutely right ordering me to stand down. He knew what he was doing, I did not."

"Are you hurt?" King asked.

Nimitz shook his head. "No, only my dignity and my uniform. Had to borrow this concoction from a sailor."

King shook his head. "I've had a hell of time moving the president and the Joint Chiefs of Staff off this 'Germany First' kick. I told them it's absolutely vital that we stop the Jap southward advance now, not a year from now. While the president has grudgingly weakened his stance on going after Germany first, we must seize the initiative right now, before minds are changed!

"So here's what we will do," King commanded. "For starters, you, Nimitz, will send a force to the Santa Cruz Islands, and where ever else you deem important in that area. MacArthur, for now, will stick to attacking and occupying Jap bases on the northeast coast of New Guinea and then, when air support is assured, proceed to attack Rabaul."

Notwithstanding all that planning, toward the end of the meeting King's aide handed him a written communication, which he read immediately. He frowned and looked at Nimitz. "Your highly efficient code-breakers at Pearl decoded a Jap message that they are sending troops and construction crews to Guadalcanal to build an airfield so that they can control the area around the Coral Sea all the way to Australia. We can't have that. So forget the Santa

Cruz Islands and go after them at Guadalcanal, before they become entrenched. What carrier support do you expect have?"

Nimitz thought for a moment. "I think I can round up three carriers, *Enterprise*, *Wasp* and *Saratoga*."

King nodded. "But we have to get there before that airfield becomes operational—before the Japs could use it as an airbase."

"I understand—all too well," Nimitz replied.

July 9, 1942, Pearl Harbor, Naval Headquarters at Makalapa, Offices of Admiral Nimitz

The Joint Chiefs, encouraged by the results at the Battle of Midway, authorized Operation "Watchtower" where the Marines would land on the beaches of Tulagi and Guadalcanal.

Nimitz turned to Vice Admiral Jack Fletcher. "Admiral Halsey is still in the hospital suffering from a very painful case of dermatitis. So Jack, you will be under the command of COMSOPAC, headed by Admiral Ghormley, but you will command this Guadalcanal expeditionary force and I expect you to be aggressive. Rear Admiral Richard Kelly will command the amphibious operations and you, Archer," pointing to Marine Major General A. Archer Vandegrift, "will command the landing force. MacArthur has promised to provide many of the troops and transports, which will be protected by his Allied Naval Force of American and Australian warships. The coordinated attack will be called 'Operation Watchtower.'

"This will be no walk in the park," Nimitz warned his assembled commanders. "The Japs, despite their defeat at Midway, still have powerful destroyers, cruisers, fast battleships, and most important, the fleet carriers *Shokaku*, *Junyo*, *Hiyo*, and *Zuikaku*, not to mention the light carriers *Hosho*, *Zuiho*, and *Ryujo*. The Jap Army has, we estimate, 5,000 tough troops on Guadalcanal—experienced jungle fighters from their battles in China, Java, Malaya, and the Philippines. They are under the command of Lieutenant General Harukichi Hyukatake."

General Vandegrift shook his head. "I hadn't expected to go into combat until January 1943. Now in a month, I must prepare operational and logistical plans, load ships for combat, and have my troops do an amphibious rehearsal in Fiji, and then set sail for the Solomon Islands to kick out the Japs. I can handle that, but this sounds like 'Operation Shoestring', not 'Operation Watchtower.' We need more Navy ships for a longer period to bombard those beaches. I don't want to lead my Marines into a slaughterhouse when they land!"

Nimitz got his back up. "This is what I have, and this is what you will have to work with. We will give you all the help within our resources. We can only stay around those beaches for a limited time before we will be exposed to the Japanese fleet."

Vandegrift shrugged. "I feel it beholden to warn you that in an amphibious landing, my experience has been that the attacker must possess overwhelming advantages—control of the air above and the sea below and require extremely heavy bombardment of enemy positions preceding the landing. That is vital. I've seen the Navy scrimp on some of these bombardments to save ammunition. That is foolish. We must, first and foremost, protect our troops in the landing and that means an unstinting heavy bombardment with all you have. More naval gunfire saves more troops in the landing, but your admirals don't seem to understand that. And after the landing is achieved, the Navy will have to stay and continue to supply my troops and give us aircover from above. You just can't deposit my troops and leave. You just told us that the Japs have 7,000 tough troops there. I know. They are not like the Germans; they'll not surrender when things are hopeless. Instead, they'll come charging out with hand grenades and bayonets. The stronger the defenses and the more dug-in the enemy is, as here, the more prolonged the bombardment we will need. And you promised me another six months of preparation."

Nimitz sighed, not answering the lecture from the Marine. "Wars don't respect schedules and we are under orders from Admiral King to proceed now. We will do what we can to bombard the beaches for your troops."

A frustrated Vandegrift frowned, raising his eyes to the ceiling. "You'd better tell that to your admirals! Furthermore, I have zilch intelligence on Guadalcanal—no maps, no photos, just some old info from former planters and missionaries who lived there years ago. I'll have to gather all this information on an island no one has ever heard of! And it would be nice if most of our equipment was not of worn-out World War One vintage!"

Nimitz paused, looking over his audience of Navy leaders, again, ignoring Vandegrift's remark.

"I have to tell you that the General, as usual, is against the strike against Guadalcanal; that we are launching Operation Watchtower well before we are ready. Just last week, this same general said he, with an amphibious force could take Rabaul."

All in the audience knew that "The General" referred to Douglas Macarthur.

Nimitz smiled. "When Admiral King heard Doug MacArthur's rant, he exploded in anger. Needless to say, gentlemen, we are moving forward with Operation Watchtower whether or not the General concurs. If we can establish airbases on Guadalcanal and Tulagi, we can neutralize the Jap airbase on Rabaul without having to sacrifice troops to take it. There's really no need to take every island occupied by Japanese troops. Some we can bypass and just let them wither on the vine by blockade and starvation."

"Where the hell is Guadalcanal?" one commander asked.

Nimitz pulled down a large map and pointed. "It's right there in the southern arc of the Pacific Ring of Fire—islands created by a whole bunch of volcanoes. Here are the Solomon Islands" he tapped his pointer, "a chain that lies just below the New Britain, New Ireland Islands, and north and east of New Guinea. The larger islands of this group form two parallel chains separated by a long, enclosed waterway some our Navy people like to refer to as 'the Slot'.

"The largest and main island in that chain is Guadalcanal, and right next to it is Tulagi, the Jap seaplane base, which we will also invade. The same volcanoes that created these islands, also created the deep trenches, some over four miles deep, in this part of the ocean. Tulagi and Guadalcanal are separated by some twenty miles across the Sealark Channel. Guadalcanal is ninety miles long and twenty-five miles wide. It has the advantage of an excellent natural harbor and a flat, smooth area called Lunga Point, ideal for all types of air operations, which the Japs are desperately trying to develop as quickly as possible. Now Guadalcanal looks lovely from the air but is a nightmare for ground forces with its dense tropical rain forests, very difficult to pass through, mountains, deep and swift rivers, heat, mud, swamps, humidity and rain. I expect we will encounter tropical diseases and fungi that should make life miserable for both sides. Other than those generalizations, we don't know much about Guadalcanal.

"The main force will land on Guadalcanal while a smaller group will attack Tulagi."

Nimitz turned to the commander of the submarine force supporting the landing on Guadalcanal. Nimitz, in his younger days, served on a submarine and understood the main purpose of the subs was sinking ship; an important part of that role included the little known but a vital part of their mission—forming a blockade around the beaches being invaded to prevent reinforcement of the enemy defenders with men and material—the failure of which would make the capture of those Islands far more difficult "Are your boys ready to blockade the supply routes?"

"Ready and anxious, sir."

After the meeting, Nimitz Satisfied himself that he had the right submarine commander but was not happy with what he considered a second team commanding the other naval force for the Guadalcanal operation. *Instead of Fletcher, I should have had Halsey,* he ruminated. *And who needed Admiral Robert Lee Ghormley? A desk admiral with no flipping fighting experience. Admiral King probably had to pick him because he's a friend of the president. Damn, what a way to fight a war!*

August 7, 1942, Just off the Coast of Guadalcanal and Tulagi, Aboard the *Enterprise*

Admiral Fletcher did not like the Guadalcanal operation and the whole concept put him in a foul mood. He doubted it would succeed. His bad temper continued when he met with his commanders. Fletcher had the seagoing command for this operation while Admiral Ghormley sat at his desk in Noumea supposedly overseeing the whole operation. *What a joke*, Fletcher thought. *Ghormley never conducted an air borne assault in his life!*

"Admiral Victor Crutchley of the Royal Australian Navy will command the ships bombarding the beaches. My air group will bomb and strafe the beaches. And just so you know, I intend to keep my carriers in this vicinity for only two days, then we will get the hell out of here before the Jap Navy catches up with us," Fletcher told his assembled senior officers. "I don't give a damn what the Marines and General Vandegrift want."

Admiral Richard Turner stood up. "That's not acceptable. The Marines going ashore need more than two days protection from your carrier planes! If you pull out that soon, the boys are going to suffer much greater casualties. I'll go over your head if I have to to protect those boys!"

"Very well," Fletcher replied, "I will stay for three days. I won't risk my carriers after that."

Admiral Turner shook his head. "That's not enough either." He sat down. *This guy Fletcher*, Turner thought, *has the reputation of not being willing to stick his neck out. This sure proves the point! And his boss, Admiral Ghormley, the head of COMSOPAC, is just as bad, hiding himself safely behind a desk on Noumea, a thousand miles away from Guadalcanal and the action! The timid hermit, that's what they call him. Why the hell isn't he here for this meeting?*

"Admiral Turner is right," Marine General Alexander Vandegrift called out. "my boys deserve more protection on the beach. Your pulling out will be a death sentence for many of them. And it will take five days to unload the transports with troops and supplies. Who will protect them and the supplies when you leave?"

Fletcher slammed his fist on the table. "That's enough! We only have three carriers in all the Pacific and all three are here. We won't be getting any new carriers from the shipyards until late 1943. I won't risk my only carriers to Jap planes. Three days it is, then we pull the carriers out."

Vandegrift sighed. *Here we go again. Ever since my days at the Officers' Training, the Navy has treated us like step children, only to be tolerated, not respected for what we can do and what the Navy cannot. When I stress the need for heavy and concentrated support from naval gunfire, a subject I cannot refrain from mentioning time and time again because of its vital bearing on the success of amphibious warfare, the Navy reacts like such a proposal is impracticable. Warships, the Navy brass claims, would always be required to carry two types of ammunition: high explosive for land bombardment and armor-piercing for action with an enemy fleet and such a double load would tax our magazine capacity. Vandegrift sighed. I'd have thought that view would have been abandoned a long time ago—but apparently not. The indecision between the job in hand and the anticipation of the threat of the Japanese Fleet resulted in ineffective naval support for his Marines.*

After a lot of grumbling in the audience, the conference broke up. As Fletcher was leaving, Admiral Turner blocked his way. In a low voice Turner growled, "You son of a bitch, if you do that you are yellow!"

Fletcher pushed past him and locked himself in his cabin. *I've had enough of these unruly admirals and generals!*

Fletcher radioed Admiral Ghormley for permission to withdraw as planned, saying his ships were low on fuel—his usual claim. Ghormley concurred.

Fletcher smiled. *Well, Ghormley and I are on the same page; he approved my withdrawal. Now my back is covered.*

CHAPTER FOURTEEN

The American Hell that was Guadalcanal

August 7, 1942, Guadalcanal

THE ALL-OUT EFFORTS OF the Japanese engineers had the airfield on Guadalcanal almost ready for fighter use. A few more days and the warplanes will be landing at the base.

But early the same morning, about 6AM, the American heavy cruiser *Quincy* moved in close to the shore and opened fire with her 8-inch guns and the Japanese knew they were a few days too late—the Americans were here.

The concussion aboard the American cruiser was terrific-and deafening as the sound of the gunfire from its 8-inch guns reverberated across Savo Sound. The first Allied offensive against the Japanese of World War II was about to begin. Four other cruisers joined in, as did six destroyers. One shell hit the jackpot—a fuel dump resulting in a tremendous explosion and a sheet of flame lighting up the ocean and the landscape. Meanwhile, across the bay, the light cruiser *San Juan* bombarded the island of north of Guadalcanal, Tulagi, and within minutes the Tulagi waterfront was destroyed, and along with it, the Japanese seaplanes.

Then the guns fell silent and gave the Wildcat fighters from the carriers the opportunity to swoop in strafing everything on the beaches, followed by the Douglas Dauntless dive bombers, going after the emplacements and the pillboxes. After the planes departed the ships offshore opened up once again. The fight for Guadalcanal and Tulagi was on!

Same Date, Guadalcanal, Behind Japanese Lines

The typical Japanese soldier on Guadalcanal likely had some prior combat experience and had been brutally trained in the code of "bushido", the way of the warrior, which meant preferring death to capture. Likewise, his prisoners would be shown little or no mercy.

The non-commissioned officer in charge of the Japanese platoon tried to teach his men about the Americans and it was clear he was completely contemptuous of the American Marines. "I hear that when subject to a surprise attack the Marines flee bawling out loud like babies."

The soldiers laughed. "That should be a sight as we pick them off one by one with our guns and bayonets!"

The non-commissioned officer continued. "I understand the Marines are a kind of naval/land unit. Ha! What do they know about fighting an army?"

"One good banzai charge should send them fleeing back to their ships like the cowards they are!" one infantryman piped up.

The whole group of soldiers then stood up and chanted "Banzai" several times. It was a good meeting and the troopers couldn't wait to confront these Marines.

In fairness, no Japanese soldier on this island ever confronted an American Marine in combat before and had no basis with which to evaluate the comments of their non-commissioned officer.

Same Date, Guadalcanal Marine Air Base, Henderson Field

Amphibious landings are an extremely complicated affair, from transferring men from the transports to the landing crafts, which then must be sent to the beach in intervals and not all at once. At the same time, the naval bombardment and air support must be coordinated to neutralize the enemy without decimating your own forces. Up to this point, command is in the hands of the Navy commander. Once the troops have landed command passes to the Marine commander. Amid all this confusion are the factors of gun and canon fire and other resistance, mines, boat breakdowns, tides, surf, and other contingencies, often unpredictable.

The first objective is to establish a beachhead which can be defended to protect the landing on the beach of needed material, food, supplies, ammunition, tanks, and artillery and creating a base to support the assaulting troops. That means securing not only the vulnerable beach, but a ways inland as well for place to move the supplies and create a base.

Different landing craft were needed for a variety of purposes. The flat-bottomed Higgins boat, with a front ramp that could be lowered disgorge troops, was fine for carrying men or light vehicles, but larger crafts were needed to land equipment like tanks onto the beach. This task fell to the LSTs (Landing Ship, Tanks). Unloading the LSTs is done through the bow doors on the lower level, or tank deck. Once these larger vehicles such as tanks are unloaded, elevators lower the smaller vehicles from the upper, or weather deck, to the lower tank deck for unloading.

There was relatively light opposition from the Japanese troops on the beach landing, and 16,000 Marines splashed ashore, established a beachhead, moved in quickly to occupy the uncompleted airfield and marched inland toward the center of the island. Here, the Japanese defenses stiffened The Marines named the captured airstrip Henderson Field, in memory of one of their ace pilots who died in the battle of Midway.

Landing with the Marines on Guadalcanal, in Operation Watchtower, was another group, the Navy Seabees, composed of officers from the Navy's Civil Engineer Corps and seamen from the Naval Construction Battalions. While their prime mission was to build, they were, like the Marines, trained to kill when necessary to protect themselves, their equipment, and the assets they had just built or were building. Unlike the Marines, they were "old" men in their thirties, men who had years of experience in civilian construction. The name "Seabees" comes from the initials CB, or "construction battalion." The Seabees had a different interpretation of those initials—wearing an amalgamation of army, navy, and marine clothing, they called themselves the "Confused Bastards."

The Navy made it possible for the best in the construction field to join *en masse*. Civilian engineers became officers, foremen became chief petty officers, and the carpenters, earthmovers, and machinists became NCOs in the naval ranks. Before they could do all this construction on land, the Seabees had to first free the waters and beaches of booby traps, mines, barbed wire, and obstructions meant to ensnare and/or sink the landing craft.

Coral was a great ally of the Seabees because its abundance in many of those Pacific islands. But coral could also be an enemy, stranding landing crafts in deep water. So one of the Seabees jobs is to survey the coral floor of the beach and when necessary, clear the coral by underwater demolition and, after being blasted from the reefs that impeded the landings, the very same coral could be crushed and used to build airstrips, roads, breakwaters, and docking facilities. Without coral, the Americans would have to transport construction materials on ships from the United States many thousands of miles through sub-infested waters.

But before the Americans can use the captured territory as bases to bomb the Japanese, the Seabees first had to go in, fight disease, mud, and Japanese soldiers, drain mosquito-infested swamps, and build airfields for the American planes, which needed to be refueled from storage tanks the Seabees had to build and camouflage. They lugged in the gasoline to fill those storage tanks, kept the troops supplied with ammunition and shells from magazines the Seabees build, construct gun emplacements to protect America's fighting men, and put up the docks and warehouses to supply and feed the troops, not to mention erecting the field hospitals to tend to the wounded, and the barracks to house the fighters. At the same time, the Seabees must build the roads through the jungles and marshes for our trucks and Sherman tanks, emplacements for our heavy guns, and seaplane ramps. It requires a hell of a lot of knowhow on many subjects. It also exposes them to extreme danger.

Initial construction of an airstrip from scratch requires clearing at least 3500 feet for runway 250 feet wide. Crushed coral is laid down followed by steel planking. The strip is built in sections so that fighter planes can use it in the minimum time. Eventually, some strips are built to 5000 feet to accommodate heavy bombers. Of course, the job is much quicker and easier when the Seabees can restore a captured Japanese airfield Henderson Field on Guadalcanal was such an airstrip in the process of being built by the Japanese. The Seabees completed the airstrip using a lot of the equipment the Japs left behind—graders, bulldozers, tractors, and flat-bottom trucks. They quickly filled in any bomb craters inflicted by Jap bombers attacking the field. In addition, the engineers and construction battalion men, recently civilians, had to learn quickly to defend themselves using hand guns and rifles.

The Seabees also did the unloading of the ships that supply the Marines with weapons, ammunition, food, and the essentials of life and combat. They were the Marines' stevedores. They unloaded the bulldozers, scrapers, amphibious tractors, and cranes that permit them to build the roads that carry the tanks and trucks into the battle; they assemble the floating piers, pontoons, causeways, and self-propelled barges that permit the supplies to come in. Of course, this stevedoring was unlike that in civilian life; the unloading of ships was a prime target for enemy bombers and artillery, and there rarely were permanent dockside piers which, even if built, also would be juicy targets of enemy bombers. This made the unloading of cargo on these islands doubly difficult and required the loading of supplies, weapons, and ammunition onto heaving barges, running them onto the beach where they are once again unloaded onto trucks—all usually under enemy fire.

As promised, Admiral Fletcher left with his aircraft carriers after three days, much to the consternation of General Vandegrift. Fletcher gave the skies over to the Japanese warplanes, at least until Henderson Field was finished enough to accommodate American aircraft.

In the meantime, the Marines dug in to protect and defend Henderson Field and the territorial gains made so far. The Marines discovered themselves ensconced in black mud in the morning, which fouled their clothes, food, and equipment. By midday, in that intense searing heat of the island, all had dried into a fine dust, covering everything, including weapons. There appeared to be no middle ground on Guadalcanal.

Near the front, troops endured the putrid smell of dead rotting Japanese. The Japanese troops left their dead where they fell. When the bodies got too numerous and the smell becomes staggering, the Marines—or Seabees—would bulldoze the Japanese bodies into long trenches in the ground.

The transport truck drivers were subject to sniper attack by Japanese perched soldiers high in the palm trees. One Marine truck driver skidded off the road in the mud, bumping a palm tree. A Japanese sniper fell out and was disposed of. After that the truck drivers made it a habit of bumping the trees to see what was up there.

Japanese troops tried frantically to retake Henderson Field. During the day, they fought only defensively but at night they used infiltration tactics combined wild bayonet charges, screaming "Banzai", their officers leading them with samurai swords drawn. In previous battles with the Chinese, Korean, and other Asian opposing troops, such tactics demoralized the enemy. But not the Marines, who stayed put in their foxholes and mowed down the charging and exposed Japanese. For the Marines, it was like a turkey shoot and the bodies of the enemy piled up in front of them. If the Marines had to fight, they liked these Banzai charges, permitting them, through carefully-placed crossfire, to bring down the Japanese troops unmercifully.

Same Date, Tulagi

Tulagi was attacked right on schedule, at 0800 hours. There was not much resistance on the beach, but it stiffened as the Marines proceeded inward to the center of the island. The Marines endured four nightly banzai attacks by Japanese troops to dislodge them and each time the Marines beat back Japanese attackers. This type of fighting became indicative of many of the nights the Marines would face on these islands. The Marines systematically cleared the troublesome terrain of caves and deep-cut trenches to clear out groups of resisting Japanese soldiers. By nightfall of August 8, Tulagi was in American control.

Same Date, Hashirajima, Aboard the *Yamato*

Yamamoto was awakened by Ugaki.

"Sir," shouted Ugaki, "the Americans are invading Guadalcanal and Tulagi. It looks serious, we count that they have at least one battleship, three cruisers, a carrier, and forty transports carrying troops."

Yamamoto, now fully awake, sat up. "Now that's serious. We must act quickly to oppose that force. If they are successful, they could threaten our large base at Rabaul."

"Yes," Ugaki said, "I have cancelled the scheduled sailing for Kure by the Combined Fleet. We must order an all-out attack now. Later, we may not be able to dislodge the enemy."

Yamamoto knew Tulagi was an important seaplane base for the Navy. "Were we able to get our seaplanes out of Tulagi?"

Ugaki shook his head. "No, they were all destroyed while on the ground by the enemy's carrier planes."

"Let's get the *Yamato* underway and get to the South Pacific as rapidly as we can," Yamamoto ordered. "Have Navy troops loaded aboard the transport *Kasuqa-maru* and order a destroyer escort to accompany us."

Yamamoto stopped Ugaki, about to leave to issue the new orders. "One more thing. Order some land-based, long-range bombers to fly to the area and drop prepared messages on our troops at both Guadalcanal and Tulagi, telling them that help is on the way and to hold out a little longer. Have the 25th Air Flotilla at Rabaul alerted to launch all-out attacks on the American fleet."

August 8, 1942, a Few Miles Off Guadalcanal, Aboard the Admiral Fletcher's Flagship *Enterprise*

Admiral Fletcher asked Admiral Ghormley for permission to withdraw his carriers, citing that they were low on fuel and also to avoid a Japanese Navy counterattack. At the end of the second day of the attack on Guadalcanal, Fletcher ordered his carriers withdrawn from the area.

With Admiral Fletcher and the protection of his carrier planes gone, the Marines were discovering that the preparatory briefing on Guadalcanal was accurate, and movement of troops through the forests, deep rivers, swamps, humidity, heat, and mud, was made very difficult. Many men were falling ill with malaria and other tropical diseases and there was a constant battle with the fungi to keep them from overwhelming the men.

August 9, 1942, Guadalcanal, The Slot at Savo Island

After Fletcher pulled out, he left only Admiral Crutchley's rag-tag force to cover the troops and supplies on the beaches.

Vice Admiral Gunichi Mikawa, whose naval force trained extensively for nighttime battles, planned a surprise nighttime raid on the American ships just off Guadalcanal.

They did indeed surprise the Allied naval force in the waters off Savo Island, between Guadalcanal and Tulagi, known as the "Slot" and later, as "Iron Bottom Sound", because of all the ships sunk there. The Japanese ships jumped the Allied force and sank an Australian cruiser and three American cruisers, with minor damage to some of the Japanese ships. Over one thousand American and Australian sailors were killed and another seven hundred wounded. For the Japanese, they received minor damage to one cruiser with a few dead. Admiral King considered that battle to be the worst defeat in American naval history.

Marines on the beach were witness to this spectacle, not far off shore, of Allied ships being blown out of the water in a wild naval battle where the opposing ships were literally on top of each other.

General Vandegrift, one of the observers, watched the burning hulks of two cruisers. He turned to one of his staff officers "What in the hell has happened to our Navy?"

The staff officer shrugged. "Sir, I don't believe the Navy has sent in the first team."

"Or it fled like frightened bunnies. We can't depend on the carrier planes for help. That's why we need to complete Henderson Field as soon as possible and get our own marine pilots and warplanes in here to deal with the Japs! Sooner or later a large Jap land force is going to show up and we will really need those planes."

✳ ✳ ✳

Admiral Mikawa, fearing a dawn attack from the three American carriers, and unaware that Fletcher had fled the scene, withdrew his forces and did not, as planned, attack and break up the invasion force and the transports at the beaches. He didn't have to. Rear Admiral Richard Turner, after the Savo battle, pulled all the transports out of Guadalcanal, some never unloaded, thereby abandoning the First Marine Division—many of the transports that left still had holds full of food, ammunition, equipment, weapons, and supplies, material desperately needed by those Marines trying to hold the beachhead and Henderson Field. The Marines reduced to a diet of field rations—hard biscuits, cold C rations, powdered eggs, and the like.

August 11, 1942, Hashirajima, Aboard the *Yamato*

Admiral Yamamoto did not have a good day. Furious at Admiral Mikawa for going against the Allied ships instead of against the American beach-side operations unloading troops and supplies, Yamamoto stamped around the ship's conference room.

"Calm down," Ugaki counseled, "be happy with the great naval victory Mikawa achieved."

Yamamoto swiveled around to face Ugaki. "The Americans are still on Guadalcanal and their transports are still supplying them. That's what matters! Not a few boats from the Australian-led force! He disobeyed my orders, and then he fled the scene like a scared rabbit. Am I the only one who understands the threat that the American Marines pose? Because neither Mikawa nor our Army seem to. The damn Army expected to clear the island of the Marines with a battalion or two. Now they are finding out that these Marines can fight and are cutting our troops to pieces while we, so far, are not budging the Americans.

"Is that really such a great victory?" Yamamoto asked.

"Our 25th Air Flotilla lost so many planes over Guadalcanal that it is no longer much of a force. And forget even the planes. We lost experienced pilots that cannot be replaced any time soon. So you'll forgive me if I don't celebrate.

"In the meantime," Yamamoto continued, "our pilots are exaggerating the Allied losses claiming twenty ships sunk. The Imperial General Headquarters deemed those exaggerations too conservative and issued a press communique declaring at least twenty-eight Allied warships and thirty transports and freighters had been sent to the bottom of the sea. An undisclosed source, supposedly in the know, boasted that the American and British naval strength has now been reduced to third-rate powers. Can you imagine? Gross inflation of the claims seems to be the norm now."

"What's up next?" Ugaki asked, trying to get his boss off the negativity and into planning.

Yamamoto paused, contemplating his answer. He approached the large wall map of the southern Pacific Ocean. "We simply can't leave Guadalcanal in American hands. They will build a large airfield there for both their fighters and long-range bombers and then they will have what amounts to an unsinkable aircraft carrier right in our midst. They would use it as a springboard to move north.

"Unfortunately, time is on the side of our enemies. Our fleet is consuming fuel at an unacceptable level and while the Americans do not have our fuel problem, the fact is that on Guadalcanal, with all the bombing and shelling of the airfield and supply dumps, the Americans have a serious fuel shortage. If we can reinforce our troops on that island, we may have a chance."

Yamamoto pointed to the Solomon Islands—specifically Guadalcanal, then swept his pointer to the islands north of there. "We must reinforce the garrison on Guadalcanal with Army troops. And now, my dear Ugaki, we know where the American carriers are because they must stay to support the invading ground troops. We won't have to search the whole Pacific Ocean; so let's hunt them down while we can.

"Here's my plan. Send to Guadalcanal a large Imperial Army landing force on four transports. That convoy will be accompanied by two of our heavy and fast carriers, the *Zuikaku* and the *Shokaku*. We will have the carriers close but out of sight until the American carriers arrive to challenge the troop ships. Then our carriers will strike. Two battleships, three heavy cruisers, and one light cruiser will accompany the carriers.

"Unfortunately, the Imperial Army leaders are very arrogant and believe they can easily sweep aside Allied resistance. They estimate only two thousand Marines on Guadalcanal. Personally, I think it is five times that number. We have been ordered to ferry these troops to the Island so that the Army, in their general's words, 'can mop up the enemy remnants, rescue the garrison and repair the airfield.' I fear they are in for an unpleasant surprise. They are going to find out they don't have enough troops to dislodge the Americans."

Same Day, Pearl Harbor, Naval Headquarters at Makalapa, Office of Admiral Nimitz

Yamamoto was not alone in his unhappiness. Nimitz angrily grumbled to his chief of staff, "With all the air and submarine reconnaissance we had available, how in the hell did we not know Mikawa's force was in the channel?"

"Admiral, sir, in defense of our seamen, they had been on duty for forty-eight hours. They are only human. They cannot go function indefinitely without rest. Fatigue must have overcome them making them vulnerable to a sneak attack."

Nimitz shook his head. "Fletcher and his air power fled the scene like a dog with his tail between his legs. He could have made the difference if he had stayed."

"But, sir, he reported running low on fuel. How could he stay?"

"That's a bunch of baloney," Nimitz retorted. "We checked, and his cruisers and destroyers were more than half full of fuel when he withdrew. To put it bluntly the report was false. Frankly, I think he's gotten gun-shy since he's lost the *Lexington* at the Coral Sea and the *Yorktown* at the Battle of Midway."

"Well, there is some good news," Nimitz declared. "The president rejected Hap Arnold's heavy presence in Washington rooting for a 'Europe-first' policy, and with support from the president's naval attaché, Admiral Leahy, Roosevelt agreed to provide twenty more cargo ships to resupply the troops in the South Pacific Listen to this memo he sent me and his other military chiefs:

'My anxiety about the S.W. Pac. is to make sure that every possible weapon gets into that area to hold Guadalcanal, and that, having held in this crisis, that munitions, planes and crews are on the way to take advantage of our success. We will soon find ourselves engaged in two active fronts and we must have adequate air support in both places even though it means delaying our other commitments, particularly to England. Our long-range plan could be set back for months if we fail to throw our full strength in our immediate and impending conflicts.'"

August 17, 1942, at Sea off the Japanese Coast, Aboard the Battleship *Yamato*

Yamamoto decided he had to be closer to the front lines and the action.

The great battleship moved regally out of the channel and into the open sea and away from the Home Islands, heading for the advance base at Truk with lookouts keeping a keen watch for the periscopes of American submarines while strict radio silence was ordered for the entire trip. As the *Yamato* picked up speed, Yamamoto leaned on the railing, looking back at the Japanese Islands. He did not know it then, but it would be the last time he would ever see them.

Then he headed for his stateroom to pen a letter, in calligraphy, to Chiyoko.

August 17 and 18, 1942, Aboard a Japanese Transport Heading for Guadalcanal

The troop ship, with 3,500 Japanese Army soldiers, moved forward at 16 knots to the southwest. Soon it would disgorge the men at Guadalcanal.

The Japanese soldiers did not seem to be preoccupied with the coming battle, some exercising on deck, other smoking and relaxing. At dinner, they were served beer, putting them in a happy state.

These men were trained night fighters and they were told that if they attack after dark, the Americans who, the cowards they were, would panic and run. At least that's what the Army Manual said. After all, the Japanese Army has been so successful up to now in routing its enemies, there was no reason to believe this battle would be any different, once there was a sufficient force on the ground.

The next day, under the cover of darkness, the transport disgorged its passengers on the island.

The Jap Army sent medium bombers, accompanied by Zero fighters from the Rabaul base, to attack the American ships near, and Marines on, Guadalcanal. The Marines dove into their foxholes—not only to protect themselves from the Japanese bombs but from the fallout of the American antiaircraft guns, which spread shrapnel across the skies to down Jap planes. But that shrapnel was a danger to American troops on the ground, as well, when it came raining down after being spent. Some unfortunate Marines were wounded or killed by falling "friendly" shrapnel.

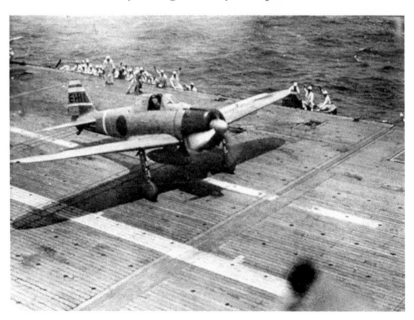

Zero Fighter on Deck

The attacking planes were met by the new American Grumman Wildcat fighters, which turned out to be a match for the vaunted Zero. The stubby Wildcat surprised the Zero pilots with its maneuverability and ability to withstand direct hits of cannon fire and keep fighting. The Wildcats were able to either shoot down the medium bombers or drive them off.

Grumman Wildcat Fighter

August 19, 1941, Guadalcanal, Japanese Army Encampment, Just Behind the Front Lines

Japanese Imperial Army Colonel Kiyonao Ichiki planned the night attack on what the defending Americans call Henderson field. "I am determined to take the airfield tonight with my reinforcements. A surprise night attack should unsettle and unseat the American troops and with a noisy bayonet attack, backed by mortars, we should be able to overrun and destroy their positions. The airfield must be taken, and I do not intend return alive if I fail. Are you clear?"

The major nodded.

"Are the men ready?"

"Yes, Colonel," the major replied. "The men are in position and anxiously awaiting the order to attack."

Ichiki looked at his watch. "It should be dark in about a half hour. Order the men to attack then."

Gripping the handle of his samurai sword, the colonel unsheathed it. "I will lead the charge."

But there would be no surprise. Across the Tenaru River, several hundred yards away, the dug in Marines were waiting—and many more than Ichiki expected—something like five times as many. The Marines had monitored the landing of the Japanese troops but held back, deciding to let the Japanese troops come to them, in the marine's fortified positions.

The first banzai bayonet attack was repulsed by the Marines. With their carefully arranged fields of fire, marine infantry cut down the Japanese troops in the open area fronting the marine foxholes. Subsequent bayonet attacks had the same result—a massacre of the Japanese who never reached the marine foxholes. Marines attempted to tend to the wounded fallen Japanese soldiers, but those wounded men would pull the pins on hidden grenades to blow up both them and the American medics who came to help them.

It was clear that this would be a war without compromise. Japanese Colonel Ichiki certainly felt that way. Though only slightly wounded in the banzai attack, after the failure of his troops to take Henderson Field, he retired to his tent, dressed himself in a white kimono, which he had packed in his duffel for just such an occasion. He burned the regimental colors, then took out his short sword and disemboweling himself, committing hari-kari, in a very painful way.

August 20, 1942, Guadalcanal, Henderson Field

The Marines tensed and manned their antiaircraft guns on hearing, in the distance, the unmistakable drone of aircraft approaching Guadalcanal. As the sound grew louder, they realized the planes were coming from the east and the Japs usually came in from the west. The gunners aimed their weapon but did not fire yet. They then recognized the planes as American Grumman Wildcats from the carriers, which made a pass overhead and prepared to land.

America's 67th Fighter Squadron, commanded by Captain D.D. Brannon, landed at Henderson Field to the lusty cheers of the Marines on the island, who desperately needed air cover in their continuing battles with Japanese troops. These planes would be based at Henderson Field. Code-named "Cactus," this rag-tag air group made a name for itself in the South Pacific as the Cactus Air Force.

CHAPTER FIFTEEN

Guadalcanal: Hell for All

Guadalcanal

August 26, 1942, Anchorage at Truk, Aboard the *Yamato*

THE *YAMATO* DROPPED ANCHOR in the harbor at Truk and was immediately visited by representatives of the Imperial Army and Imperial Navy.

The huge battleship was like a large city with thousands of crew to help keep this monster functioning like a hotel or a cruise ship. As Commander-in-Chief of the Combined Fleet, Yamamoto, per tradition, lived in luxury aboard this ship, called by others as "Hotel Yamato." His loyal chief of staff Ugaki, would be the first to admit that his boss did not work particularly hard, not being burdened with the small tasks, but left to plan, plot and develop the basic strategy for Japan's naval warfare in the Pacific He ate well and enjoyed gambling at *shogi*—a Japanese version of chess—for money with his staff officers.

The reports rolled in. "Colonel Ichiki's troops had been decimated after he tried to lead an attack across the Tenaru River. There were many more American troops on the Island than he expected," an Army representative reported. "The Americans are still holding the airfield and preparing it for use by their planes."

A Navy commander reported that while they were looking for the American carriers, apparently one of our own, the *Ryujo*, found them and was sunk by American planes.

Yamamoto took the news in stride. He knew that the *Ryujo* had been sent into harm's way as a lure to draw out the large American carriers. It worked, and despite the Americans having sunk the *Ryujo*, the American carrier, *Enterprise*, which had taken the bait was found by Japanese carrier planes. While the American planes were putting away the small Japanese carrier, the Japanese planes were able to pierce the protective screen around the *Enterprise* and scored hits with three bombs that effectively put her out of action and sending her back to Pearl Harbor for repairs. Tokyo claimed it as a great victory.

But the Americans did force our troop convoy to turn back, Yamamoto mused. *And while we put the Enterprise out of action, we lost the Ryujo aircraft carrier—and we no longer can afford to trade losses, tit for tat, with the Americans—eventually, they'll bury us with their industrial output of ships, planes, and weapons.*

Yamamoto received reports that already, the Americans brought the *Hornet* carrier into the Pacific from the Atlantic, replacing the *Enterprise*.

Ugali burst in, interrupting Yamamoto's thoughts. "It seems," Ugaki reported, "that Admiral Fletcher's poor handling of the aircraft carriers in the battle of Coral Sea and Midway put him out of favor with Admirals Nimitz and King and he was reassigned to running the Northwest Sea Frontier."

Yamamoto smiled. "Yes, I learned from my time in the United States that is the Navy's equivalent to Siberia. Fletcher is like our Admiral Nomura. Too timid for the Pacific action. We must also relieve Nomura of command."

"And the Army is having a hard time on Guadalcanal," Ugaki observed.

Yamamoto nodded. "I'm not surprised after the Army insisted on underestimating the number of troops the Americans had there to oppose it."

Army senior staff officer, General Kuroshima, and his chief of staff Colonel Tsuji, arrived aboard the *Yamato*. Tsuji begged for escorts to protect the supply convoy. "The men fighting for us on Guadalcanal are starving; they are thinner that Gandhi himself," Tsuji pleaded.

Yamamoto, clearly moved by Tsuji's heart-rendering pleas, responded, "If the boys on Guadalcanal are starving, then we should be ashamed. I tell you what. I will take the *Yamato* herself to Guadalcanal to protect our convoys and troops."

After the visitors left the ship, Ugaki pulled Yamamoto aside. "You may have forgotten, but the Naval General Staff forbids, by Imperial Command, the *Yamato* to engage in such activities when we are so short of fuel. Guzzlers like this ship must refrain becoming part of the fight at Guadalcanal."

It is ironic, Yamamoto mused, *that I am cooped up on a ship, a battleship no less, the very type that I'd convinced my superiors was useless in this age of air power!*

The Americans certainly found that out, Yamamoto thought, *after we destroyed their battleships at Pearl Harbor. So they made a remarkably rapid switch to carriers and air power and did a pretty good job of it, too! And their technology is advancing rapidly. Already they have a warplane that may be better than our Zero, and their torpedoes have been improved dramatically. But here we sit with the old weapons, good when we started the war, but not sufficiently improved now, when we need it the most. British and American radar is far superior; and they are going to build a super bomber that will fly much higher and faster than their current B-17s. But are we developing antiaircraft guns that can reach an altitude of 25,000 feet where these new bombers will fly? No!*

Why did we lose so heavily at Midway? We had more and better carriers. Our Navy leaders don't believe it. They think the Americans had many more carriers at Midway which is ridiculous. I suspect the Americans must have broken our naval code, but no one believes me!

Yamamoto made himself some tea and poured a cup, grabbing a biscuit that he knew he shouldn't have with his weight up and his exercise regime vastly scaled back. *And here I am, stuck on a battleship, because tradition says this is where I must be for someone in my position and rank. I am poised for action but can do absolutely nothing. I just can't get the thinking of the Navy leaders off their hidebound belief that the battleship is the main strength of the Navy. That attitude of theirs restrains me in too many ways from fighting the war I think should be fought. And those damn pathetic Imperial Army leaders are in a state of pure denial, with their myopic view of the China war, while at the same time, they are mired in a no-win battle with the billions of Chinese over a vast landscape.*

Yamamoto's thoughts were interrupted by a visit from Admiral Jin'ichi Kusaka. He had been on his way to his new post at Rabaul as commander-in-chief of the Southeast Asia Fleet. After an operational meeting, the two relaxed over dinner.

"So tell me," Kusaka asked Yamamoto, "what are you going to be doing?"

With an absolute straight face, Yamamoto answered, "Oh, I imagine I'll face either the guillotine or be exiled to St. Helena."

Kusaka laughed. "Not with this war on you won't."

"Let's be serious," Yamamoto said. "I am concerned about this spreading practice of suicides of captains, who think they must go down with their ships. I need those experienced captains to come back alive to take over *other* ships. I tell you, it's an utter waste! We can't hope to win this war if we keep sacrificing our best people, and that includes not only our captains, but our pilots who should be encouraged to parachute to safety and fly again against the Americans."

Kusaka nodded. "I came up against that at Midway and had a hell of a time convincing my commander and staff officers to save themselves for the good of the Empire. So I agree fully with you."

August 30, 1942, One of the Beaches on Guadalcanal

In the dead of night, the Japanese destroyer eased close to the shore of Guadalcanal. Row boats were lowered, and troops were ferried onto the beach. The surf was heavy, and many were dumped into the water with their heavy packs, making it difficult to reach the shore. Some 6,000 troops on barges never made it to the shore. The barges were sunk by planes from an American aircraft carrier.

General Kawaguchi rounded up his three thousand men and in the extreme darkness, each soldier had to hold onto the shoulder of the man in front of him. They had to cross a deep river by traversing on a fallen tree that bridged the river. It was slippery and round and certainly not easy. A few men lost their balance and were dumped into the river with their seventy-pound packs, never to be seen again. But these troops soon discovered that their trials were just beginning. A heavy rain storm soaked the men to the bone. Resting meant that they had to try to sleep in the rain and that was virtually impossible. Mosquitoes swarmed over every exposed area of skin and those bites really hurt. The trail they followed, clogged with heavy vines studded with thorns, made progress very slow, difficult and painful. This then, was their welcome to the island known as Guadalcanal.

When these Japanese troops were finally in position, that night they began a banzai bayonet attack against the dug-in Marines. After an hour of furious hand-to-hand fighting, the Japanese attack was repulsed by the Americans, themselves wracked with malaria, dysentery, fungus, and hunger. Food supplies were dangerously low forcing the Marines on a drastically reduced diet. Many of the men lost from forty to fifty percent of their body weight; they had the look of scarecrows—but they were in good condition compared to the Japanese soldiers who had already spent time on the island suffering from starvation conditions. By daybreak, the Marines counterattacked and drove the Japanese force into the sea. Many survivors admitted that the Marines had a "Yankee spirit" and loved their country as much we loved ours. The Japanese soldiers gave an appropriate name to Guadalcanal—Starvation Island.

The Marines learned an important lesson on Guadalcanal that they would carry with them for the rest of the war. The Japanese soldiers, they discovered, adhered to no form of civilized behavior in war. Surrender by the Japanese was not an option. Wounded soldiers would attempt to kill any marine seeking to give them first aid.

September 14, 1942, Tokyo, Imperial Palace, Audience Room of the Emperor

Prime Minister, head of the Army, and war secretary, Hideki Tojo, and Admiral Osami Nagano, Chief of the Imperial Japanese Navy General Staff sat stiffly in their chairs after bowing deeply when the emperor entered.

"The emperor will address you directly," the Palace secretary very formally advised.

Seating himself up on the dais, the emperor stared, not in a friendly way, at the two military men. It lasted for a few uncomfortable moments.

The two bore the silence stoically. They had no choice.

"We are in a six-week deadlock at Guadalcanal," the emperor finally began, in his high-pitched voice, "and still, you have not retaken the airfield on that island. You must go on the offense and drive the Americans off Guadalcanal! We need that 'Decisive Victory' you keep talking about and promising. That is all I have to say." The emperor stood.

Both men also stood and bowed deeply as the emperor turned and disappeared behind the screen in back of his throne.

For Tojo, after all his promises, it was indeed an intolerable loss of face for his Army. Two elite units of the Army were defeated by the Americans; Americans whom Tojo had written off as cowards and poor fighters. *I am going to commit a full division of some 20,000 troops to retake Guadalcanal, together with the Navy's Eleventh Air Fleet. Its new commander, Vice Admiral Jinichi Kusaka has been dispatched to Rabaul.*

Same Date, Pearl Harbor, Aboard the Enterprise Aircraft Carrier

The bosun blew the whistle as Admirals Nimitz and Halsey boarded the *Enterprise*, in Pearl Harbor for repairs.

Nimitz announced to the assembled crew, "Boys, I got a surprise for you, Bill Halsey's back!"

The sailors applauded loudly and whooped it up.

Halsey took the microphone. "I intend personally to have a crack at those yellow-bellied sons of bitches and their carriers."

A roar of approval arose from the seamen.

Then Nimitz spoke with Halsey in private. "We just lost the *Wasp* carrier to a Jap submarine, and with your ship and the *Saratoga* under repair, we have the *Hornet* as the only operational carrier in the Pacific. The Japs don't know about the *Wasp*. We have the survivors quarantined on Noumea so news of the carriers sinking won't be released until December, when we'll send those boys home. So we have to get the *Enterprise* out there as soon as possible."

"Believe me, Admiral," Halsey replied, "I'm chomping at the bit and I'll lean on the repair crews to finish up and get us the hell out of here."

Same Date, Aboard the *Yamato*

An angry Yamamoto sat down facing Ugaki. "I warned them repeatedly of America's growing might. I told them the Yankees won't easily relinquish their territory and that they will be just as willing to sacrifice as we are. But they don't listen and continue with this crazy false optimism about the war. That's why they send only battalions to reinforce Guadalcanal instead of divisions. Believing we are invincible doesn't mean a thing without intense preparation. Our leaders in Tokyo accept these claims from some of the military of great victories when there are none. Believe me, the men that do the fighting know the facts, but their superiors continue to believe what's happening is a 'temporary setback'. The Japanese military hierarchy is living in the world of the 1930's while we are trying to fight a war of the 1940's."

"Isn't the Army moving to reinforce Guadalcanal with a few divisions?" Ugaki asked.

Yamamoto issued a harsh laugh. "The Army is dreaming. The reality is that they can't even deliver supplies to our troops, much less a few divisions. Any shipping is driven off by American dive bombers and torpedo planes. Even forgetting the ships, since the disaster at Midway, our attrition on planes and skilled pilots has been horrendous. And, in case you haven't heard, we are running out of fuel."

September 14, 1942, Guadalcanal, Headquarters of Major General Vandegrift

Major General Vandegrift met with Lieutenant General Roy Geiger, a big fearless bull of a man and a can-do officer, commanding the Marine Air Wing stationed at Henderson Field.

"Roy," Vandegrift began, "our whole existence here on this island depends on your men hitting and destroying the Jap ships that come in after dark and disgorge troops and then fire their big guns on our guys. We call it the 'Rat Express'. You've got to hit and destroy those Jap ships before they get here. Send your planes out to find them before it gets dark and attack those ships!"

"We'll do it," Geiger responded, "but realize my Cactus Air Force flyers also have to contend with nightly raids of Henderson Field by Jap bombers from Rabaul. After dark, we have to batten down the hatches. We don't get much sleep with all those bombs the Japs drop. We're suffering the same poor food and diseases as you guys. And those Army P-400 planes are just plain lousy in aerial combat against the Japs. My guys call these planes 'nothing but a P-40 with a Zero on its tail!'"

"What about the marine Wildcat fighter?"

"Oh, they're great in a dog fight " Geiger said, "but we don't have enough of them. Let's face it, the only thing the P-400 is good for is ground support with its cannons and machine guns—strafing missions against enemy troops. They can play havoc with landing barges and troops wading through the surf. Those pilots go up early in the morning looking for Jap breakfast fires and go in with guns blazing, destroying everything in their path. When their supply of bombs runs out, they appropriate the Navy depth charges wrapped in chains and, on exploding, spray steel shrapnel everywhere. They are also good at shooting down the slow Jap reconnaissance planes. But Lord help those pilots if they encounter a Zero—then they are dead meat.

"We carved out a grassy strip that can handle the fighters," Geiger explained, "a mile from Henderson and moved the fighters there, leaving Henderson for the heavier bombers. Since the Japs are unaware that this strip exists, those boys are spared the Jap bombing runs after dark—and the falling shrapnel from our own antiaircraft guns."

September 16, 1942, Guadalcanal, Marine Headquarters

Vandegrift could sense a big battle was brewing ever since the Japs landed more troops at night. Per his instructions, the Marines dug in and armed themselves to the teeth. But, weakened by jungle disease and spread out thinly on a long loop, they simply could not be strong at every point.

Vandegrift, busy planning the coordination of the Navy ships and this Cactus Air Force, looked up in annoyance when one of his clerks interrupted him.

"Sorry, sir, but I am sure you want to see this."

The clerk handed him a letter. He tore it open. It was from Admiral Ghormley, sitting comfortably and safely all the way back in New Caledonia, writing to inform Vandegrift that "due to naval losses at sea, I cannot longer support the Guadalcanal operation." A short "up yours" message—in essence, abandoning the Marines on this island.

Vandegrift called in his staff officers and advised them of the contents of Ghormley's letter. Vandegrift, madder than hell, sputtered, "What an asshole; he abandoned us when we first landed by withdrawing his carriers leaving us stranded on the beach. Now he's doing it again, withdrawing all his naval forces. Well, if he thinks we are going to surrender, like they did on Bataan, he's got another think coming. There'll be no death march here. Not while I'm in command!"

Vandegrift pointed to the map of Guadalcanal on the plotting table. He pointed to Henderson Field. "We may have to abandon the airfield because Jap naval bombardment may make it unusable. If necessary, we may withdraw to defensive positions in the jungle. But for now, we'll just stay put."

The Japanese attacked in force that moonless night. It went from machine gun, grenade, and rifle fire to hand-to-hand combat in furious bayonet charges. In some positions, the Marines had to pull back to avoid being outflanked, reorganize, and meet the screaming enemy rushing forward over the dead bodies of their comrades.

In the morning the Marines saw the Japanese bodies stacked up all the way back to the hillside. Also in the morning, the Marines had found that Henderson Field was still in American hands while the 67th Fighter Squadron massacred the remaining enemy near the Marine positions.

General Kawaguchi looked over the hillside on the other side of the Marines' positions, now a grave yard for Japanese soldiers, that he called "Bloody Ridge". Not only had he lost so many men in the night banzai charges, but at the first dawn of light, the American planes came over strafing and bombing the survivors.

He looked sadly at his chief of staff "Our force is completely destroyed; our casualties are ruinous."

Not everything went bad for the Japanese that night. Offshore, the Japanese submarine *I-19* cruised around submerged when Commander Takaichi Kinashi, looking through his periscope, suddenly found himself inside the protective ring of the aircraft carrier *Wasp*. He could hardly believe his eyes. There, right in front of him was a large American aircraft carrier! His first torpedoes hit the mark exploding fuel and ammunition areas and blowing the large ship apart. Commander Kinashi did not retire quite yet. He put one torpedo into the battleship *North Carolina*, damaging her, and one into the destroyer *O'Brien*, sinking her.

Sinking of the Wasp

September 28, 1942, Noumea, Naval Headquarters of Admiral Ghormley

After the disastrous losses around the seas of Guadalcanal, Admiral Robert Ghormley stopped sending transports with supplies and escorting warships to Guadalcanal. Admiral Nimitz flew out to Noumea to meet with Ghormley, first making a stop at Guadalcanal itself—something Ghormley, as commander of the operation, had never done.

Nimitz wasted no time on Ghormley with preliminary niceties. "Bob, our boys on Guadalcanal are starving for lack of supplies."

Ghormley shrugged. "What can I do? We've had bad naval losses around Guadalcanal. I had to withdraw the ships."

"At the sacrifice of our Marines on shore?" Nimitz noted in a none too friendly way. He did not wait for an answer. "You are getting the *Enterprise* very soon. In the meantime, I am ordering you today to resume sending these transports to Guadalcanal with supplies you are holding here in Noumea, as well as the Army's 164th Infantry Division—and I mean right now! We need you to be more aggressive in supporting our troops on Guadalcanal. Don't dare leave them hanging in the wind again!"

October 4, 1942, Aboard the *Yamato*, in the Seas of Southeast Asia, but Well Away from the Action

Ugaki entered Yamamoto's stateroom. He had a big smile. "Some good news for a change. Our planes from Rabaul blasted the American airbase on Guadalcanal and claim to have destroyed many American aircraft. And General Hyukatake is leading a 15,000-invasion force that the Navy is continuing to move in at night to avoid American planes on Guadalcanal."

"I know. I already heard from the general. He told me he was appalled by the starving troops on that island. This was the first he knew of it. Now, I am sure, he can appreciate the situation we find ourselves in."

"I also have good news. I just heard that one of our submarines put a spread of torpedoes into the carrier *Saratoga* and sank her. With the sinking of the *Wasp* two weeks ago, the American carrier force must be in dire straits."

Yamamoto smiled. "With the *Enterprise* damaged and out of action, that's three large American carriers off the boards. The Marines on Guadalcanal now have much less air support. It's good you sent those troops to take advantage of that."

Yamamoto continued. "On my part, I have agreed with the Army's Colonel Tsuji to have the Combined Fleet escort his troop carriers to Guadalcanal. He says we need a full division with heavy artillery, ammunition, and tanks to dislodge the Americans. We will also need help from the Army Air force at their land-based fields. We can then compel the American Navy to fight us, so we can put an end to their authority in the Pacific."

October 8, 1942, Guadalcanal, Henderson Field

True to his word, Yamamoto sent two battleships, the *Kongo* and the *Haruna*, which rained 14-inch shells down on Henderson Field for an hour and a half. These projectiles were monsters and created a carnage all across the field; wrecked planes littered the field. Perhaps eight Wildcats and five SBDs remained in operable condition. Every tent and building on the field was destroyed or shredded, and most of the aviation gasoline went up in flames. Forty-one men were killed.

October 9, 1942, Aboard the *Yamato*, near Truk

Ugaki, wild with joy, rushed in to see Yamamoto. "Great news! Our bombardment by our two battleships of what the Americans call 'Henderson Field' was a great success. Our 14-inch guns devastated the airfield and most of the planes parked there. The field was turned into a massive conflagration, between the exploding planes and the flames of the aviation fuel going up in smoke. We also finally got three of our medium bombers to drop explosives on the field."

Yamamoto smiled. "Excellent! I think, for now, we have neutralized Henderson Field."

"The only fly in the ointment is that that the Army would not release its warplanes from the Kwantung Army," Ugaki advised.

"Why not?" Yamamoto sputtered.

Ugaki shrugged. "The Army says if we withdraw so many planes from Manchuria, the Soviets might be tempted to attack the Kwantung Army."

Yamamoto shook his head. "What the hell is the matter with those guys? Everyone knows the Soviet Army has its hands full with the Germans and may be totally defeated at any time!"

Yamamoto sighed. "Well, we'll just have to use our Navy planes, but our pilots are not trained in ground support like the Army flyers."

"So we will attempt to engage the American Pacific Fleet?" Ugaki asked.

Yamamoto nodded. "Yes, as soon as possible. Time is on the side of our enemies. If we cannot join the battle in ten days I am not sure we can win."

"With the American planes out of commission, we were able to land 5,000 troops in transports," Ugaki advised.

October 10, 1942, Guadalcanal, Marine headquarters

"With those additional troops the Japs were able to land last night and our supplies running low, thanks to Ghormley, we are now experiencing probing attacks by those Japs near Henderson Field," Vandegrift told his staff officers "We have to fortify our lines close to Henderson Field. Our intelligence unit is burning their documents. If necessary, I plan to have our ground units fade into the jungle and hills and live off the land, from which we can wage a guerilla war as long as is necessary. But for now, we'll defend the airfield for all we're worth!"

"Ask Ghormley for naval bombardment assistance," one officer suggested.

Vandegrift shook his head. "Not likely. He's cloistered aboard the *Argonne* in the harbor at Noumea. He's too nervous and distraught to come out and fight and this volatile South Pacific war zone is going to hell. Ghormley is even afraid the Japs might show up and attack him at Noumea Harbor!"

"Any good news?" asked an officer.

"As a matter of fact there is," Vandegrift advised. "Admiral Bull Halsey is replacing Admiral Fletcher, wounded on the carrier *Saratoga*, as commander of naval forces in this area. Halsey asked me if we can hold. I told him we could with a little more naval support. Halsey promised to send everything he had. Perhaps that can turn the tide against the Japs. He even put banners all over the place. KILL JAPS! KILL JAPS! KILL MORE JAPS!"

"We may have another ally," suggested another officer. "Some of our Solomon Island natives keeping a watch on the Japs for us report that their troops are having a very hard time in that jungle and many have come down with all sorts of diseases, especially malaria. Also, they say that the Japs have such poor communications, most of the units can't even talk to each other."

October 11, 1942, Truk, Aboard the *Yamato*, the Weather Deck

A beautiful Sunday morning dawn, and Yamamoto looked through his powerful binoculars as the Combined Fleet, slithering like a wolf pack, as it slowly moved out of its resting place in Truk. Mentally, he automatically counted them: five big aircraft carriers, four battleships, nine cruisers, and twenty-eight destroyers, heading for Guadalcanal. Objective: to eliminate, for once and for all, Henderson Field and destroy the remains of the American fleet.

Then, he thought, *the recapture of Guadalcanal can be accomplished. Imperial General Headquarters sent General Hyakutake, with whom Yamamoto had dinner last night, to assume command of the 17th Army.* Yamamoto had to smile. *Hyakutake carried with him his best dress uniform, which he intended to wear when he accepted the American surrender. I'm not so sure I have the General's confidence on defeating the Americans on that island.*

October 15, 1942, Pearl Harbor, Naval Headquarters at Makalapa

Nimitz called a meeting of his staff after returning from his tour of Guadalcanal and Noumea.

"Between Ghormley's withdrawal of the naval force at Guadalcanal," Nimitz began, "and his losses at the battle of Savo Island, and the intelligence and alertness of his staff members, he's created a big concern in our minds. Admiral King and I conferred, and we now question whether Ghormley has control of the situation out there or the guts needed to successfully run the show. Frankly, I think he doesn't have the courage to send the ships to sink the Tokyo Express supplying the Jap troops on the island. What do you guys think?"

"Admiral," Nimitz's chief of staff said, "we have been discussing this among ourselves and the consensus of the group is that Admiral Ghormley lacks the qualities to lead and we think it is time to relieve him."

Nimitz nodded. "At my request, King gave me permission to relieve him and replace him with Halsey."

Nimitz looked at his chief of staff. "Cut the necessary orders and make it so."

Same Time, Aboard the flagship *Yamato*, at Truk

"I just received word that a dozen American warplanes bombed Rabaul," Yamamoto advised Ugaki.

Ugaki frowned. "That's a first!"

"I know," agreed Yamamoto. "Admiral Kusaka reports that the raid devastated the Eleventh Air Fleet, destroying planes and killing one hundred and ten men, many of them pilots. Kusaka is demanding more planes from our carrier force. I cannot do that—deplete our carrier force simply to reinforce Rabaul. Out of the question!"

Ugaki nodded. "It seems to always be a question of too little, too late, for us in the South Pacific. Our defenses have not been built up properly."

"I'm not surprised," Yamamoto replied. "I warned Tokyo that this would happen—this change in the war—once the Americans buckled down to fight and get their factories rolling."

CHAPTER SIXTEEN

The End of Guadalcanal for the Japanese; Japan Pulls off its Own 'Dunkirk'

October 17, 1942, Aboard the *Yamato*, Somewhere in the South Pacific

UGAKI SLID INTO A chair in Yamamoto's stateroom. He did not look happy.

Yamamoto took this all in. "Well, what's the bad news now?"

"General Hyukatake has postponed the attack on Henderson field again, this time to October 22nd," Ugaki reported. "Too much jungle and disease to get his troops in position, so he says. Now he is exhorting his troops to fight gallantly on October 22 and annihilate the enemy."

Yamamoto shook his head. "Such Army bombast, with little in the way of results. If we ran the Navy like the generals run the Army, we'd have lost the war by now."

"We have had no luck in locating the American fleet in this area," Ugaki complained.

"I'm not surprised," Yamamoto responded. "The intelligence from our submarines and search planes is just plain bad, and the claims of sinkings of Allied ships is an exaggerated joke. If we believe those pilots and ship captains, the American would have no ships left in their fleet. And I know the carrier *Enterprise* is once again back in action!"

"Well," said Ugaki, "we have the *Shokaku*, *Zuikaku*, and *Junyo* in this area now. Admiral Nagumo should go find and sink the *Enterprise*."

"If he doesn't, I'm going to get rid of him," grumbled Yamamoto.

"The hero of Pearl Harbor?" Ugaki asked, smirking.

"Damn right. I am sick of his lack of aggressiveness," Yamamoto grumped.

Ugaki smiled. "You'll certainly get no argument from me. We should have gotten rid of him a long time ago."

October 23, 1942, Aboard the *Yamato*, Somewhere in the South Pacific

A furious Ugaki sputtered, "That damn General Hyukatake cancelled the attack yet again yesterday. Can you believe it?"

A much calmer Yamamoto shrugged. "Yes, but at least he attacked today. I am encouraged by the fact that at last he went on the offensive."

Ugaki's anger was not slated. "But it failed! And his excuse is not because of strong enemy resistance but because the terrain was unfamiliar! Now what kind of general would attack without sufficient preparations?"

Yamamoto looked at his Chief of Staff. "Ugaki, why are you so angry? It's the Chief of the General Staff who is in hot water because he personally promised the emperor that the Army would succeed in this attack on Guadalcanal. General Hyukatake had no choice; he had to satisfy the emperor by attacking again with an even greater force. He's been ordered to take Guadalcanal by hook or by crook!"

A few hours later, Yamamoto received the message he had been hoping for:

2100 BANZAI. THE KAWAGUCHI DETACHMENT CAPTURED THE AIRFIELD AND THE WESTERN FORCE IS FIGHTING TO THE WEST OF THE FIELD.

Finally, he thought, the airfield is ours!

Immediately, Yamammoto issued new orders. With Henderson Field no longer an American warplane threat, the Eighth Fleet will move to a position 150 miles southwest of Guadalcanal while the Second Fleet would move to a position 150 northeast of the island. A classic pincer move. Meanwhile Destroyer Squadron Four would sail down the 'Slot' to Guadalcanal to support the Japanese troops on shore with naval gunfire.

With that good news, and his orders issued, Yamamoto went to bed.

Ugaki shook Yamamoto awake. "What is it?" Yamamoto grumbled, not quite awake.

Ugaki looked serious. "Sir, I have updated news that the airfield was not taken! Our Army had only taken one position on the southern outskirts of the field, but the field itself has not been taken."

Yamamoto bolted upright. "Are there still enemy planes operating from that field?"

Ugaki nodded.

Yamamoto frowned. "So Henderson is still safely in enemy hands and the Army has failed again!"

Yamamoto sighed. "In the meantime, despite my orders, Nagumo has dithered about moving south. He wanted to refuel and feared he would be attacked from the north, so he moved north, in the opposite direction of explicit orders, and sent reconnaissance aircraft north to look for the American fleet. His planes could find none and returned to the carrier. Of course not! Because the Americans were not there! His fleet is sucking up our oil reserves so fast that tankers were siphoning fuel from the battleships! He's wasted valuable time refueling his ships and loitering in the north. Well, under my dire threats, Nagumo finally decided to turn around and move south but hesitated to get too close. But I fear he wants to avoid the battle and that might just be our swan song at Guadalcanal. I sent Nagumo a message to plan for a multi-pronged attack on the American Fleet. I told him to not hesitate or waver. But I have no confidence Nagumo will listen or become aggressive."

Finally, with Nagumo's arrival in the area of Guadalcanal, the Japanese force now outnumbered the Americans in ships and also, in planes, 212 to 172. Yamamoto ordered the fleet to move to point 150 miles northeast of Guadalcanal while Destroyer Squadron Four advanced down "the Slot" to support the Japanese troops on Guadalcanal with naval gunfire.

October 26, 1942, the Seas off Santa Cruz Islands in the South Pacific

Despite Nagumo's reluctance, the two great fleets, one American, the other Nagumo's Japanese, kept steaming toward each other, but neither knew the other's precise location. It became a deadly cat and mouse game. Then, at 3:10 AM, an American PBY spotted the Japanese carrier *Zuikaku*, and at first light, two Dauntless dive bombers found the *Zuiho* and scored with two bomb hits, not sinking her, but putting her out of action while other dive bombers badly damaged the *Zuikaku*.

Opposing admirals Nagumo and Kinkaid now sent their planes scurrying toward each other, with the fleets now about fifty miles apart. Some Enterprise avengers did not locate any carriers but found the heavy cruiser *Chikuma* and put her out of action.

The *Hornet* planes found the carrier *Shokaku* and sent three bombs smashing through her flight deck with great destructive force. In the meantime, more than one hundred Japanese planes converged on the *Hornet* and the *Enterprise*. The *Enterprise* escaped into a rain squall and disappeared from view, but not so the *Hornet*, which now bore the full brunt of all the attacking Japanese planes. But soon the Japanese pilots found the *Enterprise* again. The score: *Hornet* a blazing wreck and the *Enterprise* badly damaged. Per orders, two American destroyers sank the *Hornet* with torpedoes.

Two badly damaged Japanese carriers had to limp back to Japan and would be out of action for some time to come. Both sides lost scores of other ships in the battle.

Torpedoing the Hornet

October 28, 1942, Aboard the *Yamato*, Somewhere in the South Pacific

Admiral Nagumo broke off the engagement with the American force after he lost the *Zuikaku* and *Zuiho*.

Yamamoto shook his head. "Ugaki, if we can't do better than a standoff in these battles, then we will lose the war. Nagumo panicked and let a few American cruisers scatter our fleet. Damn fool!"

"What are you thinking?" Ugaki asked.

"I'm relieving the son of a bitch of command," Yamamoto said. "I'll stick him where he can do no harm, perhaps to command the Sasebo Naval Station on southern Kyushu. That'll keep him out of our way! I named Admiral Jisaburo Ozawa as commander-in-chief of the Third Fleet."

Ugaki nodded. "I always said that deep down, Admiral Nagumo was a coward. We should have fired him months ago."

Yamamoto nodded. "The Japanese general on Guadalcanal has just sent me a message of apology for his failure to capture Henderson Field. He is calling for a much larger force and a new offensive. But when I spoke to one of the Army leaders in Tokyo, General Imamura, he was very evasive, saying, it is 'very difficult' to supply more Army troops at this time to the South Pacific. If that is true, I fear that eventually, we shall lose Guadalcanal.

"In the meantime, the Tokyo propaganda machine is hailing the battle at Santa Cruz as a great Japanese victory. Can you believe it? The emperor even wrote an Imperial rescript praising me for the brave fight put up by the Combined Fleet."

"As many carriers as we destroy," grumbled Ugaki, "the Americans keep building second and third generation carriers. We sink one *Yorktown* and other shows up a few months later! How can we win?"

Yamamoto spread his arms in frustration. "I know, I know. I first must deal with Henderson Field still being in control of the Allies. That's my biggest problem now!"

October 30, 1942, Aboard the *Yamato* at Truk Harbor

The staff officers of the Japanese Combined Fleet met aboard Yamamoto's flagship. When Admiral Nagumo arrived, he reported immediately to Yamamoto.

Nagumo looked Yamamoto directly in the eye and reported that he had sunk three carriers and a battleship. Yamamoto knew it was not true but let it slide, so great was his disgust with this admiral.

Meanwhile, Ugaki met with Nagumo's chief of staff Admiral Ryunosuke Kusaka.

With hardly a courteous greeting, Kusaka went on the attack. "You know, our failure at Guadalcanal is all Admiral Yamamoto's fault—the way he handled the ships supporting our troops. Frankly, Admiral Nagumo does not understand why Yamamoto is still in command."

Ugaki leaped out of his chair, looking down on Nagumo's chief of staff eyes blazing. "How can you say that? It was Nagumo's cowardice—his failure to engage the American fleet left our troops hanging out without the necessary naval support. Instead of trying to shift the blame to us, you should be apologetic for the craven actions of your commander!"

November 5, 1942, Aboard the *Yamato* at Truk Harbor

"The situation is getting desperate for our troops on Guadalcanal. The planes from Henderson Field and the American Navy ships are bombarding our supply effort with impunity. Not much is getting to our troops on the island and they are in dire straits," Ugaki told Yamamoto.

Yamamoto shrugged. "I know, all too well. But I have no control over the Army whose management of the fighting on the island has been atrocious. They keep delaying any offensive, no matter how hard we or Tokyo push. Even our own fleet in is disarray. I tried sending some torpedo bombers from Rabaul to attack the American ships around Guadalcanal but the weather this month has been terrible, and the bombers failed to make contact with the enemy. In other words, nothing is going right! The Army went into Guadalcanal having great contempt for the enemy. Now they have learned the hard way how wrong they were! I am not sure there is much we can do, except to contain our losses.

"One thing I have done is convince the Naval General Staff to relieve Admiral Nagumo of operational command, after I went step by step through all his failures to engage the enemy. They were finally convinced and reassigned him to take command of the Sasebo Naval Base, where he can do no further harm to our war effort."

"So, what's next?" Ugaki inquired of his boss.

"We've got to figure out how to construct an airbase near enough to Guadalcanal so that the Americans can be attacked by air and prevented from supplying and reinforcing their troops. Rabaul is simply too far away to be effective. Our pilots are exhausted and not in top form by the time they reach Guadalcanal—and then they have to return to Rabaul! In the meantime, Admiral Koki Abe took the Eighth Fleet to Guadalcanal to bombard Henderson Field and suppress the use of their aircraft against us. The trouble with this strategy is that the damn American Seabees can restore the field within hours! And even when we suppress the Americans use of planes at Henderson Field, the Army still does not attack! What good are our efforts if the Army fails to take advantage of them?"

"We have to keep bombarding the field and keep the Americans off balance," Ugaki said. "One of the Army's difficulties is the devilish landscape of Guadalcanal itself, with its swamps and thick jungle. Our Army must move at night to avoid the American planes at Henderson Field. It had to abandon its artillery pieces because they were too heavy and cumbersome to push through the jungle trails. Also, the Army has very poor communications making a coordinated attack impossible; its men are exhausted by the time they reach the target area and no longer are an effective fighting force. I fear our Army has terribly misjudged the difficulties of moving through that terrain. By the time they get close to the field the American Marines are warned and waiting for them. Our night bayonet attacks are fierce but, in the end, the Marines hold their positions, even with heavy casualties."

Yamamoto sighed. "I'm discouraged because we have now put 23,000 men on the island, and still, no attack has begun. It's very frustrating to see that we are not receiving at least some coordination from the Army."

November 10, 1942, Brisbane, Australia, Headquarters of General Douglas MacArthur

General MacArthur pulled the corn cob pipe out of his mouth and pointed it at his intelligence chief, Brigadier General Charles Willoughby. "Charlie, it's about time we go on the offensive against the Japs. I'm tired of sitting on my duff while Nimitz hits all the islands in my territory. I want to take Buna and eliminate any threat to Port Moresby."

"Don't worry, General, our information is that there is little indication of an attempt to make a strong stand against the Allied advance," Willoughby advised. "They are understrength and badly mauled. It shouldn't take too much to push them into the sea."

MacArthur nodded. "I am going to send General Harding and the 32nd Army Division along with some Australian militia to take Buna. I don't expect it will take too long."

Willoughby looked at his chief. "The 32nd from Fort Devens? They have no combat experience."

MacArthur smiled. "Well, they have to get their feet wet sometimes, don't they? Too bad Nimitz and Halsey won't give me support. They're just interested in seeing just how much of the South Pacific his Navy and Marines can appropriate for themselves!"

"General, weren't you told by Washington and the Joint Chiefs to include some Australians and Dutch on your officer staff?"

MacArthur looked up at the ceiling taking a long drag on his corn-cob pipe. "Charlie, I don't trust those guys. I want an all-American group of staff officers and that is what I have and will continue to have. The hell with the Joint Chiefs!"

"And the president?" Willoughby asked.

MacArthur nodded. "And the president."

November 16, 1942, Aboard the *Yamato* in Truk Harbor

An aide came in with a message from the Japan's Seventeenth Army, which had established a large beachhead and built an airstrip at Buna, New Guinea, a village with native huts and a few houses, about 100 miles across the peninsula from Port Moresby, as part of the Japanese Army's plan to capture that port. The Army was able to push the Australians back thirty miles into the jungle towards Port Moresby. But after the debacle at Guadalcanal, Imperial General Headquarters in Tokyo ordered the Army to return to Buna and consolidate its position. Headquarters worried that with the long-distance supply line to Buna, the Seventeenth Army would be fortunate to just hold its position there.

"The Seventeenth Army reports it is under attack by a force of Americans and Australians. So far, our Army is holding, but requests help from the Imperial Navy in order to hold Buna," the aide said breathlessly.

"Just what I needed with my plate full with Guadalcanal!" Yamamoto complained.

If we abandon Buna, the Port Moresby invasion is finished and our hold on Rabaul would soon become untenable. Yamamoto turned this thought over in his mind. *The war was going bad more rapidly than even I expected. But I cannot leave our troops hanging in Buna.*

Yamamoto rushed to the communications room and instructed the radio operator to transmit his orders to rush the Tenth Destroyer Division to Buna with 800 troops as reinforcements.

November 21, 1942. Truk, Aboard the *Yamato*

An Army colonel from Tokyo General Staff on assignment to report back to Tokyo on the situation at Guadalcanal, visited Yamamoto.

"You can tell Tokyo for me, Colonel, that the air arms in both services are in trouble," Yamamoto said.

"Why is that?" the colonel asked.

"Because we use our best pilots daily without relief and they are being killed off especially at the battle of Midway. It's the law of averages. We are having trouble replacing them. The replacement pilots, desperately needed, don't get the training they need and lack both the skill and confidence to carry on the war in an effective manner. They used to say one Zero could take on five to ten American fighters-but that's no longer true. You tell Tokyo that they'd better release the Army planes and pilots in Manchuria if they expect us to effectively fight the Americans!"

December 9, 1942, Guadalcanal, American Garrison Headquarters

General Vandegrift smiled. "Welcome General Patch. I hereby turn over this garrison to you. I'm being shipped out and home. The malaria-ridden men of the First Marine Division will be moved to Australia, they've about had it."

"I know", replied Patch. Within the next few days, the entire division will be replaced by the Second Marine and the 25th Army Divisions. I expect by early January I'll have 50,000 troops under my command. By mid-January, I plan to commence a drive westward to mop up what remains of the Jap garrison."

December 10, 1942, Aboard the *Yamato* in Truk Harbor

Ugaki sat down facing his boss. "That move to use your destroyer fleet to supply the troops on Guadalcanal, how did it go?"

Yamamoto frowned. "Not good and nowhere near enough. The truth is that I found out that the situation on Guadalcanal is much direr than I was led to believe. Our forces are down to a quarter of what I thought they were and the men there are dropping like flies from hunger and disease. So, what's the good of putting men on the island and reinforcing the Army there if we can't supply them with food and ammunition? And with the American air force at full strength at Henderson, of the 20,000 troops I tried to land on Guadalcanal, only 2,000 made it along with 360 cases of ammunition and 1,500 bales of rice."

"I hate to say this," said Ugaki, "but it appears to me that Guadalcanal is turning into our Stalingrad!"

"I can't argue with you on that," Yamamoto replied.

December 12, 1942, Pearl Harbor, Naval Headquarters at Makalapa

"The reports I received indicate that that was one hell of a battle at off Santa Cruz," Nimitz informed his staff officers. "Apparently, the two forces met head to head in the 'Slot', the narrow waterway between the islands, now known as 'Ironbottom Sound', because of all the ships that went down in that stretch of water. Anyway, there were so many ships and no maneuvering room that they were right on top of one another. It was dark, and the Japs were coming through in two columns. I'll be damned if Admirals Scott and Callahan didn't drive the American ships right between them. What a melee! Ships a few feet apart, firing blindly at point blank, machine gun range. The shelling and gun fire were so intense and so close that both sides were also hitting their own ships! I am sure some of our ships were damaged by friendly fire. Our losses in destroyers was heavy, but so was theirs—and we managed to scatter their fleet and prevent any support troops landing on Guadalcanal which, I think, may have turned the tide of battle on that island."

"Did we lose a lot of men?" One staff officer asked.

Nimitz replied in a low, sad voice. "I'm afraid so. And it grieves me to report that, in this engagement, both Admiral Norm Scott and Admiral Dan Callahan were killed in action while manning the bridges of their ships."

Nimitz shook his head. "And typical of General Vandegrift and the Marines—he's grumbling that 'everyone is withdrawing but my Marines.'"

Same Time, Washington, D.C., the White House, Oval Office

Admiral King and General Marshall met with the president.

Roosevelt leaned back in his desk chair. "I see that General MacArthur is screaming for more ships, troops, and planes regardless of what is occurring elsewhere on the globe. Frankly, gentlemen, I am not interested in reorienting the global war toward the Pacific notwithstanding MacArthur's tantrums."

The two guests nodded in agreement.

"We've gone through this so many times, that defeat of Japan will not defeat Germany and if we concentrate our forces against Japan, it increases the chances of Germany dominating Europe and Africa. Once again, I repeat, that we cannot have. We can't be quarreling with the British or have our Army ground forces quarreling with our Army Air Force and thereby keep fumbling and bumbling toward some plan to attack the Germans. Please relay that to all under your command. Maybe this time they'll believe it!"

King and Marshall responded, "Yes, sir!" almost in unison.

Roosevelt turned to other work and the two military men showed themselves out.

Same date, Aboard the *Yamato*, in Truk Harbor

Ugaki could see Yamamoto was not happy, perhaps even depressed.

Yamamoto eyed his chief of staff. "Admiral Abe arrived at Guadalcanal with his ships and was met by an even larger American naval force, just spoiling for a fight."

"What happened?" Yamamoto's face told Ugaki that the news was not good, even before his boss even opened his mouth.

"A fierce naval battle ensued and both sides lost ships, but we lost the battleships *Hiei* and *Kirishima*. The emperor had sailed on *Hiei* and he loved that ship. The loss of both battleships is a heavy blow. I had to order one of submarines to shadow the *Hiei*—a burning hulk. I didn't want her falling into American hands. Anyway, American planes from the Henderson Field did the job for us: they had found the *Hiei* and sank her. And two of our carriers were damaged so badly they had to go back to Japan for repairs. Admiral Goto is dead. He went down with his cruiser. In the meantime, the American industrial capacity has gone into full gear and is pushing out ships at an alarming rate. Every time I turn around I get a report of our fleet encountering new ships.

"That's quite a morale buster for us and of immense propaganda value for our enemies." *In more ways than one*, Yamamoto thought.

"I served the *Hiei*," Ugaki said. "I almost wish I had gone down with her."

Left unsaid was why the battleships *Kongo* and *Haruna* were not sent also to support its mighty sister battleships.

Perhaps a failure of nerve by the Combined Fleet? Ugaki thought but did not say.

American fire-controlled radar, far more advanced in technology than we possess, thought Yamamoto, *was one of the major differences.*

I warned Tokyo about that before the war. Well, one thing our Navy learned is that the Americans can and will fight!

When Yamamoto added everything up, of the 23,000 invasion troops, the Japanese could land only 2,000 and only a fraction of their supplies. The few transports that made it to the beach had to intentionally be driven aground. In total, we lost seven transports, supplies, and men. *I must face it. This is the beginning of the end for us on Guadalcanal. My gamble at Midway failed, and what I feared about going to war with the United States is starting to happen.*

December 22, 1942, Aboard the *Yamato*, in Truk Harbor

Lieutenant General H. Adachi stopped in to see Yamamoto and Ugaki.

He and his staff had just come down from China and glibly talked about retaking Guadalcanal.

Yamamoto shook his head. "You know nothing about this area or fighting the Americans. You people are victims of your own propaganda. The Americans are neither effete nor cowardly, but very powerful soldiers with a fighting spirit that can match our own. To go in with the mistaken impression that the Americans will drop their rifle and run is the recipe for disaster. As a matter of fact, unless the Sixteenth Regiment in Guadalcanal does better, they are not going to make it out of the island or come back alive. So stop talking senselessly about retaking Guadalcanal. It's not going to happen. We'll be lucky to be able to supply our remaining troops there with the necessities of life."

The chastened general left, shaking his head.

"I agree with everything you told the general," said Ugaki. "I can't see how we can retake Guadalcanal. So many times the Army has failed. Now the Americans are reinforcing their troops almost daily. I think our position on the island is hopeless."

"We've got to get out of Guadalcanal," a sad Yamamoto said.

He got no argument from Ugaki.

December 31, 1942, Tokyo, Imperial Headquarters

At an Imperial Headquarters meeting, the chiefs of staff wanted to withdraw the Army troops from Guadalcanal and abandon the attempt to recapture the island. It was just becoming too costly and the Americans were now well entrenched with the fully functioning airfield at Henderson.

The decision was presented to Hirohito who found it "unacceptable" and demanded, "we must launch an offensive somewhere else."

Sugiyama stood. "I will take the offensive in the New Guinea area, be successful, and restore troop morale."

Hirohito liked the idea and the General Staff went along, thereby delaying for yet another time, shifting their strategy to the defense of the Homeland in the Pacific.

It would not be until February 1943, that the emperor permitted the evacuation of Japan's force on Guadalcanal.

January 3, 1943, Truk, Aboard the *Yamato*

Yamamoto walked into Ugaki's stateroom. "Just spoke to yet another staff officer from Imperial General Headquarters traveling from Tokyo to Rabaul. He says the Army plans to add seven divisions to fight for Port Moresby."

"Are you serious?" Ugaki asked.

Yamamoto shrugged. "I don't believe it for one minute. Guadalcanal is lost and probably the war also. The Navy picked up an American pilot who told them the Americans have six or seven new carriers almost ready and some of the damaged ones are back in action. He even named them: *Langley, Lexington, Saratoga, Ranger, Yorktown, Enterprise, Wasp, Hornet, Essex,* and *Bonhomie.* I fear the enemy is building these second and third-generation carriers faster than we can sink them. As much as I don't want to admit it, I fear that my prediction has come true that our successes will end in six months to a year after Pearl Harbor. Of course, the

Japanese public, thanks to Tojo's propaganda machine, thinks we are winning the war!"

"I know", said Ugaki. "A visiting delegation of Army officers did not seem to know about the dire situation on Guadalcanal."

"Guadalcanal is lost. Only the emperor, against military advice, insists we keep fighting there until at least we mount a new offensive in New Guinea—and I doubt that will happen," Yamamoto groused. "And now I just received a report from Buna that the Army has been quite capable of holding off the American troops, whom, they say, are quite disorganized and having trouble getting through the jungle to mount an attack. But our troops there are starving, and we are running out of ammunition."

Ugaki snorted. "Too bad. With a little more planning by the Army, we could have taught that MacArthur a lesson like we did in the Philippines!"

Yamamoto shrugged, "So it seems I have no choice. I ordered the Eighth Fleet near Buna to evacuate the Army troops, but so far, those troops are surrounded and cannot be reached. The garrison commander advised that he is ready to do his duty and die and wishes prosperity to the Empire and good luck to all."

Yamamoto shook his head. "And for Guadalcanal, the Army High Command in Tokyo sent some representatives down to Rabaul to see for themselves the situation on Guadalcanal and to confer. What they found out is that the troops are existing, if you can call it that, on a caramel, two crackers, and a bit of grain per day. Most of them suffer from malaria, hunger, and amoebic dysentery. The American offensive is in full swing with wholesale destruction by artillery, the typical American gambit. If you can believe it, the emperor has already issued another Imperial rescript, wishing that the Army make all efforts to recapture Guadalcanal swiftly!"

"Did you respond?" Ugaki asked.

"Of course. One does not ignore or defy the emperor. I wrote: 'We are deeply impressed with Your Majesty's gracious words. In view of the current grave situation, we, officers and men, will make further efforts and pledge ourselves to meet Your Majesty's wishes.'"

271

Yamamoto looked at Ugaki. "What else could I say? After all, he is the emperor. But it is clear we lost many of the people skills we had when we attacked Pearl Harbor."

"Such as?" Ugaki asked.

"Such as the decline of aviation skills in our air fleet We have lost too many of our best pilots in battle and our abilities are less than one-third of what they had been in the past. For example, in the last graduating class, forty-four out of sixty had no experience in a Zero fighter.

"Finally, the Tokyo chiefs, noting that the troops only had bayonets against American weaponry, decided to pull out of Guadalcanal, over the objections of the local Army commanders."

"What about the emperor and his rescript?" asked Ugaki.

Yamamoto shrugged. "The emperor better back off if does not want a blood bath!"

January 13, 1943, Truk, Aboard the *Yamato*

"The Americans have so many ships landing in Guadalcanal, we've stop keeping track of them," Ugaki reported to Yamamoto.

"Are we getting food to the men on Guadalcanal?" Yamamoto asked.

"With all the planes the Americans have at Henderson Field, it is suicide to send ships in with supplies," Ugaki explained. "Our destroyers get as close as they dare, and dump 1,500 tons of supplies in sealed fifty-gallon oil drums in the water hoping they will float to the troops, who used small boats to try to retrieve those supplies. It's a hit or miss operation with only about a third of the supplies reaching the troops."

"Tokyo ordered us to keep supplying the troops on Guadalcanal no matter what our losses," Yamamoto advised.

"The new chief of Army operations was just here—a Colonel Samada—and after inspecting the situation flew back to Tokyo to recommend abandonment of Guadalcanal and New Guinea by the Army," Yamamoto said. "He saw for himself that the men on the island were dying from dysentery and lack of food and were in such bad shape that they could not even send out patrols."

January 20, 1943, Somewhere on Bougainville in the South Pacific

Two Allied coastwatchers knew they were the subject of a determined, massive manhunt by Japanese troops. One coastwatcher covered the northern end of Bougainville, the other the southern end.

Paul Mason, the coastwatcher on the northern end learned from his native spies that a hundred Japanese troops with tracker dogs were coming after him. Mason sent a coded message to the Americans on a nearby island for help against the dogs—men he could avoid— dogs were much more difficult. He radioed the American Army Airforce on a nearby island, pinpointing the troops with the dogs.

An hour later, ten American warplanes struck the Japanese troops and killed all the dogs in their cages. With the help of loyal natives, Mason avoided the Japanese troops and lived another day to watch and report.

January 27, 1943, Casablanca, Anfa Hotel, Ballroom

President Roosevelt and Prime Minister Churchill met in the North African city of Casablanca for five days.

At the end of the conference the three Allied leaders, Roosevelt, Churchill, and DeGaulle, called a press conference.

Roosevelt took the microphone. "Gentlemen, the Prime Minister and myself have determined that peace can come to the world only by the total elimination of German and Japanese war power. The elimination of their war power means the unconditional surrender of Germany, Italy, and Japan. The letters US," Roosevelt noted, "are also the initials of one of America's great earlier presidents, Ulysses S. Grant, who first coined the phrase 'unconditional surrender' during our Civil War."

Churchill looked at the French leader, Charles DeGaulle, with a surprised look on his face. DeGaulle simply shrugged. Churchill had thought they'd agreed to keep the decision of "unconditional surrender" confidential for the time being. *Obviously, I'm wrong*, he thought. *There's no predicting Franklin!*

January 28, 1943 1943, Truk, Aboard the *Yamato*

Ugaki burst into Yamamoto's cabin. "Did you hear? Roosevelt and Churchill met in Casablanca and now they are demanding our 'unconditional surrender'—us, the Germans, and the Italians! Those are the words Roosevelt used."

Yamamoto nodded. "I already heard. Roosevelt has made ending this war by some fair settlement almost impossible. It plays into the hands of the fanatics in our military."

"Things are not going well for our ally Germany, neither in Russia nor North Africa. I am sure that is what encouraged the American president. Determined Russian resistance has stalled the German offensive and trapped a substantial portion of the German forces at Stalingrad and, in Africa, the Allies are routing Rommel," Yamamoto noted. He smiled. "It also prompted Churchill to tell the British people that 'while it was far from the beginning of the end, it was perhaps, the end of the beginning.' Churchill always had a way with words!

"It looks like our pre-war assumptions of a quick Germany victory over Britain and weak-willed Americans caving in and negotiating an early end to the war were all off the mark. The American production is churning out weapons at many times the rate of our own production."

February 2, 1943, Truk, Aboard the *Yamato*

On a moonless night, several Japanese destroyers crept close to shore and successfully evacuated 13,000 Imperial Army men from Guadalcanal. Men who were starving, wasted away, and had serious diarrhea; men who were just skin and bones in a uniform.

Yamamoto invited the commander of the operation, Admiral Koyanagi, to the *Yamato*, where he showered the admiral with praise and congratulations.

"You heard of Dunkirk, Admiral?" Yamamoto asked.

Koyanagi nodded.

"Well, this was like a little Dunkirk—right under the noses of the Americans!"

At dinner on the *Yamato*, Yamamoto became pensive and withdrawn. He knew the tide was turning against the Empire. More than a year had passed since the war started, and he knew American had already gotten its war production into full gear. They were taking civilians and turning them into soldiers and sailors. They had too many transports, and supplies were getting through to the South Pacific and Australia in great numbers.

I wonder, he thought, *whether, at the war's end, justice to me will be like that afforded to Napoleon? If we lose the war, the Allies will treat me like a war criminal because of Pearl Harbor. Will I be sent to the guillotine or exiled to Saint Helena? Well, one thing Tokyo can't blame me for on Guadalcanal is the Army's failure to send planes to the South Pacific saying the aircraft were needed in China and to repel the Russians if they attacked us. Pitiful excuses that may have cost us Guadalcanal and possibly stopped the American offensive.*

We need a new battle plan—a change in tactics to neutralize those coastwatchers on the many islands of the South Pacific who warn the Allies of the approach of our warplanes and ships. This time, I'll have our planes fly around, not over, those coastwatchers and attack in two large waves from different directions. The first wave would lure the American planes into the air. Then that wave would depart and when the American planes returned to the base and landed to refuel, the second wave would swoop in and catch them on the ground.

Same Date, Pearl Harbor, Naval Officers Club

Nimitz leaned against the bar, sipping a beer at the officers club. His chief of staff was downing a bloody mary.

"Admiral King," Nimitz said, "was not happy that we let the Japs get away at Guadalcanal."

"Hell, the Japs did a great job of disguising their operations," the chief of staff grumbled. "We thought they were preparing for a major offensive against us on Guadalcanal. The Japs sent a phony radio message, purportedly from one of our reconnaissance planes, reporting the sighting of two aircraft carriers, two battleships and ten destroyers. We took the bait and sent our planes out over the Pacific on a fool's errand while the Japs evacuated 13,000 surviving troops from Guadalcanal before our planes got back. It even fooled Halsey!"

Nimitz nodded. "That's what I told King and that seemed to calm him down. He also worried about our ship losses. I told him, 'Look, even if we lost the same amount of ships and planes, we can easily replace them. So in a battle with even losses, we come out ahead.'"

Nimitz rubbed his chin in contemplation. "One thing we did learn—the Japs are good at night naval battles, but we are improving dramatically on that score. And their advantage is now negated with our improved use of radar for range and fire control. We can land our first salvo on the unseen enemy without the benefits of flares or searchlights. It more than balances their advantage in torpedo weaponry. Even when we lose just as many planes as the Japs, we come out way ahead because our rescue and recovery of our airmen. The Japs hardly devote any effort to search-and-rescue because of their *bushido* culture, that is, the samurai warrior code of honorable death in combat. Did you know that their pilots won't wear parachutes or life vests?"

"Unbelievable!"

Nimitz pulled out a folded paper from his pocket. "We learned a lot from the actions at Guadalcanal. Listen to this note from Marine General Vandegrift: 'I have never heard or read of this kind of fighting. These people refuse to surrender. The wounded will wait until the men come up to examine them and blow themselves and the other fellow to pieces with a hand grenade. You can readily see the answer to that.' So that's what we're up against. Kill or be killed and take no prisoners."

Captain Rochefort, the head of the code-breakers at Naval Intelligence came into the club and headed directly for Admiral Nimitz. "Sorry to break in on you, Admiral, but this is the latest tidbit we decoded. The Japanese propaganda machine is telling its people that Guadalcanal is merely a tactical redeployment and that the Army decided to turn toward another sector of the front, advancing in a new direction, so to speak."

Nimitz laughed. "I understand that they had over 150,000 men killed, compared to our fatalities of just under 1,600. To me, it's more like 'advancing backwards'—so to speak!"

Nearby, Major Cochrane, an Army doctor stationed at Tripler Army Hospital on Oahu, overheard the conversation. "Excuse me for interrupting, Admiral, but I have seen many of our soldiers and Marines sent back from these islands which, I must say are home to terrible sanitary conditions and some of the most malignant insects and microorganisms causing dozens of varieties of malaria, lymphatic disease, dysentery, typhus, and even bubonic plague. Nearly half our casualties are from illness and disease!"

Nimitz sighed. "I know all too well, doctor. I get the reports."

"The fighting in the Pacific is a totally different animal from that in the European theater," said Nimitz's Chief of Staff. "Aside from the diseases—and the suicidal Japs—which are unique to the Pacific, the troops here spend most of their time waiting and maybe twenty percent of their time fighting. In Europe, the troops often spend months on the battle line."

CHAPTER SEVENTEEN

Americans Decode Yamamoto Plan for a Trip to the Front; Do We, or Don't We?

March 3, 1943, Pearl Harbor, Naval Headquarters, at Makalapa; Guadalcanal, Henderson Field

"OUR AIR FORCE IN the Pacific has been supplied with the new powerful twin-engine P-38 lightnings. They'll be part of the newly formed Army 339th Fighter Squadron," Nimitz announced to his staff officers "They are supposed to be able to handle the Jap Zeros."

"Finally! General Arnold stubbornly refused to provide us with those great fighters. They all went to Europe. The P-39s we were using are crap. They could not stand up to the Zeros—just hopelessly outclassed. Tell me, who is going to lead the squadron?" Nimitz's chief of staff asked.

"One of their aces, Captain D.D. Brannon, now promoted to a major. The squadron has already been sent to Henderson Field at Guadalcanal."

At Henderson Field, Major Bannon looked with pride at their new, hard-to-come-by, possessions, the P-38 Lightning fighter planes. They looked nothing like any fighters he'd ever seen. They had large twin-tail fuselages with a pair of large engines on each fuselage. The pilot looked like a bug, sitting in an elongated oval pod of a cockpit between the two fuselages and attached to the middle of a long, thin wing that ran through the fuselages, kind of like a "flying H".

Bannon climbed into the cockpit. *The manufacturer,* he mused, *boasts that I'm protected by two-inch bulletproof glass on my front windshield and when I fire the guns these guys spit out bullets tightly focused, which they tell me, gives amazing accuracy. This baby has self-sealing gas tanks and is supposed to be able to fly very long distances. The engineers assure us that the Lightning can go higher and faster than any known fighter, including the Zero. It bristles with armament, sporting a 20-mm cannon plus four .50-caliber machine guns. Well, we and the Jap pilots will soon find out if this plane can live up to its hype!*

Major Bannon and his boys took the P-38s up to join a big dogfight and, sure enough, flying faster and higher than either the Zeros or their own marine colleagues in the Wildcats sped, with all their guns blazing, through the Japanese formations. One after another of the Zeros dropped out of the skies, victims of this new, awesome plane. The P-38 was in the South Pacific to stay.

About time! thought Bannon. *No doubt, it's living up to the manufacturer's claims.*

✸✸✸

Major Bannon called in one of his pilots. "You have a lot of explaining to do."

The pilot looked at him quizzically.

"One of our coastwatchers reported that over Munda, a P-38 "bombed" a Jap twin engine bomber and brought it down. Said it was the most amazing thing he ever saw—one plane bombing another. You were the only one with a reported kill in that area. How in the hell did you bomb a plane in the air? Do you mind explaining?"

The pilot laughed. "I guess that was what it looked like to the coastwatcher. I spotted this medium Jap bomber below me—it was a Nell—so as I dove down on it and found my plane wasn't responding very well. Then I realized why—I still had my extra range external fuel tank attached to my plane's belly! So I released the damn fool thing just as I hit the plane with my cannon gun and the fuel tank tumbled through the air right onto the Nell. What an explosion. Damnedest thing I ever saw!"

Bannon smiled. "I think I'll leave the report as it is. Should make some General scratch his head and wonder!"

Bannon assigned fighter ace Captain John Mitchell to lead five P-38s on a mission to escort several Allied bombers. Mitchell, a commander determined to inflict maximum damage on the Japanese, and an ace himself, having earned the Distinguished Service Cross, trained his men to pull so close to the enemy plane that they could almost read the Jap's instruments. "That way," he told his men, "you can't miss when you fire."

Twenty-five Zeros attacked them from above and although outnumbered five to one, the powerful P-38s tore through the Japanese formation downing three Zeros plus three more "probables".

Mitchell downed one of the Zeros himself. He loved the P-38! In the meantime, several experienced pilots in the P-38s joined Mitchell's team: Tom Lanphier, Rex Barber, and Doug Canning. They were the 339th Fighter Squadron.

While all these heroics were going on, Admiral Marc Mitscher, an experienced carrier captain, commanding the entire Allied air operations at Guadalcanal, moved himself into a canvas tent and endured the life of the other militaries on the island—the rain, the sun, and, of course, the mosquitoes.

March 4, 1943, Truk, Aboard the Yamamoto's New Flagship, the Battleship *Musashi*

Yamamoto's new flagship, the magnificent battleship *Musashi*, was even more splendid that her sister ship, *Yamato*. Yamamoto transferred over to her after ship entered the protected anchorage at Truk. She was as long as the Chrysler Building was tall and weighed three times as much as one of his large aircraft carriers. Her eighteen-inch guns, all six of them, were unmatched by the Americans. Her armor was eighteen-inches thick.

Yamamoto, piped aboard, took time to stroll around his new home. *She is big,* he thought, *like the Yamato, and very impressive looking. But his fight against building her got him nowhere. He knew that she and the Yamato would be useless in modern naval warfare. He had no doubt that bombers and torpedo planes could sink her. But his superiors would not listen and spent all this time, money, and labor that could have gone into a multitude of aircraft carriers, which he so desperately needed. The Musashi and Yamato will be little more than floating fuel barges for other real fighting ships!*

Yamamoto sighed. "The Lord Keeper of the Privy Seal Kido informed me that the emperor was very displeased with the latest loss at Guadalcanal and expected us halt the enemy's advances."

Ugaki uttered a harsh laugh. "Did Kido have any suggestions?"

"No, but I do have some ideas. I want to force a major battle with the American Navy before their new carriers arrive in the Pacific and make things impossible for us," Yamamoto explained.

Ugaki frowned. "But sir, we are already having trouble supplying our troops in the Pacific southwest on places like New Georgia and nearby islands."

Yamamoto sighed. "I know. Their sea and air power is very strong. In the Bismarck Sea, their B-24 heavy bombers from Australia discovered our convoy of twenty-two ships and sank the destroyers *Murasame* and *Minegumo* in the Shortlands while those ships were trying to protect supplies and transports—and their new P-38 fighters are playing havoc with our Zeros assigned to protect that shipping. In the end, we lost all the troop-carrying transports. Of the twenty-two ships, not one remains afloat! Now the Army, at

Imperial General Headquarters in Tokyo, directed its commanders to concentrate on New Guinea. I sent Tokyo a wire telling them that so long as the big airbase on Guadalcanal was in operation, the Eleventh Imperial Naval Air Fleet was under constant threat, as were all my operations in the entire South Pacific.

"But with Tojo in office, the Army still holds the reins of power in Tokyo and wants to take the offensive again in New Guinea."

"So what are you planning to do?" queried Ugaki.

"I have now ordered the carriers *Shokaku, Zuikaku, Zuiho, Junyo,* and *Hiyo* down here to the South Pacific as quickly as possible. It will be the largest force of aircraft we've ever assembled. Their mission is to decimate the Allied air forces in the Solomons and New Guinea."

"How?" Ugaki asked.

Yamamoto smiled. "That's the puzzling question, isn't it? They first want us to regain control of the air far away from our current bases. We simply can't do it. Yet I've been instructed to 'clear the skies of enemy planes'.

"One other thing. I have decided to go to Rabaul myself to supervise operations, which I have called Operation I-Go. Here is the detailed agenda and schedule of my trip to Rabaul."

Ugaki shook his head vigorously. "That's not smart. The Commander-in-Chief of the Combined Fleet should not be anywhere near the front lines. You could be killed!"

Yamamoto straighted up in his chair and stood. "I think it is essential for me to go there for morale purposes. I'm convinced I'm not going to survive this war anyway, so what's the difference?"

"Then I am going too," Ugaki insisted.

Yamamoto did not argue the point.

Same Time, Military Hospital, Oahu, Hawaii

While Yamamoto was planning his trip to the front lines, Admiral Nimitz, recovering from a bout with malaria, was discharged from the hospital. Not much had changed while he was laid up. In fact, he retained command control as Commander-in-Chief of the Pacific Fleet from his hospital bed and, with the military successes on Guadalcanal, he felt that hastened his recovery.

While Admiral Bull Halsey predicted an early end to the war over these Japanese "bastards" and "monkeys", General George Kenney, commander of the Fifth Air Force in General MacArthur's Pacific Northwest area, was not so sure. He warned that the Japanese were not going to be a "pushover" after Germany falls. He told his men in no uncertain terms, "We will have to call on all our patriotism, stamina, guts, and maybe some crusading spirit or religious fervor thrown in, to beat them. No amateur can take these boys out. We have got to turn professional. Another thing: there are no quiet sectors in which troops get started off gradually, as in the last war. There are no breathers in this schedule. You take on Notre Dame, every time you play!"

Rabaul, is a city located on the northeast end of New Britain Island, in the Bismarck Archipelago, not far off the eastern end of New Guinea. Seven weeks after Pearl Harbor, Japanese troops crushed the small Australian force in Rabaul. The city has a magnificent harbor from which supplies and troop reinforcements were sent to the other islands. A bastion of strength, the Japanese had built five airfields there in support of its war efforts.

March 28, 1943, Pearl Harbor, Naval Headquarters at Makalapa

Nimitz addressed his assembled staff officers in the large conference room.

"Gentlemen, I have just heard from on high. The Joint Chiefs have adopted Admiral King's plan to bypass most of the Solomons and Rabaul. We plan to take Bougainville, just off the coast of New Guinea."

Nimitz, with a long wooden pointer tapped a spot on the wall map.

"We will land a force in the Admiralty Islands, west of Rabaul. That way, we can neutralize that Japanese stronghold and naval base without having to expend lives to take it. The same will hold true for many of the islands in the Solomons, except for Bougainville. We'll just let the Japs there rot on the vine, making sure that none of those troops are resupplied by Japanese shipping. I am not happy about bypassing many of these islands, and MacArthur is furious about cancelling an assault on Rabaul, but that is what we have been ordered to do.

"We will aim our sights on the Marianas, the Carolines, and the Volcano Islands, eventually reaching the Ryukyus."

"The Ryukyus?" someone asked.

"That's where Okinawa is located."

"Wow, I have heard that the Japs consider that part of their homeland," the voice from the audience said.

Nimitz just nodded.

April 7-13, 1943, Rabaul, the Main Airfield

Admiral Yamamoto, in his dress whites, stood beside the runway as he launched his pilots on a series of raids against Guadalcanal and other American bases, including those in New Guinea. He saw over 150 planes take off on this first day of Operation I-Go.

During that week, on four separate days, Yamamoto stood at the runway and waved farewell, as he watched a total of 486 fighters, 114 carrier-based bombers, and 80 land-based attack planes go up against the American forces. Each day he waited anxiously for the pilots to return with their reports. He totaled up the claims. They claimed 134 American planes shot down and only 42 of their own. He took those reports with a grain of salt, knowing the pilots' tendency to exaggerate.

After that week, Yamamoto announced, to the Navy and Army commanders, his intention to fly to the forward bases at

Bougainville, specifying the date for the visit as April 18. The punctilious Yamamoto followed that up with a secret memorandum, prepared by his meticulous administrative staff officer Watanabe, who was well aware of his boss' penchant for precise timing. So he detailed the exact times of arrival at each stop—and the admiral fully expected his staff and pilots to comply with the schedule—to the minute!

April 13, 1943, Truk Officers' Dining Room at the Airbase

Lieutenant General Hitoshi Imamura, commander of the Japanese Eighth Army in Rabaul flew in to meet and dine with Yamamoto on the admiral's arrival.

Yamamoto give Imamura a penetrating look. "General, there is no sense in not being very frank with each other at this stage. The American air forces are beginning to overtake us. At the beginning, they used to say that one Zero could take on five to ten American planes; now they say maybe two American aircraft. But it's irrelevant, because the enemy's replacement rate is three times ours, and we have lost most of our experienced pilots. It comes down to this: things are looking bleak for us now.

Imamura stared at Yamamoto. "If that's true, then we certainly cannot afford to lose you."

Yamamoto shrugged, seemingly unimpressed with the General's point.

This angered Imamura. He slapped his napkin down on the table hard. "It's utter madness," he growled angrily. "I came that close to death when I took the same flight to Buin, on the southern tip of Bougainville. We barely escaped an American fighter plane."

Imamura raised his hand to close to Yamamoto's face with his right thumb and index finger almost touching to show how close he came to dying. "I know you are planning to fly to Buin and Ballale. Please, don't go."

Yamamoto's long-time friend, Admiral Takaji Joshima, who flew in when he heard of Yamamoto's plans and had joined the dinner group. "I wholly agree with General Imamura. The plan is absolutely insane and an open invitation to the enemy, especially with his air bases so close to where you want to go."

Another diner, Admiral Jisaburo Ozawa, Commander-in-Chief of the Third Fleet also objected to the trip. "It's pure craziness for our Combined Fleet Commander-in-Chief to expose himself like this."

Yamamoto smiled. "I appreciate your expressions of concern, but I think it's important and I have no intention of changing my plans. If the weather is good, I am going, and that's that."

Later that evening Yamamoto met with his chief of staff Ugaki. "Our pilots report great losses suffered by the Americans. That may or may not be true. But what is true is that the power of the Americans grows day by day, no matter what we do. Our resources are spread too thin and our efforts to sustain Operation I-Go will be almost impossible. I-Go has failed simply because our forces were too small and our efforts too brief. We lost too many good and experienced pilots at Midway. Let's face it—the attrition rate is appalling—we are left with too many inexperienced pilots; and their morale is low. This is one of the reasons I feel I have to visit the men at the front and show the units at Ballale, Buin, and Shortland that I have confidence in the ultimate outcome and encourage them to greater valor in the name of the emperor."

Yamamoto looked at Admiral Ugaki. "Do you still insist on going with me?"

Ugaki nodded.

"Very well, but we must go in separate planes."

"Agreed," replied Ugaki.

Earlier, Yamamoto, as was his wont, wrote out the precise schedule of his visit, minute by minute. Commander Watanabe of the

Eleventh Air Fleet, had tried, in vain, to discourage the visit, but with no success.

Watanabe copied the schedule by hand and took it to the communications officer.

"I want this delivered by courier," Watanabe said.

The communications officer shook his head. "Sorry, sir, but protocol, and my orders, require us to send this by radio as a coded message."

"I don't like it," Watanabe protested. "The Americans can intercept the message and maybe, decode it."

The communications officer smiled indulgently. "Commander, we know it is impossible for the enemy to decode it. The new naval code went into effect two weeks ago and it is impossible to break in that time period. If we send it by courier, many things can go wrong, including having him shot down by the Americans. Rest assured, Commander, this is the safest and quickest way to deliver this schedule."

Watanabe, was not persuaded, but gave no further argument.

Yamamoto retired, feeling the strain of planning a battle he did not want to conduct. It affected his health and he took shots to alleviate the numbness he felt in the fingers of his right hand. His ankles and feet hurt badly, requiring him to change shoes several times a day. His doctor suggested that his swollen joints may be the result of beriberi, perhaps from a lack of vitamin B in his diet.

Things such as this depressed Yamamoto. *These days*, he thought, *the only good news I receive are reports from some friends who visited my beloved geisha, Chiyoko, and sent me back a lock of her hair.*

He sat down in his cabin and wrote to his beloved, using a writing brush. "Tomorrow, I go to the front for a short while. I will write you when I return. Be well. Love." Chiyoko was very special to him and he always wrote to her with a Chinese writing brush and rarely, with an ordinary pen.

Yamamoto wasn't yet ready to go to sleep. He called in his senior aide, Commander Yasuji Watanabe, and played *shoji*, a Japanese board game. Yamamoto won two out of three games, while strategically maneuvering the black and white pebbles.

Watanabe, an old friend of the admiral, wondered about the wisdom of being too close to the front lines. "After all, you yourself, have condemned the time-honored practice of the captain going down with the ship. This is almost the equivalent!"

Yamamoto looked up from the board. "To tell you the truth, I'm not too keen on going, but I think my presence there will boost the morale of the pilots—and believe me, those men need it."

Same Time, Pearl Harbor, Hypo Station Offices and Admiral Nimitz's Quarters

Commander Watanabe worries were indeed justified Moments after sending the coded message, the Americans intercepted it and sent it to Combat Intelligence Headquarters in Pearl Harbor.

Those men in the basement, the Hypo team, struggled throughout the night with the coded radio message and by dawn of April 14, Rochefort raced over to the quarters of Admiral Nimitz.

Rochefort had the Admiral's orderly wake up Nimitz.

Nimitz rubbed his sleepy eyes. "What's so important, Commander?"

"Sir, Admiral Yamamoto is making a trip by plane from Rabaul to Ballale. The radio intercept we just decoded gives the exact time and schedule for his visit! We figured out that RYZ was Ballale, an island off Bougainville, RXP was Buin, and RR was Rabaul."

Nimitz nodded, took the decoded message, and studied it.

✳ ✳ ✳

TO: COMMANDER, 1ST BASE FLOTILLA COMMANDER, 11TH AIR FLOTILLA

COMMAMDER, 26TH AIR FLOTILLA

COMMANDER, 9S8TH AIR DETACHMENT

CHIEF, BALLALE DEFENSE UNIT

C-IN-C, 8TH FLEET, SOUTH-EASTERN AREA FLEET

INFORMATION: C-IN-C, COMBINED FLEET

C-IN-C, COMBINED FLEET WILL INSPECT RXZ, RXE, AND RXP ON "SETSUA" AS FOLLOWS:

AT 0600 LEAVES RR BY "CHUKO," A LAND-BASED MEDIUM BOMBER (6 FIGHTERS ESCORTING)

AT 0800 ARRIVES AT RXZ

AT 0840 ARRIVES AT RXP BY SUB CHASER (COMMANDER, 1ST BASE FORCE WILL ARRANGE ONE CHASE IN ADVANCE)

AT 0945 LEAVES RXP BY SAME SUBCHASER

AT 1030 ARRIVES AT RXZ (AT RXZ A "DAIHATSU" WILL BE ON HAND AND AT RXE A "MOTOR-LAUNCH" FOR TRAFFIC)

AT 1100 LEAVES RXZ BY "CHUKO"

AT 1110 ARRIVES RXP

LUNCHEON AT HQ, 1ST BASE FORCE (ATTENDED BY COMMANDANT 26TH AIR SQUADRON AND SENIOR STAFF OFFICERS)

AT 1400 LEAVES RXP BY "CHUKO"

AT 1540 Arrives AT RR

2. OUTLINE OF PLAN

AFTER THE VERBAL REPORT ON THEIR PRESENT CONDITIONS BRIEFLY BY EACH UNIT, UNIT

MEMBERS WILL BE INSPECTED (1ST B.F. HOSPITAL WILL BE VISITED). THE COMMANDING OFFICER OF EACH UNIT ALONE SHALL WEAR THE NAVAL LANDING PARTY UNIFORM WITH MEDAL RIBBONS.

IN CASE OF BAD WEATHER, IT WILL BE POSTPONED FOR ONE DAY.

Nimitz called in his orderly. "Tell my chief of staff I want a meeting of my top staff for eight hundred hours in the main conference room."

Later that Day, Pearl Harbor, Naval Headquarters at Makalapa, Main Conference Room

Nimitz began the meeting by pointing to the small island on the large wall map of the Pacific. "As you can see, it is close to Bougainville. That's where Admiral Yamamoto, the planner of the Pearl Harbor attack, is going to fly to on April 18. We have a real problem—a true dilemma. In the face of the great need to protect the fact that the enemy's code has been broken, we must now face the question: Should the information so obtained be acted upon if the action would reveal our capability to decode?

"To put it another way, shall we ambush the son of a bitch? The blood of thousands of Allied and American soldiers, sailors, Marines and airmen has been spilled because of him. Here, we have an opportunity to get rid of him for once and for all."

"Isn't he the one who arrogantly planned to dictate the peace terms in the White House?" an officer asked.

"He's the one," Nimitz responded.

"Is it wrong, under the rules of war, to target your equivalent enemy officer for assassination? I don't think Ulysses S. Grant would have ordered a hit on Robert E. Lee."

Nimitz rubbed his chin. "Probably not, but here, we have Yamamoto, who is the beating heart of the Japanese Navy, embodying their unwavering Bushido fighting spirit. He comes from a long line of samurai, you know.

"I guess," continued Nimitz, "the real question is do we really want to kill the person who lost the Battle of Midway and badly mismanaged the Guadalcanal campaign?"

Commander Edwin Layton from Naval Intelligence, and part of the code-breaking team, offered the following: "I think the loss of Yamamoto would be a serious blow to the Japs. He's the best they have. His death could demoralize the Japanese Navy and shock the nation. He is exceptionally able, forceful, and quick-thinking. Don't forget, at Midway, he was the victim of our secret code-breaking, not shortcomings on his part. I view it the same as if they shot you down! But to protect the secrecy of the code-breakers, we can attribute our source to the Australian coastwatchers."

Layton continued. "But there's the other side of the ledger on Yamamoto."

Nimitz looked intently at his sharp intelligence man, with great interest.

"While we know that the Admiral planned the Pearl harbor attack, we also know that Yamamoto is a calming influence amidst fanatics like Tojo. We know he always believed Japan could not win a war with the United States and was against a war with us. Some of my intelligence analysts believe he might be a moderating factor in Tokyo, a voice of reason around which a peace faction could form and just perhaps, bring an end to the fighting."

Nimitz shook his head. "That's too speculative. You have all raised good questions. I'll need to sleep on it and confer with Admiral Halsey."

Nimitz wired Halsey, setting forth the facts of Yamamoto's upcoming trip.

Halsey wired back that Marc Mitscher on Guadalcanal advised him that his Army Air Force P-38 fighters had the range to make the interception of Admiral Yamamoto at Bougainville and that Mitscher's team relished the opportunity to go after him. Halsey ended his wire with, "TALLEYHO X LET'S GET THE BASTARD X."

That did it. Nimitz agreed, and gave Halsey the go-ahead. The hunt for Yamamoto was on.

Southern Bougainville lay about 400 miles from Guadalcanal's Henderson Field. The new P-38s had the necessary range to make the round trip. They were our longest-legged fighter aircraft. The pilots would have to be careful not to burn too much fuel. But with fuel drop tanks, they could wait for Yamamoto's plane and still make it back, particularly if they use a lean fuel mixture.

John Mitchell would be the leader of the flight He would designate four planes as the "killers"—the ones that would attack Yamamoto's plane. The others would fly cover to protect against the escorting Zeros. Mitchell would be the backstop. He'd oversee the operation and if all else failed, he would go in himself for the kill.

Mitchell pointed to the map showing the area of the attack, including the islands of Balalle and Buin. "According to his schedule, Yamamoto is flying into Balalle, then taking a subchaser to Buin. The question we have to decide is whether to attack Yamamoto in his aircraft before he lands or wait and bomb him on the subchaser?"

Lanphier objected to bombing the subchaser. "As an Army pilot, I don't know one boat from other, much less a subchaser—I don't even know what it is! Bombing and strafing a boat is much less sure of a kill and, even if you sink the boat, who's to say he won't survive on a raft, or swim to shore in a life jacket? And we'd be facing antiaircraft guns blasting away from every ship."

Mitchell rubbed his chin. "I tend to lean toward going after the plane. What if there are several boats? Which one do we attack?

If we go for the ship, we'll be very close to Buin and the Japs have seventy-five fighters not more than 15 miles away. Fuel will become a problem because we'd have to be over the target too long to strafe and bomb a boat on the water. And that'll give Japs enough time to send up those fighters to protect the admiral and, being at such a low altitude, we'd be in a poor position to defend ourselves from Zero attack, not to mention that they'd outnumber us in fighter planes, five to one."

He took arguments for another half hour and then put up his hand. "I've heard enough. Look, we are all fighter pilots and that's what we do. We should take him out in the air."

CHAPTER EIGHTEEN

P-38s Catch Up with Yamamoto

April 17, 1943, Rabaul Airbase

As YAMAMOTO AND UGAKI approached the dinner table, Rear Admiral Takoji Joshima buttonholed Yamamoto before he could sit down.

Once again, he pleaded with the Admiral. "Please cancel your trip, Admiral, because I am fairly certain your itinerary might have been intercepted by the enemy. It was foolish to send it out over the radio."

Yamamoto glanced at Ugaki, who seemed to be just staring at the ceiling. Then he smiled at Joshima. "I appreciate your concern but so what? They can't break the navy code. I must go on this trip to the front. All the arrangements have been made. It would be bad for morale if I, the commander-in-chief, of all people, cancelled. I have a duty to visit the units at Ballale, Buin, and the Shortland Island to encourage them on to greater glory for our emperor. Showing up at the front will prove to my men that I have confidence in the ultimate outcome of this war."

"I just wish you hadn't been so detailed and precise," Joshima grumbled.

Yamamoto gave him a pat on the shoulder. "It's all right. I'm perfectly safe and will return here at dusk tomorrow after the trip is over and then we can laugh at those concerns. You will see."

Yamamoto turned to his chief of staff. "Ugaki, because we are going up to the front, I don't think our white dress uniforms are appropriate. My aides have convinced me it is too conspicuous. So I am switching to the new dark green simplified field uniform with my samurai sword. Then, we will blend it better with the battle uniforms of the men we are flying out to visit."

Ugaki nodded his agreement.

April 18, 1943, Rabaul Airbase and Airspace Over Ballale

The day before, April 17, a bright and sunny day greeted Yamamoto as he left his flagship and traveled to the airbase on Truk.

Two Japanese twin-engine medium bombers, Bettys, as the Americans called them, were warming up on the tarmac. He, Yamamoto, would take one Betty and his chief of Staff, Admiral Ugaki, would take the other. It was a strict policy of Yamamoto to assure that the loss of a single plane would not get them all.

Japanese "Betty" Bomber

The trip to Rabaul, escorted by three Zero fighters, was uneventful. Yamamoto slept most of the way, and the planes arrived exactly a time. A known stickler for punctuality, this pleased him.

On this morning, April 18, the two admirals, at Yamamoto's insistence, dressed in their green field uniforms with all medals attached, black airmen boots, and white gloves, boarded different brand-new Betty medium bombers of the 705th Naval Air Squadron for the trip to Balalle. Before leaving his room, Yamamoto stuffed his pockets with a handkerchief, some folded toilet paper, and a diary with some poems of the Emperor Meiji, which he copied in the back of the book. He then attached his samurai sword. It had been a gift from his deceased elder brother. The Fleet surgeon and a staff officer, Yamamoto's secretary, joined him on the first plane while the Fleet Paymaster and two staff officers accompanied Ugaki on the second plane. Each plane had five crewmen. Betty was the name given to these bombers by the Americans. Yamamoto called them "flying cigars."

These two land-based Mitsubishi G4M assault bombers, numbered on their tails as 323 (Yamamoto's plane) and 326 (Ugaki's), roared off from Vunakanau Air Base at precisely 5:45AM (Tokyo time), climbed to 6500 feet and were met by six Zeros of the 204th Naval Air Squadron led by First Lieutenant Morisaki, who followed closely in two three-ship Vs above and a little behind the bombers. None of the Zeros carried radios which, as far as Morisaki was concerned, were nothing but static-producing devices and added more weight which would make the plane less nimble and reduce its airspeed.

Vice Admiral Ozawa, with great trepidation, stood on the tarmac and watched the planes disappear into the haze. He looked at his watch. They left precisely on time. Ozawa smiled. *That was Yamamoto for you!*

And they would arrive on time, the pilots assured Yamamoto. He watched as the planes flew in a tight formation at about 5,000 feet. Behind and above them flew six Zero fighter planes—their protective cover.

Yamamoto's pilot, Lieutenant Hayashi, when told the night before that for today's mission, he had to dress up properly in a regulation flying uniform instead of the comfortable jacket he liked, he had objected. When told his passenger was the Commander-in-Chief of the Combined Fleet and other high-ranking officers, he relented.

The weather was clear and the trip smooth. Yamamoto settled back in his seat, his sword cradled between his legs.

Morisaki, in the lead Zero, thought to himself, *I wonder why more Zeros weren't assigned as protective cover? After all, this was Admiral Yamamoto himself!*

John Mitchell was up at 4:30 A.M. It was Palm Sunday. *What a day to set out to stalk and kill a man!* he thought. There was still a shortage of P-38s, and the Army P-38s at Guadalcanal were shared with the Navy pilots. At the base, there was a continual shortage of vital supplies such as ammunition, aircraft parts, and oxygen, supplies vital to P-38s on long, high-altitude missions. But for this mission, all the supplies were pooled to provide everything the pilots needed.

Admiral Mitscher, who had commanded the carrier *Hornet*, which had, last year, launched Jimmy Doolittle on his celebrated raid on Tokyo, arrived at the base to give the pilots a pep talk, reminding them that the Japs had tortured and starved captured American airmen and they should be pleased with being the ones given the rare opportunity to shoot down Yamamoto in retaliation.

"We selected you boys, the best shots in the squadron, to do the job, knowing your P-38s, with the added fuel tanks, were the only fighters we have that could fly the distance from Guadalcanal to Bougainville. You will be led by your commander, Major John Mitchell."

Mitscher pointed to Mitchell, the popular, confident, and efficient leader of the Army Airforce's 12th Fighter Squadron. Mitchell smiled and waved to his men.

"The Navy's 339th is coordinating with the Army Airforce's 12th Fighter Squadron on this joint mission," Mitscher reminded, "so don't disappoint us!"

✵✵✵

Mitchell selected his best shooters, Army Captain Tom Lanphier, and Lieutenants Rex Barber, Jim McLanahan, and Joe Moore, to be the killers, that is, the planes that would actually attack Yamamoto's aircraft. He knew it would be a very dangerous mission and had the rest of his squadron, the other fourteen P-38s, flying cover for the killers.

"Yamamoto will be flying in a Jap medium bomber, probably a 'Betty'," Mitchell advised, "and our decoded intercepts give the exact time he is scheduled to land at Ballale. Some our own officers had been acquainted with Yamamoto when he was in the United States and they say he is punctual to a fault."

"Major, how come you are not in the 'killer' group?" Joe Moore asked.

"Because there'll be a swarm of Jap Zeros trying to stop us and I can't pass up such an opportunity to shoot down their fighters!"

For Captain Lanphier, the name Yamamoto rang a bell. *Why do I know that name?* he thought. *Of course! Pearl Harbor! Son of a Bitch! I'll get him! The mission of ultimate revenge!*

Mitchell outlined the plan. "All eighteen aircraft will fly the entire route at about 50-100 feet off the water. When we approach land, which is when we should meet up with Yamamoto's plane, on my orders, all of us will skin off our drop tanks and the four designated killer planes will attack the bomber while some of us will engage the Zeros protecting the bomber, and some will climb to 18,000 feet to protect against Jap fighters coming from land. Besby Holmes and Ray Hine, you will be the backup to the four killer planes and should be prepared to move into any position in the killer formation should one of its pilots be in trouble and is forced to turn back,"

"Why can't we all attack the bomber?" one of the pilots asked.

"Because," explained Mitchell with a little growl in his voice and trying to maintain his patience, "the rest of you will need altitude to protect against the enemy fighters and besides, too many attacking planes would only get in each other's way and with everyone firing some of us are bound to get hit with friendly fire.

"This mission is of supreme importance and you will not, I repeat, will not, attack any other target on land or sea, not associated with Yamamoto's flight plan. We will maintain strict radio silence. If anyone has to abort, use hand signals. Don't get on that radio."

"Isn't flying that low for such a distance dangerous?" one pilot asked.

"We can't fly over land because if we are seen by Jap soldiers or radar, we'll lose Yamamoto," Mitchell replied. "So the entire route will be over open water. And yes, it's dangerous because there is a tendency to start daydreaming and get sleepy on a long trip like this. You're going to be hot. You're going to be bored. Once we leave Guadalcanal, we won't see land until Bougainville. There'll be no landmarks, so I'll have to fly by clock, altimeter, airspeed indicator, and compass readings—and intuition. I'll fly in the lead plane. Keep within sight of at least one other plane. You don't want to get separated and disoriented. It could be fatal. And just don't stare at the water. Remember, your depth perception goes to shit fly low like this. If you're careless, you'll end up in the drink! You are all volunteers, so if anyone is now having second thoughts, this is the time to express them."

The room became as quiet as a tomb.

"One more thing. Just before we approach the target I'll give you a signal and you will spread out."

With that, Mitchell stood up to go out to the tarmac. *How the hell am I supposed to find a dot in the sky—that's all Yamamoto's plane will appear to be to us. While Yamamoto could fly a straight route from Rabaul to Ballale, me and my men have to take a circuitous route to avoid all land. And we must arrive at about the same time as Yamamoto. I have no idea how fast his plane flies. I have set it at 180 miles per hour. I hope the hell I'm correct and we can catch the bomber when it is low and slowing down to land. One minute or one mile off and my P-38s might never see Yamamoto's plane. Suppose the code-breakers misinterpreted the message and the plane landed elsewhere but on Ballale?* Mitchell shook his head. *Our odds of find him are probably 1,000 to 1.*

The airfield was made ready as workers toiled through the night cleaning the runway and sprinkling it to hold down the dust. After all, it isn't everyday they were visited by the Commander-in-Chief of the Combined Fleet! As the arrival time approached, officers and men, in clean and pressed uniforms, lined the edges of the strip at attention. The airstrip commander smiled. *It was a sight to behold!*

The pilot handed Admiral Yamamoto, seated behind him, a note. "Expect to arrive Ballale at 7:45." Yamamoto nodded and smiled. He looked at his watch. 7:28 now. *Right on time!*

In the same instance, the lead pilot in his Zero, who'd been scanning the skies above him for Americans because that's where they always attacked from—a high altitude, suddenly spotted P-38s climbing from below, heading for the two bombers. He dipped his wings and pointed down, then he nosed the fighter down into a steep dive. His two wingmen immediately followed him down.

In the lead bomber, suddenly, Yamamoto was pushed back hard back into his seat as the plane dived at a steep angle, leveling off at treetop level, just above the jungle.

"What just happened?" Yamamoto shouted.

"I spotted several enemy fighter planes below us and climbing!"

The pilot had liked the Bettys as a bomber but certainly not as a passenger plane; for a bomber, it could carry a large bomb load and had an incredible range of almost 2,000 miles. But to achieve that range, the Betty had the reputation of being mostly a flying fuel tank and could turn into a flaming fireworks when hit. So to carry a passenger like the commander-in-chief, it was not recommended.

The Betty crew scrambled to their gun positions, opened the ports, and began firing creating such cacophony of sound, combined with a screaming wind, that Yamamoto thought his eardrums would burst. But that, as it turned out, would be the least of his problems.

The two Betty bombers, taking evasive action, separated. The first bomber veered to the right and the other, to the left. But the enemy planes stuck with them, boring down unrelentingly.

Yamamoto's plane, swept with cannon fire from one or more of the P-38s, crashed in the jungle.

Ugaki, in the other plane, awakened by all the noise, rubbed his eyes, glanced out the window and screamed, "My God, look, the commander-in-chief's plane has crashed. See the smoke in the jungle?" He shook the arm of the staff officer sitting next to him, pointing to the ground. But then Ugaki's plane turned sharply to avoid an enemy fighter and Ugaki lost sight of Yamamoto's plane for good.

A red tracer bullet passed over the pilot's head.

"Hang on," the pilot shouted, "now they are coming after us."

The pilot made sudden turn of ninety degrees and put the bomber in a steep dive. Ugaki felt himself thrown around as the plane went through many violent maneuvers. The plane finally leveled off at 150 feet and, having lost sight of the other plane, which was on fire, the pilot headed out to sea. But he did not get very far when a P-38 shot away his flaps and shattered his cables. The pilot had no choice but to ditch the plane, now uncontrollable, into the sea.

It's a good thing I'm belted in, Ugaki thought. But things, he'd discover, would get much worse. He felt bullets hitting the fuselage and the right wing and saw one of the staff officers slump over, face down on the table with his arms outstretched. Suddenly, Ugaki heard the plane's engines throttled back as the pilot tried to glide the plane easily into the sea, but with no controls, the plane landed hard into the water. Ugaki's seat, with him still in it, pitched forward, torn out of its mooring and into the passageway; everything went black for Ugaki.

The takeoff of the 337th Squadron was uneventful except for McLanahan, whose left tire, just about the time of reaching flying speed, hit a piece of pierced metal, flattened and caused him to veer off the runway to a complete stop. In the air, Ray Hine slipped into his spot.

Mitchell circled around slowly until all his planes were in the air and joined up on him. There was no chatter and the pilots, Mitchell was pleased to note, were able to keep absolute radio silence. It was a simple instruction but a hard one to maintain in the excitement of flying into battle.

With all planes joined up, Mitchell slowly descended toward the water, leveling out at 750 feet. He looked at the clock on his dashboard: 0725. When Mitchell signaled, all the pilots switched to fuel fed by their belly tanks. They'd use up that fuel first and drop those tanks before the battle. Joe Moore's belly tank would not feed fuel and he signaled he would return to the base. Besby Homes took his place among the "killer four". Mitchell now had only sixteen P-38s.

Once Mitchell was down to an altitude of about sixty feet above the water, he signaled, with his wings, for the planes to spread out. After that, he could only spot of few of the planes, but if each stayed within sight of his own wingman, that should not be a problem.

Four hundred and ninety miles later, Mitchell rocked his wings, signaling it was time to test their guns and then get into close formation.

The sky was hazy and bright with sunlight, and Mitchell could see no land, no nothing, not even a breeze. Calm as a cucumber up to now, he began to get a case of the nerves. *Where the hell were the hills of Bougainville. I should be seeing them by now!*

Then he saw them—the beaches of Bougainville. He realized he was just where he had wanted to be. The eleven planes he was leading climbed to a higher altitude to provide cover for the killer flight.

As Mitchell reached the altitude and leveled off one of his flyers broke radio silence.

Doug Canning shouted into his mike, "Bogeys! Seven o'clock!"

Mitchell looked down, searching the sky—*there, at seven o'clock, were two Jap bombers at about 4,000 feet and descending in preparation for a landing.*

302

The sight surprised Mitchell because there were two Betty bombers, not one. *Which one carried Yamamoto?* He spotted six Zeros behind and above the bombers.

"Roger that," Mitchell called out. "I have the Zeros. Boys, skid off your external tanks, let out the throttle, and dive! Go after both those bombers!"

The low flying killer group had problems. Holmes radioed he could not drop his external tanks and pulled away out over the water. His wingman, Hine, followed Holmes to protect him, as protocol required. Holmes climbed to a higher altitude and dove at 350 miles per hour, pulling such high G's (gravity) that he almost blacked out. That maneuver finally ripped away the external tanks.

"He's all yours, Tom," Mitchell radioed to Lanphier.

But Mitchell was ready to barrel in, even if it meant ramming Yamamoto's plane. His orders were to do anything to down that plane and that was just what he intended to do.

Lanphier and Barber, the only two of the killer group left, turned upward toward the two Bettys. Lanphier reported the bombers on fire.

As Mitchell dropped down along with the other P-38s into the flight of Zeros, he saw Hine's aircraft smoking from one engine. But Mitchell had his hands full with several Zeros around him and lost sight and track of Hine.

Barber caught up with one of the bombers and pounded it with bullets. The plane burned but refused to go down. Then Barber dove at the target, banked sharply and spit cannon shells and bullets in a line over the fuselage and into the right engine, destroying the vertical fin and the rudder. Barber pulled up as the bomber staggered onward. Now he had several furious Zeros on his tail, so Barber never saw the plane go down. He was peppered with machine-gun bullets as he twisted and dodged to escape. Fortunately, the armor plate covering his seat protected him from any serious injury.

Holmes, now rid of his external fuel tanks, finally caught up and pulled behind the Yamamoto's stricken bomber and while the

Zeros were preoccupied with Barber in a dogfight. Holmes' cannon fire ripped off the wing of the plane and he saw it crash in flames into the jungle below. Mitchell also saw the smoke in the jungle but couldn't tell what type of plane had crashed.

P-38

Lanphier pulled behind the other bomber but had several pesky Zero diving toward him. He knew he had time for one burst of his machine gun. It was a long burst and the bullets shredded the right wing and the engine on that wing burst into flames. Lanphier, almost on top of the bomber, watched as the right wing ripped off and the plane crashed into the sea. By now, Mitchell and his group were into the Zeros hounding Lanphier and he escaped the enemy planes.

Finally, as fuel was getting low, Mitchell, eyeing several smoking crashes radioed, "Let's go home. Mission accomplished—get your ass out of here—all of you!"

The entire attack, from the time the Japanese bombers were spotted to when John Mitchell ordered the American fighters home, lasted less than ten minutes.

Ugaki regained consciousness, choking and stunned, finding himself floating in the cold water. *I'm alive!* he thought unbelievingly. He looked around. Only the right wing was standing in the sea behind him and that was burning fiercely. He knew Yamamoto died. No one could have survived that crash and the flames in the jungle. Before they hit the water, Ugaki remembered seeing his fellow passengers bullet-ridden corpses.

Ugaki hung onto a wooden crate. He saw the pilot in the water, who either ignored him or did not see him. The pilot swam strongly for the shore. Ugaki, hanging onto that crate and kicking with his feet, eventually made it to shore, though badly wounded.

The body of Admiral Yamamoto, discovered in the jungle, was thrown clear of the plane and still strapped in his seat, gripping his sword. An autopsy found that he had been hit by two bullets, one in his lower jaw that exited through his temple, and another in his left shoulder that never exited. The doctors concluded he was probably killed instantly while his plane was still in the air. No one on his plane had survived. The diary in his breast pocket confirmed that it was Yamamoto.

Yamamoto died in the crash—the planner of the crushing attack on the American base at Pearl Harbor was destroyed by the very same navy and army he'd devastated!

The code breakers at Pearl Harbor were very apprehensive of the Yamamoto venture for fear that the Japanese would discover their decrypting abilities. It was almost blown handling information on Midway and Guadalcanal. But it was not their decision to make.

Indeed, as the code-breakers feared, the Japanese began to suspect that that the Americans were aware of their plans and it could only have come from the coded telegram concerning Yamamoto's visit to Ballale. Fortunately for the Americans, the Japanese ultimately gave up pursuing the possibility of a code break.

EPILOGUE

UNTIL THE END OF 1942, Japan and Germany simply let their American opponent, then on the defensive, get on-the-job training. By mid-1943, America achieved what its enemies, except for Yamamoto, thought was not possible. America started fighting offensively—and successfully—a war on two fronts—in Europe and the Pacific—as Admiral Yamamoto of the Japanese Imperial Navy had predicted and General Erwin Rommel, of the German Wehrmacht, could have attested, had he survived the war. Volume Two, will pick up where Volume One left off, with the events of the Pacific War after the killing of Admiral Yamamoto.

Did the Americans know of the Japanese attack on December 7, 1941? A fairer question would be, did they know the attack would be against Pearl Harbor? Based on my research, it is clear to me that the leaders in Washington had no idea Japan would attack Pearl Harbor. The Philippines, yes, but no one envisioned the Japanese bold enough to travel over 5,000 miles of ocean undetected to attack Pearl Harbor. But having said that, after decoding the Japanese 14-part diplomatic message to its ambassador in Washington, American leaders, including Roosevelt, really knew war was imminent and though Hawaii was not the expected area of attack, there seemed to be little sense to withhold that information from our military leaders in Pearl Harbor, the largest American Navy and Army base in the Pacific Ocean, the same ocean it happened to share with the Japanese. Thus on the morning of the seventh, what our Washington leaders already knew, our local commanders, Admiral Husband Kimmel and General Walter Short did not. Some say America pushed Japan into the war; that Roosevelt just did not want to fire the first shot because his isolationist Congress simply could not be pushed into declaring war. Perhaps Roosevelt hoped the Japanese were bluffing and he could get on eventually to confronting what he considered to be a greater nemesis, Hitler.

Even after the Pearl Harbor attack and the Congressional declaration of war against Japan, our senators and representatives dug in their heels and were not about to declare war on Hitler too, regardless of what Roosevelt wanted. Hitler and his toady, Mussolini, obliged Roosevelt by declaring war on the United States. Congress, then, had no choice and America was in a two-front war, whether the politicians liked it or not.

For Yamamoto, it was Japan's fighting spirit pitted against America's overwhelming industrial military might. Many Japanese fervently felt that, with their overriding spirit, the Japanese both at home and on the front lines could endure hardships that the Americans could never withstand and, if the Japanese worked harder, ate less, and faced death willingly, with a samurai-like indifference, they could win the war. Yamamoto was one Japanese who rejected that idea. He was a stubborn opponent against not only the war against America, but the one against China, as well. Yet he was picked by Japan's military leaders to plan the start of the aggressive war against America.

And Yamamoto was right about America's industrial might. Between 1940 and 1943, Britain tripled its war production, Germany and Russia doubled theirs, and Japan's increased fourfold. America? Its war production increased twenty-five times!

Washington leaders looked not in the mirror but all around for someone to blame. And they found him, or I should say them— Admiral Husband Kimmel and General Walter Short—the respective Navy and Army commanders at Pearl. Admiral William F. Halsey later said that Kimmel and Short were "our outstanding military martyrs." And blamed for something about which they were powerless to do anything. Well, not quite. Kimmel could be faulted for not conducting long-range air reconnaissance around Oahu. He could also be blamed for not having the antitorpedo nets in place around the battleships. And the fleet's movements were totally predictable, enabling Japanese agents to report to Tokyo which major vessels would be in port over the weekend. Just plain luck found America's two aircraft carriers in the Pacific out of Pearl Harbor on assignment and one in drydock in San Diego. Short could be faulted for parking those planes wingtip to wingtip, making their destruction by Japanese planes rather easy. True, it was suggested by his superiors, but he should have known better.

Halsey, commanding one of those aircraft carriers, *Enterprise*, took no chances and ordered his ship on a war footing, even before the sneak attack.

In the end, the American public began to realize that the Japanese destroyed only a lot of old hardware, with the shallow waters of the harbor preserving most of the ships to fight another day. What the Japanese did accomplish is to wake up the American Navy with a good swift kick in the butt!

Admiral Ugaki, in the second plane, survived with serious injuries. He spend many months in the hospital recovering. He had a compound fracture of his arm, wounds on his right biceps, and bled profusely from his lower thighs and his right eye. One staff officer and the chief pilot also survived. Ugaki's diary of that day stated; "[The enemy plane] gunfire caught us splendidly, and bullets could be seen on both sides of the plane. He made many hits. Several of the people aboard had already been killed..."

John Mitchell, the ace pilot with many Japanese kills and the leader of the aerial attack on Yamamoto, was awarded the Distinguished

Service Cross. The squadron lost one plane in the attack, the one piloted by Lieutenant Raymond Hine. He was last seen going down near the Shortland Island his left engine on fire. His remains have never been found. Three enemy Zeros were seen to be destroyed.

But not all participants in the attack were so honored. It seems that the American military leaders had their own problems, trying to keep their citizens from learning about the broken Japanese naval code. They censored several reporters and threatened prosecution if they reported anything about the broken code. Such action was necessary because Lanphier, Barber, and another had spoken to reporters when they had returned. Admiral Halsey called those three into his office On his desk lay the recommendations for Medals of Honor, with stirring prose, from Admiral Mitscher. The pilots, expecting some form of adulation, received the surprise of their lives. He picked up and crushed in his fist the paper with the recommendations. "As far as I am concerned, none of you deserve even the lowest air medal for what you did." He then proceeded to give the men a profanity-laced tongue lashing, accusing them of being traitors and so stupid, they didn't deserve to wear the American uniform. "I'm not going to court-martial you, but I will reduce these citations down to the Navy Cross. You men are horrible examples of pilots in the military service. You deserve to be court-martialed and reduced to privates or seamen for talking to reporters about the mission and code breaking. You three are out of this war and remanded to stateside duty! Now get the hell out of here!"

If anyone needed to be court-martialed, it was the leaders of Imperial Navy Headquarters. Members of Yamamoto's staff insisted that the Americans must have broken the naval code because the attack was carefully planned, and they knew precisely where the admiral would be at the exact time. But at headquarters, its own communications experts assured the leaders the naval code was unbreakable, and the arrival of the P-38s off Bougainville must have been "pure coincidence". Imperial Headquarters just brushed aside the Yamamoto staff s theories in happy ignorance.

✯✯✯

The Japanese war cabinet appointed Admiral Mineichi Koga to replace the slain Yamamoto as Commander-in-Chief of the Combined Fleet.

✯✯✯

Since the successful Manchuria venture and up to December 1941, the Japanese military had known nothing but easy victories. But in taking on the British, Dutch and Americans, many citizens in Japan were not so sure and had severe apprehensions. Then, easy victory followed easy victory: at Pearl Harbor, in the Philippines, and in southeast Asia, surprising greatly many of the doubters. So by the time of Midway, you could almost say most of the Japanese were downright arrogant and overconfident.

The feeling of invincibility also infected the Imperial Navy planning of the Midway operation and there did not seem to be consideration of what the Americans would do or anticipation of what they might do, or what they were capable of doing. The American capabilities seemed simply to be dismissed from the Imperial Navy leaders thinking.

✯✯✯

Marine General Vandegrift was awarded the Congressional Medal of Honor for his skills as commander of the Marine forces on Guadalcanal.

Several writers and historians have also alleged that Nimitz received personal approval for the Yamamoto killing from both Secretary of the Navy Frank Knox and President Roosevelt, but my study of those references turned up no credible or substantial evidence, merely speculation and gross hearsay. As a matter of fact, Roosevelt, at the time of planning the attack, was out of Washington, making a goodwill train trip to Monterrey, Mexico.

Yamamoto was cremated, his ashes were divided with half of them buried in Tama Cemetery in Tokyo and half in his home town of Nagaoka.

The ashes interred in Tokyo rest alongside that other Japanese naval hero, Admiral Togo. In an impressive state funeral where there was a nation-wide outpouring of grief, Emperor Hirohito bestowed upon him posthumously the Grand Order of the Chrysanthemum, first class, and promoted him to the rank of fleet admiral.

Ugaki, still in the hospital recovering from his wounds and injuries, did not attend the cremation. Extremely depressed, Ugaki blamed himself for his commander's death. Friends feared he might commit suicide sometime in the future. Were they prescient?

Ugaki's further actions in the war will appear in Volume Two.

BIBLIOGRAPHY

Bassett, James, *Harm's Way*. World Publishing Co, Cleveland, 2010.

Batty, David, *Japan in the Second World War in Colour*. Andre Deutsch, London, 2004.

Bell, Frederick J., *Condition Red: Destroyer Action in the South Pacific*. Longmans, Green and Co., New York, 1943.

Belote, James H. and William M. Belote, *Titans of the Sea, The Development of Operations of Japanese and American Carrier Task Forces During World War II*. Harper & Row, New York, 1975.

Bergamini, David, *Japan's Imperial Conspiracy, Vol I*. William Morrow and Company, New York, 1971.

Bix, Herbert P., *Hirohito and the Making of Modern Japan*. HarperCollins, New York, 2000.

Borneman, Walter R., *The Admirals, Nimitz, Halsey, Leahy, and King-The Five-Star Admirals Who Won the War at Sea*. Little, Brown and Company, New York, 2012.

Charles River Editors, *Amphibious Warfare In World War II; The History and Legacy of the War's Most Important Landing Operations*. Create Space Publishing, Charleston, S.C., 2017.

Charles River Editors, *The Battle of the Coral Sea: The History and Legacy of World War II's First Major Battle Between Aircraft Carriers*. Create Space Publishing, Charleston, S.C., 2016.

Charles River Editors, *The Samurai: The History and Legacy of Japan*. Create Space Publishing, Charleston, S.C., 2018.

Cook, Blanche Wiesen, *Eleanor Roosevelt, the War Years and After, 1939-1962, Vol. 3.* Penguin Books, New York, 2016.

Davis, Donald A., *Lightning Strike, The Secret Mission to Kill Admiral Yamamoto and Avenge Pearl Harbor.* New York, St. Martin's Griffin, 2005.

Dower, John W., *Embracing Defeat, Japan in the Wake of World War II. W.W.* Norton, New York, 1999.

Dull, Paul S., *The Imperial Japanese Navy (1941-1945).* Naval Institute Press, Annapolis, MD, 1978.

Eichelberger, Robert L., *Our Jungle Road to Tokyo.* Viking Press, New York, 1950 (reprinted 2017).

Fischer, James D., *Neptune's Inferno: The U.S. Navy at Guadalcanal.* New York, Bantam Books, 2010.

Frank, Gerold and James Horan, *U.S.S. Seawolf: Submarine Raider of the Pacific.* G.P. Putnam & Sons, New York, 1945.

Frank, Richard B., *Downfall, The End of the Imperial Japanese Empire.* Random House, New York, 1999.

Fuchida, Mitsuo and Masatake Okumiya, *Midway, The Battle That Doomed Japan, the Japanese Navy's Story.* Annapolis, MD, Bluejacket Books, 1992.

Glines, Carroll V., *Attack on Yamamoto.* New York, Orion Books, 1990.

Harris, Brayton, *Admiral Nimitz, the Commander of the Pacific Ocean Theater.* Palgrave MacMillan, New York, 2011.

Hiroyuki, Agawa, *The Reluctant Admiral, Yamamoto and the Imperial Navy.* Tokyo and New York, Kodansha International, 1979.

Hoffman, Jon T., *From Makin to Bougainville: Marine Raiders in the Pacific War.* Didactic Press, San Diego, 2015.

Hornfischer, James D., *Neptune's Inferno: The U.S. Navy at Guadalcanal.* Bantam, New York, 2011.

Hoyt, Edwin P., *The Last Kamikaze, The Story of Admiral Matome Ugaki.* Praeger, Westport, Ct, 1993.

Hoyt, Edwin P., *Yamamoto, The Man Who Planned Pearl Harbor*. McGraw-Hill, New York, 1990.

Huie, William Bradford, *Can Do! Story of the Seabees*. Kessinger publishing LLC, Whitefish, Montana, 2010.

Kenney, Gen. George C., *Air War in the Pacific: The Journal of General George Kenney*. Uncommon Valor Press, 2015.

Kenney, Gen. George C., *The Saga of Pappy Gunn*. Duell, Sloan & Pearce, New York, 1959.

Leckie, Robert, *Okinawa: The Last Battle of World War II*. Penguin Books, New York, 1996.

Lord, Walter, *Incredible Victory*. Burford Books, Shorthills, N.J., 1967.

McClain, James, *A Modern History-Japan*. W.W. Norton Company, New York, 2002.

Nimitz, Admiral Chester, *Refections on Pearl Harbor*.

O'Reilly, Bill and Martin Dugard, *Killing of the Rising Sun, How America Vanquished World War II Japan*. Henry Holt & Co., New York, 2016.

Parshall, Jonathan and Anthony Tully, *Shattered Sword, the Untold Story of the Battle of Midway*. Washington, D.C., Potomac Books, 2005.

Potter, E.B., *Nimitz*. Naval Institute Press, Annapolis, MD, 1976.

Prange, Gordon W., *At Dawn We Slept, The Untold Story of Pearl Harbor*. McGraw-Hill Book Co., New York, 1981.

Samurai, a Real Look into the Lives of the Last Samurai. The Web.

Smith, Holland and Percy Smith, *Coral and Brass*. Bantam Books, New York, 1987.

Spector, Ronald H., *Eagle Against the Sun, The American War with Japan*. New York, Vintage Books, 1985.

Stille, Mark, *Yamamoto Isoroku, Leadership, Strategy, Conflict*. Osprey Publishing, Oxford, 2012.

Thomas, Evan, *Sea of Thunder, Four Commanders and the Last Great Naval Campaign 1941-1945*. Simon & Schuster, New York, 2006.

Tillman, Barrett, *Clash of the Carriers, the True Story of the Marianas Turkey Shoot of World War II*. NAL Caliber, New York, 2005.

Toland, John, *The Rising Sun, The Decline and Fall of the Japanese Empire, 1936-1945*. The Modern Library, New York, 1970.

Toll, Ian W., *Pacific Crucible, War at Sea in the Pacific 1941-1942*. W.W. Norton, New York, 2012.

Toll, Ian W., *The Conquering Tide, War in the Pacific Islands, 1942-1944*. W.W. Norton, New York, 2015.

Ugaki, Matome, Admiral, *Fading Victory, The Diary of Admiral Matome Ugaki, 1940-1945*. Naval Institute Press, Annapolis, Md., 1991.

Walsh, George, *The Battle of Midway: Searching for the Truth*. Create Space Publishing, Charleston, S.C., 2015.

Willmott, H.P., with Tohmatsu Haruo and W. Spencer Johnson, *Pearl Harbor*. Cassel& Co., London, 2001.

OTHER BOOKS BY AUTHOR

Print Editions and Kindle

Wallenberg is Here!: The True Story About How Raoul Wallenberg Faced Down the Nazi War Machine and the Infamous Adolph Eichmann and Saved the Tens of Thousands of Jews in Budapest.

Righteous and Courageous: How a Japanese Diplomat Saved Thousands of Jews in Lithuania from the Holocaust.

Improbable Heroes: The True Story of How Clergy and Ordinary Citizens Risked Their Lives to Save Jews in Italy.

Barred!: The Shameful Failure of FDR's State Department to Refuse to Save Tens of Thousands of Europe's Jews from Extermination.

We Shall Be Called Israel!: How David Ben-Gurion, Chaim Weismann, American school teacher Golda Meir, President Harry S. Truman, and a Kansas City haberdasher fostered the birth of the Jewish State, in the face of Arab violence and British Foreign Minister Bevin's fanatic obstructionism.

Wily Fox: How King Boris Saved the Jews of Bulgaria from his Axis Ally Adolf Hitler and the German Army.

The Outfielder (co-authored): How the dreadful secrets and lies of an Auschwitz death camp survivor almost destroyed his American-born son, the outfielder that never was.

Now What?: The Irreverent Memoirs of a Daydreamer, Counterspy, Prosecutor, Defense Attorney, and Adventurer.

Villains or Heroes? True Story of Saving Jews in Occupied France Where There were Heroes and Villains and sometimes, You Could Not Tell the Difference.

Kindle Only

Harassment, A Law Firm Killing and Glass Ceiling Legal Thriller.

Extreme Malice, The Desperate Battle to Avoid Female Genital Mutilation. HIV Killer Preys on Women Executives and Lawyers.

CPSIA information can be obtained
at www.ICGtesting.com
Printed in the USA
LVHW032031220419
615089LV00003B/325